Reading Faster and Understanding More

W. M. Miller
El Camino College

Sharon Steeber
Oxnard College

Anne G. Dye
Santa Monica College

Doris Ladd

Reading Faster and Understanding More

Book

Winthrop Publishers, Inc.
Cambridge, Massachusetts

17 Dunster Street, Cambridge, Massachusetts 02138

10 9 8 7 6 5

HIJ Reading Level

Cover design by David Ford
Interior design by Phil Carver & Friends, Inc.

Acknowledgments appear on page xxi

Library of Congress Cataloging in Publication Data

Miller, Wanda M
Reading faster and understanding more.

1. Rapid reading. I. Steeber, Sharon, joint author.
II. Title
LB1050.54.M54 1979 428′.4′3 78-10351

ISBN 0-87626-729-0 (v. 1)
ISBN 0-87626-731-2 (v. 2)

Contents

Preface *xiii*
Introduction *xvii*
Acknowledgments *xxi*

PRETESTS

Comprehension and Rate Pretest **2**
Vocabulary Pretest **7**

LESSON 1

Directions for Letter Perception **12**
Exercise 1A—Letter Perception ***13***
How to Improve—Letter Perception **14**
Exercise 1B—Letter Perception ***15***
Directions for Word Perception **16**
Exercise 1C—Word Perception ***17***
How to Improve—Word Perception **18**
Exercise 1D—Word Perception ***19***
Directions for Word Comprehension **20**
Exercise 1E—Word Comprehension ***21***
How to Improve—Word Comprehension **22**
Exercise 1F—Word Comprehension ***23***
Words in Context **24**
Theme for Reading Selections: Looking Back **26**
Directions for Short Readings **26**
Exercise 1G—Short Reading
"The New Dress," Maya Angelou 27

How to Improve—Short Readings 29
Exercise 1H—Short Reading
"from *The Autobiography of Mark Twain*," Samuel Langhorne Clemens 29
Directions for Long Readings 31
"from *The Story of my Life*," Hellen Keller 31
How to Improve—Long Readings 35

LESSON 2

Exercise 2A—Word Perception 38
Exercise 2B—Word Perception 39
Directions for Phrase Perception 40
Exercise 2C—Phrase Perception 40
How to Improve—Phrase Perception 42
Exercise 2D—Phrase Perception 42
Exercise 2E—Word Comprehension 44
Exercise 2F—Word Comprehension 45
Finding the Main Idea 46
Practice Paragraphs—Main Idea 47
Words in Context 51
Theme for Reading Selections: Feeling Good 52
Exercise 2G—Short Reading
"Research Debunks Old Myths About Mind's Decline" 52
Exercise 2H—Short Reading
"Pain in the Neck Is All in Your Head," George Alexander 54
Exercise 2I—Long Reading
"Is Your Sex Life Going Up in Smoke?" Genell J. Subak-Sharpe 56

LESSON 3

Exercise 3A—Phrase Perception 62
Exercise 3B—Phrase Perception 64
Exercise 3C—Word Comprehension 66
Exercise 3D—Word Comprehension 67
Directions for Phrase Comprehension 68
Exercise 3E—Phrase Comprehension 68
How to Improve—Phrase Comprehension 70
Exercise 3F—Phrase Comprehension 70
More Practice Paragraphs—Main Idea 72
Words in Context 74
Theme for Reading Selections: Sports in Society 74

Exercise 3G—Short Reading
"Baseball on My Mind," Jacques Leslie 75
Exercise 3H—Short Reading
"Tim Gallwey's 'Inner Game'," Jacques Leslie 77
Exercise 3I—Long Reading
"Track Star," Dick Gregory with Robert Lipsyte 79

LESSON 4

Exercise 4A—Phrase Perception 86
Exercise 4B—Phrase Perception 88
Exercise 4C—Word Comprehension 90
Exercise 4D—Word Comprehension 91
Directions for Sentence Comprehension 92
Exercise 4E—Sentence Comprehension 92
How to Improve—Sentence Comprehension 93
Exercise 4F—Sentence Comprehension 93
Retaining Details 94
Practice Paragraphs—Details 98
Words in Context 103
Theme for Reading Selections: Creatures, Strange and Common 104
Exercise 4G—Short Reading
"A Chimp Learns a Language," Joyce Dudney Fleming 105
Exercise 4H—Short Reading
"The Unicorn in the Garden," James Thurber 107
Exercise 4I—Long Reading
"The Yahoos and the Houyhnhnms," Jonathan Swift 109

LESSON 5

Exercise 5A—Phrase Perception 116
Exercise 5B—Phrase Perception 118
Exercise 5C—Word Comprehension 120
Exercise 5D—Word Comprehension 121
Exercise 5E—Phrase Comprehension 122
Exercise 5F—Phrase Comprehension 124
Practice Paragraphs—Details 126
Words in Context 129
Theme for Reading Selections: Tracing Our Roots 130
Exercise 5G—Short Reading
"from *Roots*," Alex Haley 131
Exercise 5H—Short Reading
"from *One Flew Over the Cuckoo's Nest*," Ken Kesey 133

Exercise 5I—Long Reading
"Carnival Queen," Jeanne Wakatsuki Houston and James Houston 135

LESSON 6

Exercise 6A—Phrase Perception 142
Exercise 6B—Phrase Perception 144
Exercise 6C—Word Comprehension 146
Exercise 6D—Word Comprehension 147
Exercise 6E—Sentence Comprehension 148
Exercise 6F—Sentence Comprehension 149
Scanning for Specific Answers 150
Exercise 6G—Scanning 152
Exercise 6H—Scanning 154
Exercise 6I—Scanning 156
Exercise 6J—Scanning 158
Words in Context 160
Theme for Reading Selections: Study Skills 160
Exercise 6K—Long Reading
I. "How to Prepare for a Test," Anne Dye 161
Exercise 6L—Long Reading
II. "How to Take a Test—And Pass," Anne Dye 165

LESSON 7

Exercise 7A—Phrase Perception 172
Exercise 7B—Phrase Perception 174
Exercise 7C—Word Comprehension 176
Exercise 7D—Word Comprehension 177
Exercise 7E—Phrase Comprehension 178
Exercise 7F—Phrase Comprehension 180
SQ3R—How the Pros Study-Read 182
Words in Context 185
Theme for Reading Selections: The Sciences 185
Exercise 7G—Long Reading
"The Migration of the California Grey Whale," Tom O'Neill 187
Exercise 7H—Long Reading
"The Day the Dam Burst," Dietrick E. Thomsen 192

LESSON 8

Exercise 8A—Phrase Perception (Variation) 200
Exercise 8B—Phrase Perception (Variation) 202
Exercise 8C—Word Comprehension 204

Exercise 8D—Word Comprehension *205*
Exercise 8E—Sentence Comprehension *206*
Exercise 8F—Sentence Comprehension *207*
Skimming for Overview **208**
Words in Context **210**
Theme for Reading Selections: Tales of Imaginary People **210**
Exercise 8G—Short Reading
"The Creation of Man and Woman," Miriam Cox 211
Exercise 8H—Short Reading
"The Creation of the First World," recorded and translated by Oswald White Bear Fredericks 215
Exercise 8I—Long Reading
"The Descent from the Sky," a story from the Yoruba People 218

LESSON 9

Exercise 9A—Phrase Perception (Variation) *226*
Exercise 9B—Phrase Perception (Variation) *228*
Exercise 9C—Word Comprehension (Variation) *230*
Exercise 9D—Word Comprehension (Variation) *231*
Exercise 9E—Phrase Comprehension (Variation) *232*
Exercise 9F—Phrase Comprehension (Variation) *233*
Words in Context **235**
Theme for Reading Selections: Tales of Real People **235**
Exercise 9G—Short Reading
"Elvis Presley's First Concert," by Red West, Sonny West, and Dave Hebler as told to Steve Dunleavy 236
Exercise 9H—Short Reading
"from *Golda: The Life of Israel's Prime Minister,*" Peggy Mann 239
Exercise 9I—Long Reading
"from *Lyndon Johnson and the American Dream,*" Doris Kearns 242

LESSON 10

Exercise 10A—Phrase Perception (Variation) *248*
Exercise 10B—Phrase Perception (Variation) *249*
Exercise 10C—Word Comprehension (Variation) *250*
Exercise 10D—Word Comprehension (Variation) *251*
Exercise 10E—Sentence Comprehension *252*
Exercise 10F—Sentence Comprehension *253*
Determining Inference **254**
Practice Paragraphs—Inference and Logic **256**
Words in Context **258**
Theme for Reading Selections: Beyond Sex Roles **259**
Exercise 10G—Short Reading
"Men's Liberation from Etiquette," Jack Smith 259
Exercise 10H—Short Reading
"from *The Hazards of Being Male,*" Herb Goldberg, Ph.D. 261

Exercise 10I—Long Reading
"Click!" Jane O'Reilly 263

LESSON 11

Exercise 11A—Phrase Perception (Variation) 270
Exercise 11B—Phrase Perception (Variation) 271
Exercise 11C—Word Comprehension (Variation) 272
Exercise 11D—Word Comprehension (Variation) 273
Exercise 11E—Phrase Comprehension (Variation) 274
Exercise 11F—Phrase Comprehension (Variation) 275
More Practice Paragraphs—Inference 277
Words in Context 280
Theme for Reading Selections: Conflicts in Literature 280
Exercise 11G—Short Reading
"Amelia from *Vanity Fair,*" William Makepeace Thackeray 281
Exercise 11H—Short Reading
"Rebecca from *Vanity Fair,*" William Makepeace Thackeray 283
Exercise 11I—Long Reading
"The Sacrifice from *Vanity Fair,*" William Makepeace Thackeray 285

LESSON 12

Exercise 12A—Phrase Perception (Variation) 290
Exercise 12B—Phrase Perception (Variation) 291
Exercise 12C—Word Comprehension (Variation) 293
Exercise 12D—Word Comprehension (Variation) 294
Exercise 12E—Sentence Comprehension (Variation) 295
Exercise 12F—Sentence Comprehension (Variation) 297
Words in Context 298
Theme for Reading Selections: Interpreting Literature 298
Exercise 12G—Long Reading
"The People Next Door," Pauline C. Smith 299

HOMEWORK

Lesson 1	**How to Use the Dictionary**	**309**
Lesson 2	**Twenty Ways to Compliment Your Friends**	**315**
Lesson 3	**Twenty Ways to Insult Your Enemies**	**319**
Lesson 4	**Word Analysis: 20 Common Greek and Latin Roots**	**321**
Lesson 5	**20 More Greek and Latin Roots**	**327**
Lesson 6	**Even More Greek and Latin Roots**	**331**
Lesson 7	**Still More Greek and Latin Roots**	**335**
Lesson 8	**Prefixes**	**339**

Lesson 9	20 More Prefixes	343
Lesson 10	Suffixes:	
	25 Noun Suffixes	347
Lesson 11	Seven Verb Suffixes	353
Lesson 12	19 Adjective and One Adverb Suffixes	357

POSTTESTS

Comprehension and Rate Posttest 362
Vocabulary Posttest 366

APPENDIX

"The Process of Reading" 372
Checklist of Observable Clues to Vision Problems 374
Perceptual Drills 1–6 376
Personal Vocabulary List 381
Prefix/Root/Suffix List 382
Rate (WPM) Chart for Long Readings 388
Progress Chart—Short and Long Readings 391
Progress Chart—Pretests and Posttests 392

Preface

Reading Faster and Understanding More, Book II is an intermediate-level reading improvement workbook designed for the young adult or mature adult reader whose vocabulary and comprehension need to be improved. It is especially suited for a teacher-led group; however, it is self-instructional enough to be used for individual study in a learning center or at home.

This book is a revision of *Reading Faster and Understanding More* by Wanda Miller, Anne G. Dye, and Doris Flood Ladd, which was first published in 1976. It has grown out of the authors' collective experience teaching English and reading, from remedial to rapid reading, in public and private high schools, learning centers, and community colleges. We have drawn on our own and our students' reactions to different kinds of textbooks, workbooks, commercial kits, reading machines, and teacher-made materials. Like all reading instructors, we know that no single workbook or program answers every need. Nor can it, since the reading process is composed of dozens of factors, and every problem reader is a unique case.

Ideally, of course, each reader should receive individual diagnosis and prescription for his or her reading difficulties. Yet the reality is that much of our nonclinical instruction occurs in groups, whether small or large, and also, many reading problems are sufficiently common that they *can* be dealt with in groups.

Therefore, *Reading Faster and Understanding More,* Book II presupposes that in most cases students will move as a group through each Lesson (or chapter) during a class period. Also, the book focuses on two major reading skills—perception and comprehension—and attempts to train students in these thoroughly, paying some attention to developing *methods* of vocabulary building. (Rather than spread this workbook too thin, the authors recommend a supplementary vocabulary book.)

Distinguishing Features

The authors' goal for this book is to provide a well-organized, stimulating, and useful developmental reading workbook for both the teacher and the student. Besides its pragmatic acceptance of group teaching and the desirability of focusing on the most crucial reading skills, the design of *Reading Faster and Understanding More* is based on certain other premises that we feel are often ignored by other books:

1. This text is Book II in a series of three workbooks which introduces basic reading skills in the first book and progresses to 13th grade reading level in Book III. (Books I of the series is also in print. Book III is to follow.) These workbooks are designed with the same format so that they may be used concurrently in the same classroom.

Basic reading classes usually consist of students whose reading abilities vary as much as seven grade levels. There is a need to instruct and time these students simultaneously in group drills, yet at the same time accommodate the differing reading levels. The format of the *Reading Faster and Understanding More* series enables the instructor to combine the efficiency of group teaching with the individualization required by sound educational methods.

On the other hand, those teachers who prefer that all the students in the same classroom use the same book will find this series of three graded workbooks meets the need of the typical reading program: Book I can be used for an entry-level reading class, Book II for an intermediate level, and Book III for a higher level.

2. Another premise of *Reading Faster and Understanding More* is that most students, although they may have a low reading level, are nevertheless too informed and worldly-wise to be enthralled by reading material aimed at the preteen or 1950s teenager. Also, the student population in higher education, and therefore in reading classes (whether developmental or advanced), has changed dramatically in the last five years. Studies show an ongoing trend toward a higher percentage of mature adults in college—men and women returning to education; senior citizens; men and women who wish to or are forced to change jobs; and part-time, career-motivated young adults. These persons as well as teenagers may need to sharpen their reading skills, but neither group will be engaged by material designed for the adolescent. Rather, they express interest in mental and physical health, expanding roles of the sexes, discoveries in science, national leaders, even in the art of reading itself. The short and long reading selections in this book have been chosen to appeal to these adult interests.

3. Eye perception is a basic first stage of the reading process often ignored in reading instruction. A growing body of research by neurologists, optometrists, and others, much of it published within the last few years, points to undiagnosed perceptual disorders as a common cause of reading disability. Through special drills and suggestions for improvement, this workbook increases quick and accurate perception.

4. We have accepted the premise that timing *any* task improves the performer's concentration and efficiency. Furthermore, a time score provides the reader with a second indicator of progress besides the usual comprehension check. The majority of today's students are acutely aware of efficiency—they want to study and read more quickly in other courses, and they wish to learn *how* more quickly. Hence we have included timing instructions for all drills and reading selections. Any part of the book may be used for discussion or power (untimed) practice.

5. We believe that students are the final best critics of classroom lessons. They seldom miss an ambiguity, inconsistency, or self-defeating shortcut. Thus, most of the exercises have been field tested by the authors. We hope that we and our students have corrected most of the errors that all too commonly occur in this type of book.

Objectives for Students

1. to improve visual and perceptual skills;
2. to improve comprehension of phrases, sentences, and longer readings;
3. to gain flexibility in rate and technique through directed attack on various reading problems, from slow careful sentence analysis all the way to speeded techniques of skimming and scanning;
4. to create interest and enjoyment in the act of reading, by the use of carefully chosen, lively selections on adult topics (no platitudes from *Boys Life* or the Greater Boise Chamber of Commerce);
5. to provide useful techniques for vocabulary development (such as Greek and Latin roots, prefixes, suffixes; dictionary use; and contextual clues) while leaving intensive vocabulary study to supplementary books.
6. to offer directed reading in a variety of prose styles progressing from the literal to the affective doman.

Objectives for Instructor

1. to package the features listed above in one workbook, eliminating many supplemental texts, drills, handouts, and so on;
2. to ensure an adult interest-level in the comprehension exercises;
3. yet at the same time, to ensure an easy readability level (using Edward Fry's formula);
4. to provide twelve pre-planned Lessons, easily adaptable to the average 1 – 1½ hour class session, and to either the quarter or semester system;
5. to offer a compact instructor's manual with keys to homework exercises and tests to both Books I and II, a list of other reading software and hardware, and a graded guide to those materials.

Introduction

How to Use the Text

The most effective use of the text is to work through one entire Lesson (or chapter) in one continuous study period—either as a class or individually. We recommend that a class or individual work through each Lesson in the order of its arrangement.

The exercises may be timed independently or by an instructor. The answer keys to all the timed exercises are at the bottom of the page following each exercise. It will be necessary for the student to turn the page to see the key; this lessens the temptation to look before answering the questions.

The Homework sections in the back of the book are to be done outside of class. (The keys are in the teacher's manual.) Also, some untimed portions (such as discussion of the main idea, details, and inference) in several Lessons may require more careful and time-consuming study than can be accomplished during class time.

It is important for the student to take both the Pretests and the Posttests and to record the results of the Short and Long Readings in the Progress Charts in the Appendix. It is good positive reinforcement to see the improvement in skills.

General Description of Text

A helpful first assignment is to survey the Contents to see where you are going in the book and how you will get there. Now, if you surveyed the Contents well, you saw that each of the twelve Lessons begins with perception drills (for seeing more accurately). Most of the Lessons end with three timed prose readings; two of the readings are short (about 200 – 500 words); one of them is long (about 1000 – 2000 words). All the readings increase in length from Lesson to Lesson to provide a continuing challenge in speed. The drills are scored for time and errors; the readings are scored for rate (WPM) and percent comprehension.

The material in the twelve Lessons is organized according to two principles: (1) *repeated reinforcement,* and (2) a *progression from simple to complex.* Reinforcement operates within each Lesson; for example, a perceptual skill is introduced and practiced with suggestions following, then practiced again. The same is true for the comprehension skills: word, phrase, sentence, and longer prose comprehension is practiced several times. Reinforcement also operates throughout the book from Lesson to Lesson: most skills are picked up and repeated in several Lessons, rather than being dropped after one Lesson.

The second principle, progression from simple to complex, is seen within each Lesson. The reader begins with simple perception drills and goes on to perception plus comprehension in word, sentence, and longer reading exercises. It is also seen in the overall organization of the book: perception drills change from simple letter and word perception in Lesson 1 to the longer phrase drills in later Lessons. Reading skills range from reading for main idea to reading for details and for inferences, then on to skimming and scanning. As you progress through the book, you learn flexibility of purpose; that is, you learn to adapt your technique to the reading task.

Most of the later Lessons combine both reinforcement and growing complexity, leading to cumulative reading skills. The authors feel that the ultimate goal of any reading course or book is the intelligent, efficient reading of long expository selections. The various skills that go into this process can, of course, be taught more or less separately. However, it is logical to stress that they must be retained and made to operate together, in the final act of reading.

For example, while Lesson 2 introduces finding the main idea, *all* the following comprehension checks include one main idea question. Lesson 12 reinforces most of the earlier skills, while providing the challenge of interpreting literature. Since speed and comprehension are necessary for good performance, the book reminds students again and again that they must continue to use quick, accurate perception for all reading tasks.

The Lessons have an additional feature: the Short and Long Readings in each Lesson are grouped around the same general topic given in a brief Introduction preceding the reading selections in each Lesson. Too often, reading books ask the students to practice a new skill while expecting them to adjust their mental set every few minutes from one subject to another—hypnotism, grandma's pet cow, life in the year 3001 A.D., and so on. (This feature should interest any instructor who takes the "tune-in" aspect of the SQ3R method seriously.)

The Pretest and Posttest each have two parts. The first part is a Comprehension and Rate test. It is like one of the Long Readings and, in both Pretest and Posttest, is about some aspect of reading. The second part contains a Vocabulary test using words from the "Words in Context" sections, from the Word and Phrase Comprehension exercises, and from the Homework section (including some roots, prefixes, and suffixes).

The Homework sections have material on the dictionary, special vocabulary words, Greek and Latin roots, prefixes, and suffixes. (The answer keys to the Homework exercises are in the teacher's manual.) An additional aid to vocabulary is the "Words in Context," preceding the reading selections in each Lesson. They contain words from the readings that students might find difficult.

The Appendix has a discussion of the reading process, a rate table for the timed prose readings, a progress chart for the Short and Long Readings, supplementary perceptual drills, space for a personal vocabulary list, and a reference list of alphabetized prefixes, suffixes, and Greek and Latin roots.

Acknowledgments

Alexander, George. "Pain in the Neck is All in Your Head." Adapted from *The Los Angeles Times,* October 24, 1974. Reprinted by permission.

The American Heritage Dictionary of the English Language, paperback edition. Copyright 1969, 1970, 1973, Houghton Mifflin Company. Reprinted by permission of the publisher.

Angelou, Maya. Adapted by permission of Random House, Inc. from *I Know Why the Caged Bird Sings,* by Maya Angelou. Copyright 1969 by Maya Angelou.

Clemens, Samuel. From *The Mark Twain Autobiography,* edited by Charles Neider. Published by Harper & Row, Publishers, Inc.

Courlander, Harold. "The Descent From the Sky." From *A Treasury of African Folklore.* Copyright 1975 by Harold Courlander. Reprinted by permission of Crown Publishers, Inc.

Cox, Miriam. "The Creation of Man." From *The Magic and The Sword.* Copyright 1960. Reprinted by permission of Harper & Row, Publishers, Inc.

Dye, Anne. "How to Prepare for a Test," and "How to Take a Test—And Pass." Copyright 1976 by Winthrop Publishers, Inc. Reprinted by permission of the author.

Flagler, J. M. "I Was a Speed-Reading Dropout." Copyright Cowles Communications, Inc., 1969.

Fleming, Joyce Dudney. From "State of the Apes." Reprinted from *Psychology Today* Magazine. Copyright 1973 by the Ziff-Davis Publishing Company.

Goldberg, Herb. From *The Hazards of Being Male.* Nash Publishing Corporation, copyright 1977. Reprinted by permission of the author.

Gregory, Dick. "Track Star." From *Nigger: An Autobiography,* by Dick Gregory with Robert Lipsyte. Copyright 1964 by Dick Gregory Enterprises, Inc. Reprinted by permission of the publishers, E. P. Dutton & Company, Inc.

Guomo, George. "How Fast Should a Person Read?" Adapted from *The Saturday Review,* April 21, 1962. Copyright 1962 by the Saturday Review/World, Inc.

Haley, Alex. From *Roots.* Copyright 1976 by Alex Haley. Reprinted by permission of Doubleday & Company, Inc.

Houston, Jeanne Wakatsuki, and James D. Houston. From *Farewell to Manzanar.* Copyright 1973 by James D. Houston. Reprinted by permission of Houghton Mifflin Company.

Kearns, Doris. From *Lyndon Johnson and the American Dream.* Copyright 1976 by Doris Kearns. Reprinted by permission of Harper & Row, Publishers, Inc.

Keller, Helen. From *The Story of My Life.* Published by Doubleday, Page, & Company, copyright 1903.

Kesey, Ken. From *One Flew Over the Cuckoo's Nest.* Copyright 1961 by Ken Kesey. All rights reserved. Reprinted by permission of Viking Penguin, Inc.

Leslie, Jacques. "Tim Gallwey's 'Inner Game'," and "Baseball on My Mind." Used by permission of the author.

Mann, Peggy. From *Golda: The Story of Israel's Prime Minister.* Copyright 1971 by Peggy Mann. Reprinted by permission of Coward, McCann & Geoghegan.

O'Neil, Thomas. "The Migration of the California Grey Whale." Used by permission of the author.

O'Reilly, Jane. "Click!" Adapted from "The Housewife's Moment of Truth," by Jane O'Reilly. *Ms.* Magazine, Spring, 1972. Copyright, *Ms.* Magazine Corp.

"Research Debunks Old Myths About Mind's Decline." Adapted from *UCLA Monthly,* October, 1974. Reprinted by permission.

Smith, Jack. "Men's Liberation from Etiquette." Adapted from "Goodby Amy, Hello Jane," by Jack Smith. *Los Angeles Times,* September 12, 1972. Reprinted with permission.

Smith, Pauline C. "The People Next Door." Copyright 1952 by Grace Publishing Company, Inc.

Subak-Sharpe, Genell J. "Is Your Sex Life Going Up in Smoke?" Adapted from an article first published in *Today's Health,* August, 1974. Copyright 1974 by American Medical Association. As condensed in *Reader's Digest,* January, 1975.

Thomsen, Dietrick E. "The Day the Dam Burst." Adapted from *Science News,* October 19, 1974. Reprinted with permission from *Science News,* the weekly news magazine of science and applications of science. Copyright 1975 by Science Service, Inc.

Thurber, James. "The Unicorn in the Garden." Copyright 1940 by James Thurber. Copyright 1968 by Helen Thurber. From *Fables In Our Time,* published by Harper & Row, Publishers, Inc. Originally printed in *The New Yorker.*

Waters, Frank. "The Creation of the First World." From *Book of the Hopi,* copyright 1963 by Frank Waters. All rights reserved. Reprinted by permission of Viking Penguin, Inc.

West, Red; Sonny West; and Dave Hebler. "Elvis Presley's First Concert," as told to Steve Dunleavy. Published by Ballantine Books, a division of Random House, Inc. Copyright 1977 by World News Corporation.

Reading Faster and Understanding More

Pretests

COMPREHENSION AND RATE PRETEST

LENGTH: 1571

Read the following selection as rapidly as you can but with good comprehension. Wait for a signal from your instructor before you begin reading. (This reading should be timed.)

How Fast Should a Person Read?

George Guomo

It's probably useless to hope to talk sensibly any more about so-called speed reading. The extremists have overrun the field and, as usual, ridiculous statements and foolish misconceptions make good copy. Amidst the din, quieter voices go unheard.

The extremists of the left—using such effective platforms as television talk shows—tell us that we should be reading at ten thousand words a minute, fifteen thousand, twenty thousand. . . .

Their right-wing counterparts thunder back with equal irrelevance. George Stevens's piece in the August 26, 1961, issue of this magazine, entitled "Faster, Faster!" is typical. Why not, he suggests, keep reading faster and faster until we can read all of Gibbon's *Decline and Fall* over a cup of instant coffee?

Why not, one could suggest in turn, carefully train ourselves to read slower and slower until it takes us a minute to read a single word? We could then blissfully spend something like 21,000 solid hours—or 2,625 eight-hour days—reading *Decline and Fall.*

To some, not knowing their reading rate is a source of pride. They don't want to know. One's reading rate is God-given, and to measure or question it or, heaven forbid, to try to improve it, is blasphemy. The assumption, of course, is that everybody's reading rate is just dandy as it is. Perhaps. But the facts scarcely encourage such a carefree attitude.

At the other end of the scale, we have those whose pride springs from rates measured in rapidly multiplying tens of thousands. Bosh and foolishness, I say. Up in the rare heights of twenty or thirty thousand words a minute, a person is skimming, or surveying, or "getting the gist of the thing." But he isn't reading with anything resembling full or specific comprehension. With few exceptions most people cannot read effectively at much better than two thousand words per minute. Perhaps it would pay us to leave the extremes where they belong and look at the whole question realistically. The average adult, for instance, reads about 250 words a minute. This is also the average I've found among college freshmen. But the variations in my classes run from 125 to 900. This means that some students were reading over *seven* times as fast as others. There's probably an even greater spread among the general public.

All right, one is tempted to reply, some people are simply faster readers than others, as they may also be taller, fatter, or better looking. But speed itself does not tell the whole story. And no one except the figure-worshippers of the left and the figure-haters of the right is concerned with speed alone. What counts is a person's overall reading ability. But in this, speed plays an important and usually misunderstood part. Every reputable study has shown that reasonably fast readers perform not only as well as slower readers, but often better.

Probably the most common and groundless misconception about reading is the one that equates even moderate speed with sloppiness. Actually, the slow readers are the sloppy ones. They read aimlessly and passively and have more trouble concentrating than do faster readers. In addition, they do not understand as much, do not evaluate as well, and do not remember as effectively. The person who says he always reads slowly because he is being careful is just fooling himself. He is neither as careful nor as diligent as he likes to think. He is simply inefficient. He's driving along a smooth, clear highway in the same low gear he uses to get his car out of the mud.

The fast reader is fast because he is alert and skillful. He has been trained—or has trained himself—to use his ability and his intelligence effectively. Thousands of persons, including President Kennedy, have proved that such training is both possible and practical.

The methods used cannot be fully explained in a brief article, but they are based on sound principles and have been approved by many respected and conservative educators. More important, they have consistently worked. A person is taught, for instance, to read several words, or a phrase, or perhaps a whole line, at a single eye-stop, instead of making such a stop for every word.

A person with a rate of less than 250 words per minute almost always reads word by word. This method is so slow and inefficient that it actually hinders comprehension. In learning to read by meaningful word groups, a person enables his brain to function much closer to its capacity and almost invariably improves his comprehension.

No matter how hard some people try to ignore the fact, reading is a learned process, in which certain techniques operate more successfully than others. No one is born knowing how to read; he must be taught. He can be taught well or poorly. What most often happens, however—and this seems to be what the "slower, slower" people are fighting for—is that he is not taught at all. Left to his own devices, he typically develops a surprising number of bad reading habits, among which is the habit of reading too slowly for maximum comprehension or enjoyment.

The real issue here is not whether a person should or shouldn't read twenty thousand words a minute, or even whether he can or can't. The real issue is much more mundane than that, and much more important. It is whether the average person—now reading 250 words a minute—would not be a better reader in every way if he learned to read effectively at 600, 800, or a thousand words a minute. The evidence is quite convincing that he would.

A person whose rate is 250 words a minute is not only kept from reading well, but is often kept from reading at all. Let's take another look at *Decline and Fall.* At 250 words a minute, a person will take eighty-three hours to read it. How often does he, faced with such a task, simply decide he hasn't got time for it? Rightly or wrongly, this is often his decision, for he has only two alternatives: to spend eighty-three hours on it, or no hours.

And this brings us to an important and generally neglected point. In actual fact, a person does not have a single reading rate. He has—or should have—many rates. He should be able to read as fast or as slow as he wants, or as the situation warrants.

But all people have what can be considered a "base" rate—the rate at which they normally read more or less average material. It is from this base rate that they should speed up or slow down in accordance with the demands of the material.

However, the reader with a low base rate—around 250—rarely does this. He reads Shakespeare and Spillane at essentially the same pace. And even when he does try to shift gears, he isn't very successful. He can't get much faster because he's too unskilled, and he can't get much slower without coming to a dead halt.

The reader with a better base rate—say 800 words a minute—has a far broader range of differing speeds. He can easily move up to a thousand words or better for casual reading. And he can always slow down as much as he wants for studying, or for the reading of difficult or specialized material. The rapid reader is not a slave to speed. The slow reader *is* a slave to slowness.

Thus it's absurd to argue about "speed reading." The term is meaningless, because critics insist on interpreting it to mean that a person must read everything as fast as he possibly can. He must race headlong through Yeats and Milton and Donne and dash madly through *Moby Dick.* Quite the contrary. If a person learns his lesson well, he will not be limited in reading a good-sized novel to a choice of either no hours or ten hours. He can spend on it any number of hours in between. He can spend on it as much time and effort as he feels it deserves. More than that no writer, not Gibbon, nor Shakespeare, nor Spillane, can fairly ask of any reader.

Now, for the life of me I can't see why encouraging sensible reading techniques, and pointing out that most people read too slowly for satisfactory comprehension or appreciation, should be considered evil or anti-intellectual. Perhaps the explanation lies in the startling emotional investment most people have in their reading habits. Almost everyone who has worked in the field has noticed this. You can criticize a person's ignorance of arithmetic or spelling or sex or politics, but mention his reading techniques and immediately he's insulted. Good, bad, or indifferent, they're his and he loves them.

The whole question can really be put quite simply. If someone can prove to me that a reasonable increase in a person's reading rate causes disadvantages—such as loss of comprehension, or a lessening of that person's appreciation or enjoyment—I'll happily throw the whole business over and learn all the chants of the "slower, slower" crowd.

By the same token, I'd like to see these people agree that if a person *could* read faster—without any such losses, and usually with appreciable gains—then the increase in speed would be a desirable good, and worth working for.

This doesn't seem too much to ask. But the radicals will probably howl anyway.

TOTAL READING TIME _______

Immediately answer the questions below without referring to the selection.

1. Choose the statement that best expresses the main idea.
(a) People cannot read effectively when reading over 2000 words per minute.
(b) The average reading speed is 250 words per minute.
(c) Readers can be trained to read faster and more effectively.
(d) An increase in reading speed means a decrease in comprehension for most readers.

2. We can assume that the author disagrees both with the extremists who encourage speed reading and those who encourage slow reading. **T** **F**

3. One's reading rate, like a big nose, is God-given and should not be changed. **T** **F**

4. The author found that the college freshmen in his classes read at about the same speed—slow. **T** **F**

5. The fast reader usually comprehends more because he is alert and skillful. **T** **F**

6. The author recommends a base reading rate of
(**a**) 250 (**b**) 500 (**c**) 800 (**d**) 1000 words per minute.

7. The author suggests that most people are defensive about their reading habits. **T** **F**

8. Readers can read Shakespeare as fast and as effectively as they can read Spillane if they have trained properly. **T** **F**

Check your answers with your instructor. Then turn to page 388 to get your words per minute for this selection. Finally, record your scores below and on the progress chart on page 392.

WORDS PER MINUTE ______

% COMPREHENSION ______

Percentage Chart for Comprehension Check

Errors	0	1	2	3	4	5	6	7	8
% Right	100	88	75	63	50	38	25	13	0

VOCABULARY PRETEST

This test is made up of words taken from the Homework sections, Word Comprehension exercises, and Words in Context in this book. Since you have not yet begun to study these vocabulary words, you probably will not know as many as when you take the Posttest at the end of the book. You should then be able to score much higher. (Your instructor may want you to take this test in class using a separate answer sheet.)

A. Matching, 1–5

In the blank before each word, write the letter of the best definition.

______	**1.** synonymous	**(a)** servant
______	**2.** crevice	**(b)** young
______	**3.** juvenile	**(c)** prank
______	**4.** valet	**(d)** similar
______	**5.** caper	**(e)** crack

B. Short Definitions, 6–15

In the blank at the left, write the letter of the word that is being defined.

______ **6.** save
(a) finesse **(b)** pseudonym **(c)** seclude **(d)** salvage

______ **7.** cat
(a) wench **(b)** feline **(c)** amateur **(d)** oculist

______ **8.** rude
(a) surly **(b)** prominent **(c)** sufficient **(d)** oblivious

______ **9.** dictator
(a) physician **(b)** politician **(c)** tyrant **(d)** sultry

______ **10.** rubbish
(a) casualty **(b)** horde **(c)** delinquent **(d)** debris

______ **11.** overturn
(a) nominate **(b)** capsize **(c)** smudge **(d)** accumulate

______ **12.** guard
(a) sentinel **(b)** pedestrian **(c)** replica **(d)** scoundrel

______ **13.** therefore
(a) nevertheless **(b)** moreover **(c)** consequently **(d)** finally

______ **14.** sarcastic
(a) devious **(b)** formidable **(c)** snide **(d)** ornate

______ **15.** secret
(a) grotesque **(b)** boisterous **(c)** listless **(d)** cryptic

C. Context—Phrases, 16–30

In the blank at the left, write the letter of the best definition for the italicized word.

______ **16.** was *inexpressibly* glad
(a) can't be talked about **(b)** can't be described **(c)** inexcusably **(d)** obnoxiously

______ **17.** persisted in *confounding* the two
(a) forgetting **(b)** remembering **(c)** writing **(d)** confusing

______ **18.** due to old age or *senility*
(a) a serious disease **(b)** occasional forgetfulness **(c)** physical and mental weakness because of old age **(d)** giving up on life

______ **19.** grass and dirt that *evoke* the countryside
(a) are similar to **(b)** are different from **(c)** call to mind **(d)** are near to

______ **20.** *comparable* to the earliest combinations of children
(a) different from **(b)** similar to **(c)** bigger than **(d)** leading up to

______ **21.** a *proportionate* degree of reason
(a) balanced **(b)** sufficient **(c)** tremendous **(d)** small portion

______ **22.** to my everlasting *mortification*
(a) delight **(b)** amusement **(c)** embarrassment **(d)** anger

______ **23.** inside in that *squalor*
(a) miserable filth **(b)** small dwelling **(c)** dense forest **(d)** abandoned nursery

______ **24.** trying to *mediate*
(a) listen **(b)** make a fresh start **(c)** act quickly **(d)** help people reach an agreement

______ **25.** of super-*colossal* size
(a) frightening **(b)** insignificant **(c)** gigantic **(d)** colorful

______ **26.** can *divine* the meanings of all things
(a) foretell **(b)** soothe **(c)** hasten **(d)** forget

______ **27.** with an *impassive* stare
(a) showing no emotions **(b)** hostile **(c)** angry **(d)** deceptively sweet

______ **28.** in cartoon *imagery*
(a) lies **(b)** characters **(c)** designs **(d)** funny stories

______ **29.** in a *solicitous* tone
(a) expressing concern **(b)** hypocritical **(c)** sarcastic **(d)** harshly critical

______ **30.** so *guileless* and good natured
(a) smiling **(b)** simple **(c)** foolish **(d)** passionate

D. Context—Sentences, 31–40

In the blank at the left, write a *T* if the statement is true; write an *F* if the statement is false. (Emphasis is on the correct use of the *italicized* word rather than on facts.)

______ **31.** If you get *tangible* results from your efforts, you won't be able to see or feel those results.

______ **32.** A successful bank robber would probably feel *repentance* for his actions.

______ **33.** The dragon is a *mythical* beast.

______ **34.** Strong friendships are based on mutual *antipathy.*

______ **35.** A graceless dancer *lumbers* across the floor.

______ **36.** An inept *neurologist* could do a lot of damage to your garden.

______ **37.** Mules are known for their *obstinance.*

______ **38.** Because of our *infinite* nature, we must all one day die.

______ **39.** Their marriage is so *complacent* that they fight all the time.

______ **40.** He certainly is a *precocious* child; at eleven years old he still cannot tie his shoelaces.

E. Roots, Prefixes, and Suffixes—Matching, 41–50.

In the blank at the left, write the letter of the best definition for the root, prefix, or suffix.

Roots

______ **41.** ocul	**(a)** to lead
______ **42.** vers, vert	**(b)** eye
______ **43.** duc, duct	**(c)** earth
______ **44.** terra	**(d)** wishing, willing
______ **45.** volens	**(e)** to turn

Prefixes and Suffixes

______ **46.** arch-	**(a)**	one who (noun)
______ **47.** -esque	**(b)**	chief, principal
______ **48.** bi-	**(c)**	two
______ **49.** -cide	**(d)**	having the quality of (adj.)
______ **50.** -ster	**(e)**	killing (noun)

Check your answers with your instructor. Record your score below and on the progress chart on page 392 in the Appendix.

% CORRECT ______

Lesson 1

DIRECTIONS FOR LETTER PERCEPTION

These drills consist of a meaningless unit of letters on the left, followed by five units of letters on the right. The key unit is repeated once among the five groups printed at the right. Find the identical unit as quickly as you can and cross it out, as in the following example:

key unit

ist	ism	sti	~~ist~~	irt	tis

Continue until you finish all twenty-five items. Look up and your instructor will indicate your time in seconds.

Check your work for errors; then write your time and number of errors at the bottom of the drill.

Exercise 1A — Letter Perception

key unit

1. ane	ena	anc	ane	ame	nea
2. zle	zel	zle	sle	zlc	zte
3. wth	tmh	hwt	twb	wth	fwh
4. jec	ecj	cej	eci	ecy	jec
5. ick	kic	ikn	ihm	cik	ick
6. cor	ccr	cro	cor	ocr	roc
7. jub	yub	jup	jub	yup	buj
8. zex	zcx	zex	xez	sxe	exz
9. nas	nse	sen	nas	nza	nsa
10. qui	qrt	qin	qrt	qni	qui
11. dub	bdu	dbu	ubd	dub	bdv
12. pim	pin	pjm	piw	pim	bim
13. ocl	col	loc	lco	oel	ocl
14. sti	stj	sti	sfi	rti	ist
15. fre	fre	fpe	erf	feq	ref
16. dth	thd	thb	tdh	dth	dht
17. alk	blk	glk	pkl	kla	alk
18. bub	buz	bub	zud	sub	zub
19. ach	acb	ach	aeh	cah	aoh
20. gif	gif	igt	igf	iqf	igl
21. uey	uey	vey	wej	wey	yew
22. une	uui	enu	une	iuu	iui
23. ond	onb	onp	bno	dno	ond
24. sor	rso	srg	sro	srq	sor
25. ght	thg	hth	ght	hht	tth

TIME _______

ERRORS _______

HOW TO IMPROVE—LETTER PERCEPTION

Remember that these drills are not like reading. They are designed to help you see faster and more accurately. The letter units obviously have no meaning. So relax; let your eyesight do most of the work. React quickly to each unit as a whole. Develop an easy but accurate left-to-right eye motion along the line. Coordinate your marking hand with your eyes, and make a fast return sweep to the next item.

Don't say the letters to yourself, and don't examine other choices after you have located the answer. Expect to make a few errors. Trust yourself and your eyes. As you move through these exercises, your perception will become surer and your choices more accurate.

Exercise 1B—Letter Perception

key unit					
1. deg	beg	deg	daq	deq	ged
2. asm	asm	azn	azm	ezm	axm
3. bef	bet	beh	bed	bef	baf
4. nop	nop	ncp	mop	nob	nod
5. cix	ciz	oix	cxi	xic	cix
6. ver	wrv	ver	mvr	evr	rev
7. yul	yvl	uyl	yul	jul	ywl
8. ste	sle	sta	sfe	set	ste
9. ign	ign	igm	ing	jgn	gin
10. fas	faz	fes	tas	fas	has
11. hob	boh	hob	hcb	hod	hcp
12. ruw	rvw	rwu	ruw	wur	rum
13. kez	kex	kaz	kze	kcz	kez
14. que	qvy	quy	equ	que	qvj
15. jim	jim	ilm	jlw	jlm	jln
16. ine	ihe	ine	nie	ein	hne
17. ust	usf	uzt	usj	usl	ust
18. daf	abf	daf	adf	apf	edf
19. str	rts	trs	sto	str	sbr
20. ims	imr	inr	irm	jmr	ims
21. ish	shi	ist	ish	hse	sih
22. gea	gae	gac	ped	gca	gea
23. wie	wei	mie	wie	iwe	wic
24. oth	oht	ofh	cth	oth	olh
25. nex	ncx	nex	mcx	ucx	nxc

TIME ________

ERRORS ________

DIRECTIONS FOR WORD PERCEPTION

These drills consist of a key word on the left, followed by five words on the right. The key word is repeated once in the words at the right. Find the identical word as quickly as you can and cross it out, as in the following example:

key word

superb suburb super stupor barber ~~superb~~

Continue until you finish all twenty-five items. Look up and your instructor will indicate your time in seconds.

Check your work for errors; then write your time and number of errors at the bottom of the drill.

Exercise 1C — Word Perception

key word					
1. bedroll	bedrest	rollick	bedroll	bedrail	bedside
2. observe	obsess	observe	servant	obstruct	obscure
3. permit	permeate	permute	remit	permit	permissive
4. scream	screech	scratch	cream	screen	scream
5. unison	uniform	unison	union	universal	nestle
6. switch	switch	swatch	witch	swathe	watch
7. learned	leaven	earned	learned	leather	lectern
8. pupil	papal	puppet	pilfer	pupil	pulpit
9. turnspit	turnplate	turret	spittle	turnstile	turnspit
10. spindle	spinal	spindle	spindly	poodle	spinet
11. virtuoso	virtuoso	virtuous	virulent	riotous	virtual
12. rotation	rotary	nation	rotation	rotate	notation
13. whisker	whistle	skirt	whisper	whisker	whist
14. hustle	bustle	hustle	hurtle	hurried	nestle
15. aversion	avenue	aviation	version	average	aversion
16. cartilage	cartilage	cartridge	carriage	partition	cartwheel
17. devout	devour	devote	devout	evoke	devoid
18. foundry	founder	foundling	foundry	laundry	fountain
19. ulterior	interior	ulterior	ultimate	ulcerate	exterior
20. engrave	engrain	gravity	engrave	engross	enhance
21. glitter	litter	glister	blister	glitter	glimmer
22. pension	tension	pensive	pensioner	pennant	pension
23. queen	queen	queer	quench	twain	spleen
24. vesture	vestry	vesture	future	veteran	vestige
25. zealot	harlot	zebra	zealot	zero	jealous

TIME ________

ERRORS ________

HOW TO IMPROVE—WORD PERCEPTION

The letter perception drills have helped train you to react to size and shape rather than to meaning or sound. These word perception drills continue this training. You are not expected to know the meanings of the words, nor should you sound them out to yourself. This will only slow you down unnecessarily.

Of course slight changes in a word can affect the meaning. A *trail* is very different from a *trial,* and a *fiancé* is different from *finance.* But in actual reading, you see the word in context, and your brain usually makes the necessary corrections as you follow the thought of the sentence.

So do not be afraid of making errors. Do not go back to correct any errors. Do not linger over any word. Form a picture in your mind of the whole key word; then find the identical word as fast as possible.

Exercise 1D—Word Perception

key word					
1. blanket	blank	blanket	bland	strand	blankly
2. conviction	convection	victory	conviction	convention	convince
3. foliage	foliage	folio	folder	tollgate	folk
4. natal	natural	nation	fatal	natal	nasal
5. merely	mercy	surely	mercury	merrily	merely
6. jackal	jabbed	jacket	jackal	tackle	jackpot
7. party	partial	partly	party	poorly	rapidly
8. honor	honey	honor	honest	honed	boner
9. passion	fashion	passive	passerby	passion	passenger
10. shame	shame	sham	tame	shank	share
11. transcribe	transform	transcend	ascribe	transcript	transcribe
12. warlock	warhorse	warrant	warlock	locket	warpath
13. yokel	yodel	yoke	yogurt	token	yokel
14. gymnast	gypsum	gymnast	gypsy	nasty	gyrostat
15. hatchet	hatchway	hateful	patch	hatchet	hatter
16. jigger	jigger	jigsaw	trigger	jiggle	jiffy
17. manage	mangle	manacle	manage	marriage	mandate
18. obtuse	obtain	obtuse	obstruct	truck	obtrusive
19. quarrel	quarter	quarry	quartz	laurel	quarrel
20. slither	slipper	slinky	lithe	slither	sliding
21. amatory	amatory	amateur	tolerance	mature	amaze
22. billion	bilious	billiards	billion	million	billet
23. extortion	extrovert	extortion	external	contortion	exhortation
24. heathen	hearken	hearty	earthen	hearth	heathen
25. militia	military	malaria	lottery	militia	militate

TIME ________

ERRORS ________

DIRECTIONS FOR WORD COMPREHENSION

These drills are similar to the preceding perceptual drills. In these, however, you must also know the *meaning* of the words. Look at the key word on the left and comprehend its meaning. Next, quickly locate the *synonym,* or the word with the closest meaning, among the five words on the right. Then cross it out, as in the following example:

key word

man woman main boy ~~male~~ mail

Continue until you finish all twenty items. Look up and your instructor will indicate your time in seconds.

Check your work with the answer key on the bottom of page 22. (You must always turn a page to find the answer key.) Write your time and number of errors at the bottom of the exercise.

Exercise 1E—Word Comprehension

key word					
1. swerve	grow	turn	swear	question	allow
2. salvage	friendly	guess	save	different	family
3. quench	search	satisfy	wrench	write	thirst
4. slack	loose	lose	goose	limb	tight
5. fatigue	fang	rest	dangle	guest	tire
6. hoist	haul	foist	pearl	raise	lower
7. synonomous	reach	order	similar	ignorant	learn
8. rely	independent	depend	real	left	lie
9. gag	paper	rag	serious	smell	joke
10. depart	leave	arrive	deport	devil	partition
11. victor	vicious	veal	winner	vice	loser
12. site	study	place	still	movement	help
13. spry	dream	inactive	perfect	active	lead
14. nuisance	nestle	pest	helpful	seclude	whim
15. gigantic	huge	gentle	bribe	tiny	lost
16. anxiety	ancient	carefree	anger	hurl	fear
17. victim	visible	prey	threat	prevent	toss
18. submerge	dunk	itch	struggle	afflict	above
19. alias	alas	catch	pseudonym	finesse	benumb
20. ajar	awash	closed	mourn	open	bottle

TIME _______

ERRORS _______

HOW TO IMPROVE—WORD COMPREHENSION

These exercises are more complex than the perceptual drills. You are working to develop not only rapid eye movement and reaction, but also a quick grasp of meaning.

The exercise requires some familiarity with the key words and corresponding *synonyms* (words similar in meaning). However, do not agonize over a word you do not know; go on to the next item. Also, do not look for fine distinctions between synonyms. Look only for the one word that is closest in meaning.

As soon as you find the correct answer, go on to the next item. Trust your judgment. Don't waste time double checking with the other possible answers. Concentrate! Do not be distracted by *antonyms* (words opposite in meaning) or look-alike words. Use an active approach—know what meaning you are looking for. Do not wait passively for the meaning to occur to you.

Remember too that in English a single word may have several different meanings.

Example: The *bear* went into hibernation. (noun)
He will *bear* a large part of the cost. (verb)

No attempt has been made to confuse you, but keep your mind open to a definition other than the one you are more familiar with.

Note: The words in these exercises have been taken from a basic list of words appropriate to your reading level. It is important for you to know them. If you miss any item, circle both the key word and the correct answer for that item and enter both words in your "must learn" Personal Vocabulary List in the Appendix on page 381.

Answer Key: Ex. 1E
1. turn **2.** save **3.** satisfy **4.** loose **5.** tire **6.** raise **7.** similar **8.** depend **9.** joke **10.** leave **11.** winner **12.** place **13.** active **14.** pest **15.** huge **16.** fear **17.** prey **18.** dunk **19.** pseudonym **20.** open

Exercise 1F—Word Comprehension

key word					
1. excursion	trip	extreme	trite	exclaim	curse
2. boulder	rancid	bolder	mould	rock	holding
3. furious	first	angle	angry	great	pleasant
4. chef	chief	cook	cheese	felt	oven
5. amateur	amass	professional	mature	tourist	beginner
6. stench	wench	smell	inch	start	small
7. contrast	control	opinion	opposite	similar	cannon
8. pose	pretty	positive	hose	pretend	raid
9. suitable	appropriate	table	shined	adorable	unfit
10. sly	fly	slide	sort	snake	sneaky
11. fearless	fist	unafraid	afraid	feat	uncle
12. barren	fruitful	barrel	empty	bared	entire
13. assassinate	session	assign	nation	last	kill
14. shame	humiliate	share	humid	moisture	certain
15. revise	write	revel	reveal	modify	modern
16. starving	striving	starring	famished	fabulous	forest
17. physician	precise	doctor	physical	docile	deprive
18. seclusion	icicle	include	isolation	section	plume
19. purify	appeal	putrid	craft	ruin	cleanse
20. feline	lady	worst	mental	cat	omen

TIME ________

ERRORS ________

WORDS IN CONTEXT

The following sentences are taken from the reading selections in this Lesson. They contain words that may be new to you. This exercise introduces them now so they will not slow you down while you read the selections.

Without using your dictionary, try to determine the meaning of each word in **boldface** print. Choose the meaning below that best fits the context—the way it is used in the sentence or phrase.

Short Reading 1G

1. The dress I wore was lavender taffeta . . . it sounded like crepe paper on the back of **hearses.**
   (a) horses **(b)** girls dressed up for church **(c)** an old-fashioned buggy **(d)** a vehicle for carrying a dead body

Short Reading 1H

2. It was the first time I had ever had a chance to tell anything on him, and I was **inexpressibly** glad.
   (a) can't be talked about **(b)** can't be described **(c)** inexcusably **(d)** obnoxiously

Long Reading 1I

3. Have you ever been at sea in a dense fog, when it seemed as if a **tangible** white darkness shut you in?
   (a) invisible **(b)** brilliant **(c)** able to be touched **(d)** imaginary
4. When I finally succeeded in making the letters correctly, I was **flushed** with childish pleasure and pride.
   (a) embarrassed **(b)** glowing from excitement **(c)** tired **(d)** on the verge of tears
5. Earlier in the day we had had a **tussle** over the words "m-u-g" and "w-a-t-e-r."
   (a) struggle **(b)** joke **(c)** exercise **(d)** agreement
6. Miss Sullivan had tried to impress it upon me that "m-u-g" is mug and that "w-a-t-e-r" is water, but I persisted in **confounding** the two.
   (a) forgetting **(b)** remembering **(c)** writing **(d)** confusing

Answer Key: Ex. 1F
1. trip **2.** rock **3.** angry **4.** cook **5.** beginner **6.** smell **7.** opposite **8.** pretend **9.** appropriate **10.** sneaky **11.** unafraid **12.** empty **13.** kill **14.** humiliate **15.** modify **16.** famished **17.** doctor **18.** isolation **19.** cleanse **20.** cat

7. In the still, dark world in which I lived there was no strong **sentiment** or tenderness.
(a) wrong-doing **(b)** feeling **(c)** power **(d)** gloom

8. Then my eyes filled with tears; for I realized what I had done, and for the first time I felt **repentance** and sorrow.
(a) sadness **(b)** happiness **(c)** repetition **(d)** regret

Check your answers with the key on the bottom of the next page.

THEME FOR READING SELECTIONS: LOOKING BACK

The two Short and one Long Readings that follow are taken from three autobiographies. The three famous authors are from different backgrounds but had the same kind of growing pains we all have had. Maya Angelou, also a well-known performer, tells about being a black girl growing up in a small Southern town in the days before she learned Black is beautiful. Mark Twain was a nineteenth century author from a small town in Missouri. Helen Keller, a celebrated writer who also grew up in the nineteenth century, relates a key episode from her life that helped her overcome her blindness and deafness. The three excerpts are about their feelings of being different when they were children.

Imaginary Situation

You will be able to concentrate better when you read if you have a particular purpose for reading something. It helps even more to have a personal interest in what you're reading. This is hard to do in an unnatural situation like doing timed readings in a classroom. This reading situation is not typical of how you will be reading most of your life.

To help you tune in to the reading selections in each Lesson, you will be given an imaginary reading situation. Put yourself mentally in that situation before you start reading. Your pretended purpose may become a reality someday.

To prepare yourself for these readings, pretend that you are at home in an easy chair reading about people who fascinate you. Think about what you already know about them, and make a connection between their feelings about growing up and your own.

DIRECTIONS FOR SHORT READINGS

Read the following short selections rapidly. Try to finish in one minute and still understand as much as you can. When the minute is up, circle the number to the right of the last line read. This number is your total words read per minute (wpm).

Immediately go on to the four questions below the selection, and underline the correct answer. Occasionally, there will be bonus questions; they need not be counted in your comprehension percentage. Turn the page and check your answers with the key on the page following the questions. If you made an error, review the reading to find the correct answer.

Then record your words per minute and percent correct at the bottom of the exercise.

Answer Key: Words in Context
1. (d) **2.** (b) **3.** (c) **4.** (b) **5.** (a) **6.** (d) **7.** (b) **8.** (d)

HOW TO IMPROVE—SHORT READINGS

In these exercises, practice reading whole phrases at a glance. Read for ideas, not for single words. If you find you still think of each word separately, or move your lips, you are reading word-by-word. As a result, you will have difficulty reading more than 150–200 words per minute. Turn to page 376 in the Appendix for additional drills in using your peripheral vision (what you can see around the point of focus) and in widening your eye span. Many readers find it helps to focus on the space just above the line of print (or to practice on the dots printed in the later phrase exercises). Try to speed up your rate, even if you miss a few words or details.

Note that question 1, marked with a circle ○, deals with the main idea of the selection. Sometimes question 2 will ask for inference and be marked with a triangle △. Questions 3 and 4 usually deal with details related to the main idea. When you read, you will be able to follow the writer's thought better if you find the main idea as quickly as possible and relate additional information and details to it.*

In all of the short readings try to read faster and faster while making fewer errors.

Exercise 1H—Short Reading

Try to read the following selection in one minute.

from *The Autobiography of Mark Twain*

Samuel Langhorne Clemens

WPM
My mother had a good deal of trouble with me, but I 12
think she enjoyed it. She had none at all with my brother Hen- 25
ry, who was two years younger than I. I think that the unbro- 37
ken monotony of his goodness and truthfulness and obedience 45
would have been a burden to her but for the relief and variety 58
which I furnished in the other direction. I was a tonic. I was 71
valuable to her. I never thought of it before but now I see it. I 86
never knew Henry to do a vicious thing toward me or toward 98
anyone else—but he frequently did righteous ones that cost me 109
as heavily. It was his duty to report me, when I needed report- 122
ing and neglected to do it myself. He was very faithful in dis- 133
charging that duty. 136
[Once I had an opportunity to report Henry.] Henry 145
never stole sugar. He took it openly from the bowl. Mother 156
knew he wouldn't take sugar when she wasn't looking, but she 167
had her doubts about me. Not exactly doubts, either. She knew 178
very well I *would*. One day when she was not present Henry 190
took sugar from her prized and precious old-English sugar 199

*For a discussion of different types of organization, see "Retaining Details" in Lesson 4.

bowl, which was an heirloom in the family. And he managed to 211
break the bowl. It was the first time I had ever had a chance to 226
tell anything on him, and I was inexpressibly glad. I told him I 239
was going to tell on him but he was not disturbed. 250
When my mother came in and saw the bowl lying on the 262
floor in fragments, she was speechless for a minute. I allowed 273
that silence to work; I judged it would increase the effect. I was 286
waiting for her to ask, "Who did that?"—so that I could fetch 299
out my news. But it was an error of calculation. When she got 312
through with her silence she didn't ask anything about it. She 323
merely gave me a crack on the skull with her thimble that I felt 337
all the way down to my heels. Then I broke out with my in- 350
jured innocence, expecting to make her very sorry that she 360
had punished the wrong one. I expected her to go something 371
remorseful and pathetic. I told her that I was not the one—it 384
was Henry. But there was no upheaval. She said, without emo- 395
tion, "It's all right. It isn't any matter. You deserve it for some- 407
thing that you are going to do that I shan't hear about." 418

Mark the number of words read (or the number to the right of the last line read). Then immediately answer the questions below without referring to the selection.

1. The mother's attitude toward the author is one of
   (a) suspicion. **(b)** trust. **(c)** pride. **(d)** hatred.

2. The two brothers loved each other too much to report on each other's misdeeds. **T** **F**

3. Henry broke the sugar bowl. **T** **F**

4. The mother apologized to her son for punishing him unjustly. **T** **F**

Check your answers with the key on the bottom of page 32, and record your scores below and on the progress chart on page 391.

WORDS PER MINUTE ______

% COMPREHENSION ______

Answer Key: Ex. 1G
1. (d) **2.** T **3.** T **4.** F

HOW TO IMPROVE—LONG READINGS

The suggestions for these exercises are similar to those for "How to Improve—Short Readings." But the Long Readings present specific challenges: (1) to concentrate for longer periods of time, and (2) to follow a main idea through more complicated development. We have helped you "tune in" and concentrate by grouping the readings in each Lesson around roughly one general subject.

As you work through the book, be alert to the principles of reading being stressed.

Again, increase your speed with each Long Reading. Read faster and faster, and don't regress (or reread).

Note: As in the Short Readings, the circle symbol ○ is used for questions involving main idea, and the triangle symbol △ for questions involving inference.

Answer Key: Ex. 1I
1. (c) **2.** T **3.** F **4.** F **5.** T **6.** F **7.** T **8.** T

Lesson 2

Exercise 2A—Word Perception

key word					
1. geology	geography	geometry	geology	radiology	genuflect
2. pickle	picked	pickup	nickle	pickle	picket
3. repellent	repealer	repellent	excellent	repentant	replicate
4. extrovert	extrovert	extricate	extravagant	convert	expletive
5. glide	gilt	slide	glade	gild	glide
6. notation	nation	ovation	notation	vacation	notional
7. scurry	scurvy	scurry	curry	scruffy	scuffle
8. financial	fineness	pension	finagle	financial	finality
9. hayrick	hayrick	hayrack	rickets	haywire	hayseed
10. metaphor	metaphase	euphoric	metamorphic	meteor	metaphor
11. kidney	kindle	kinder	hinder	kidnap	kidney
12. generic	genesis	generic	genetic	regenerate	general
13. hamster	sterile	hamper	hamster	hammer	handler
14. cricket	cricket	ricket	crinkle	critic	crinkly
15. breadth	breach	bread	break	breadth	reach
16. appeal	appear	pealed	appall	appeal	appease
17. flotation	rotation	flotation	flotsam	notation	fluoridated
18. grumble	humble	crumble	grunter	grunion	grumble
19. wastrel	waster	wasteful	wastrel	minstrel	wassail
20. sprig	sprig	spring	string	prig	sprite
21. expert	expiate	expire	expense	expert	spurt
22. beagle	beadle	beagle	legal	beacon	beaker
23. retort	retired	torte	retort	retract	restored
24. totality	mobility	torture	focal	locality	totality
25. electric	eclectic	laxative	efficient	effective	electric

TIME ______

ERRORS ______

Exercise 2B — Word Perception

key word					
1. graduate	gradient	graduate	radiator	gradual	radical
2. equality	equalize	quality	equality	equal	qualify
3. mean	middle	men	main	mean	level
4. sensation	soaring	sore	sensitive	sensible	sensation
5. tactile	tactile	traction	attractive	track	contact
6. politic	pompous	pills	politic	politician	radical
7. whip	which	whip	whit	hipster	wick
8. penalty	penalize	purify	legality	penalty	petrify
9. approve	prove	applaud	poverty	approval	approve
10. leopard	lioness	partner	leopard	jeopardy	lizard
11. revenue	revenue	reveal	avenue	renew	revel
12. exalt	exit	exalt	solid	excite	salt
13. dreariness	dearness	nearness	harness	dreariness	dreadful
14. anyone	someone	known	anybody	annoy	anyone
15. origin	original	rigorous	origin	orifice	artificial
16. titillate	titular	titillate	titled	scintillate	stifle
17. quaint	quantity	saint	quality	quandary	quaint
18. borough	borough	borrow	thorough	brought	through
19. paragon	paragraph	antagonize	parallel	paragon	paraffin
20. shipboard	overboard	shiftless	shipboard	shipment	shipbuilder
21. territory	terrible	territory	tertiary	terror	terse
22. hypocrite	hypnosis	critical	hypodermic	hypothesis	hypocrite
23. rejoin	rejoice	revolve	joint	rejoin	join
24. vermin	vermin	vernal	verbal	ermine	vertical
25. wealth	weal	weasel	wealth	worthy	health

TIME _______

ERRORS _______

DIRECTIONS FOR PHRASE PERCEPTION

These drills consist of a key phrase on the left, followed by five phrases on the right. The key phrase is repeated once among the five phrases on the right. Find the same phrase as quickly as you can and cross it out, as in the following example:

key phrase			
bed rest	red vest	best vest	dead bird
	~~bed rest~~	led there	

Continue until you finish all twenty items. Look up and your instructor will indicate your time in seconds.

Check your work for errors. Then write your time and number of errors at the bottom of the page.

Exercise 2C—Phrase Perception

key phrase			
1. prepared for	program for	four pastels	prepared for
	a peppercorn	perfect day	
2. those flowers	rose bowers	those flowers	these fingers
	florid nose	that flourish	
3. does need	red toes	those weeds	did bleed
	does need	do lead	
4. to be as	to see us	to breach	have been to
	are being as	to be as	
5. our own	our own	four gowns	on loan
	are grown	down on	
6. first year	third gear	white yeast	yellow bird
	fine dear	first year	
7. also ran	also ran	false run	sole reason
	unfair ruse	ran also	
8. my turn	his churn	my turn	too stern
	slow burn	to discern	
9. has enjoyed	joyful noise	have rejoiced	has enjoyed
	pass underneath	joyous pastime	
10. practical joke	radical plan	heavy yoke	praying jockey
	practical joke	hockey player	

11. as you are	are you as at your arm	you are as as you are	your orange
12. for rent	for rent fourth dent	poor recital formal retort	recent file
13. last week	very meek few weeds	last week fine beads	lost wine
14. is new	as new will win	as few is him	is new
15. their car	they're here that war	are there their car	this tar
16. about noon	about nine about noon	nice abbot not able	almost abate
17. onto the floor	out the door under the flower	into the flour on the foyer	onto the floor
18. near home	rear tire her mother	home free neither one	near home
19. empty mug	empty mug extant bug	dug into much exercise	entry rug
20. demand more	reprimand him more sand	demon rum demand more	mandatory act

TIME ________

ERRORS ________

HOW TO IMPROVE—PHRASE PERCEPTION

Like the Letter and Word Perception drills, these exercises require you to react to the size and shape of the phrase *as a whole,* not as separate letters or words. The exercises are designed to widen your eye span and get you used to longer units of print.

If you find yourself reading each word in a phrase separately, try focusing on the dot above each phrase. You should be able to see the entire phrase through your peripheral vision, without moving your eyes. If you cannot, turn to the Peceptual Drills in the Appendix for additional help in increasing your eye span.

Soon you will be able to see, perceive, and think in phrases, and eventually to read faster and more intelligently. These drills can help you cross the gap between reading word-by-word and reading phrases and ideas.

Exercise 2D—Phrase Perception

key phrase			
1. rock singer	rock salt rock song	rock singer jam session	jazz singer
2. up a creek	sip a coke in a creel	sup on cake in a crack	up a creek
3. over the hill	over the hill under the hill	into the hat out of the hill	took the pill
4. the bird nest	the brown nest the third nest	the red vest the bird nest	the best word
5. good reader	good reading good and ready	book reader red goods	good reader
6. having shot	have a shot hearing shots	having shots having shot	having pots
7. dirty glass	dirty grass dirt and grass	dirty glass tidy glasses	dusty glass
8. loud noise	crowd noise louder noises	loud voice loud noise	long nose
9. fast foods	finest foods fast foods	first foods fasten hoods	fresh food
10. bad news	sad news better news	bad news cat mews	bad and new

11. hungry dog	hunted dog hungry dog	hunting dog greyhound dog	hungry god
12. bright shirt	bright shorts eight shirts	right shirt bright shirt	bright shift
13. high heels	high peals tight heels	high heels high hills	higher heels
14. lift weights	lift weights weigh the lifts	lose weight lost weight	lifting weights
15. for a price	four prices for a price	for the rice from a price	found a price
16. a hard course	a heavy course a hard curse	a hard cause have a course	a hard course
17. a dream house	a daydream house a dread house	a dream horse a dream house	a dreary house
18. foreign leader	friendly leader frightful leader	fleeing leader foreign leader	foreign reader
19. traffic jam	traffic cop traffic in jam	traffic jam mad traffic	trifling jam
20. go to court	gone to court good, a court	go to count go to court	go to the coast

TIME ________

ERRORS ________

Exercise 2E—Word Comprehension

key word					
1. stylish	clothes	fashionable	sock	wicked	dated
2. clad	clod	form	clothed	closet	undressed
3. era	time	mistake	enter	routine	wreck
4. venture	venal	squirrel	denture	try	cliff
5. aware	snare	adorn	wear	oblivious	alert
6. acute	pretty	scissors	roar	dull	sharp
7. bliss	bent	joy	sadness	blend	horn
8. humane	cruel	weird	slack	kindly	humble
9. prominent	promenade	noticeable	aroma	permit	obscure
10. tyrant	discourse	semblance	dictator	rural	affection
11. crave	carve	devil	crass	desire	view
12. accurate	incorrect	right	acorn	render	account
13. puncture	toured	paralyze	touch	plunder	hole
14. altitude	alcove	trite	height	hope	hinder
15. appropriate	affected	inappropriate	suitable	administer	geared
16. absurd	about	blank	serious	drudge	foolish
17. sufficient	recall	enough	scant	locate	sustenance
18. crevice	crack	wobble	place	home	crest
19. blunder	pence	desist	mistake	blotter	clod
20. dismay	joy	diligent	volt	grief	physic

TIME ______

ERRORS ______

Exercise 2F—Word Comprehension

key word					
1. apologize	criticize	rules	excuse	respect	unique
2. conflict	peaceful	clash	speed	across	different
3. basic	eye	black	manipulate	paisley	primary
4. disposition	chowder	chops	tendency	dissenter	return
5. distinguished	dizzy	divulged	notified	excellent	pennant
6. situated	border	located	conform	torn	exuberant
7. pillar	column	pumpkin	division	mirage	wheedle
8. policy	insurance	death	proceeds	taxes	course
9. criticize	lead	gonad	evaluate	emulsify	glue
10. customary	decay	gong	sugar	usual	rarely
11. alteration	ambush	fight	borrow	change	extreme
12. apparent	gifted	obvious	invisible	marvel	father
13. allegiance	mission	unfaithful	flag	bind	loyalty
14. brittle	crisp	peanut	fragile	soft	brusque
15. balk	magazine	cooperate	stop	gyrate	banquet
16. climax	brake	penal	winter	high point	clement
17. snarl	dog	usage	entry	snail	tangle
18. moderate	relent	middle	costly	wheeze	stare
19. majority	honest	remote	over half	clincher	mob
20. melancholy	gloomy	disease	canteloupe	flag	brain

TIME _______

ERRORS _______

FINDING THE MAIN IDEA

What do we mean by a *main idea* in writing? It is a general statement about the topic of the paragraph, article, chapter, or book.

So, first of all, you must know what the topic is: for example, "Vitamin A," "Talking to Your Plants," or "Television in the 1970s." Second, you must discover what main point the writers are making about their topic. Examples:

> "Vitamin A is essential for normal bone growth, vision, and skin."
> "Plants are sensitive to sound."
> "The 1970s have seen a rise in high quality movies made expressly for television."

These are examples of the *main idea* statement that gives more information about the topic and introduces the article.

Announcing a topic is much like the introductory words of a comedian who, with a little bow, says, "Now I'm going to do a skit about bicycle clubs." He may or may not go on to state his main point about bicycle freaks, but, as you watch the skit unfold, you soon realize what it is. "They go in for special costumes," perhaps, or "They are a snobbish bunch."

Like the entertainer, writers usually state their topic at the beginning, often in the title. Writers of a textbook—non-fiction, explanatory, informative prose—usually state their main idea about the topic at the beginning of the unit. For example, the topic of this section is announced in the title "Finding the Main Idea," and the main point is stated in the second sentence of the first paragraph. Whether you are reading a paragraph or a whole chapter, 70 to 90 percent of the time you will find the main idea(s) at the beginning. The rest of the time you will find it in the middle or end of the unit. Sometimes it is stated at the beginning, then repeated in a conclusion or summary at the end.

In a short unit like a paragraph, the main idea may be clearly stated in a *topic sentence.* In a longer work such as an essay, article, speech, or textbook chapter, the main idea is usually called a *thesis.* And a one- or two-sentence statement of that main idea is a *thesis statement.* Sometimes, of course, the writer does not conveniently provide you with a topic sentence or thesis statement. Then you must infer, or judge, from the details or organization just what the main point is.

Answer Key: Ex. 2E
1. fashionable **2.** clothed **3.** time **4.** try **5.** alert **6.** sharp **7.** joy **8.** kindly **9.** noticeable **10.** dictator **11.** desire **12.** right **13.** hole **14.** height **15.** suitable **16.** foolish **17.** enough **18.** crack **19.** mistake **20.** grief

Answer Key: Ex. 2F
1. excuse **2.** clash **3.** primary **4.** tendency **5.** excellent **6.** located **7.** column **8.** course **9.** evaluate **10.** usual **11.** change **12.** obvious **13.** loyalty **14.** fragile **15.** stop **16.** high point **17.** tangle **18.** middle **19.** over half **20.** gloomy

Whether stated for you or implied, the main-idea statement is like an umbrella. It covers all the details, but does not introduce any new ones. The other sentences in the paragraph function as supporting details, developing or holding up the main idea.

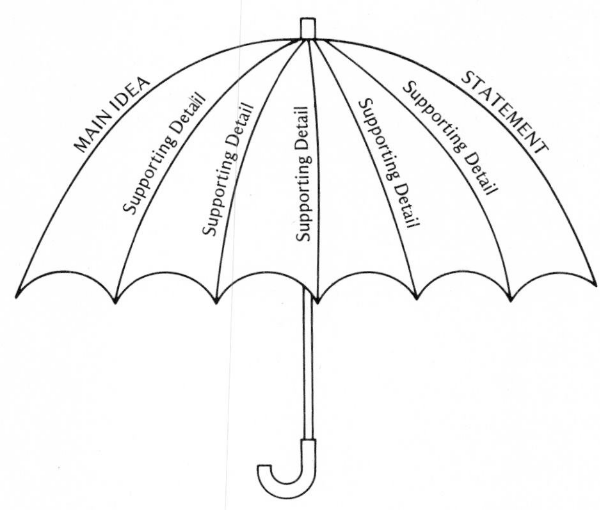

Finding the main idea in your reading is probably the first and most essential skill. Yet most readers have more trouble with this skill than they do with others, such as understanding and remembering colorful details. This skill is the key to increasing understanding and speed because once you have that main idea in mind, everything that follows seems to click into place. You see the parts (details, minor points, inferences, and so on) in relationship to the whole (main idea). In every reading selection in this book you will be asked to locate the topic and the main idea before anything else. Main idea questions are marked with a circle: ○.

PRACTICE PARAGRAPHS—MAIN IDEA

Read the following paragraphs to find, first, the topic or subject being discussed. Second, find the writer's main idea about that topic. Remember that the main idea is not always stated clearly in one sentence. After answering the questions for each paragraph, check with the key on the bottom of the next page.

A. (1) I have a friend who will go to any lengths to achieve what she calls Total Beauty. (2) Three years ago, when she first moved to Los Angeles, land of many Total Beauties, she had rhinoplastic surgery (a nose job). (3) She had a distinctive Roman nose that perfectly suited her rather long, thin face. (4) Now she has a cute little snub nose which seems to belong to someone else's cute little pixie face. (5) Last year she decided she must have Inner Peace to achieve Outer Beauty. (6) She, in turn, immersed herself in Transcendental Meditation, Yoga, EST, Bio-

Energetics, and Biofeedback. (7) She became so peaceful, as a result, that she lost her high pressure sales job—thereby suspending funds for other important beauty projects like facials and manicures. (8) Finally, this year she abandoned Inner Peace to look like Farrah Fawcett-Majors, one of the media's favorite sex kittens. (9) She tortured her lovely, shiny, straight brown hair through two permanents (the first wasn't curly enough), a bleaching, and a streaking. (10) Her fine hair overreacted, and she appears most of the time these days with a colorful peasant scarf over her frizzled blond Afro. (11) If the fashion this summer calls for a tranquil snub-nosed gypsy with yellow Brillo-pad hair, she is definitely *in*.

1. What is the general topic of the paragraph? ____________________
2. In your own words, what is the main idea about this topic? (State the idea in a complete sentence.) ____________________

   ____
3. Is the main idea stated in a topic sentence? ______

   If so, what is the number of the sentence? ______

B. (1) What is good driving technique? (2) It means that one must avoid jackrabbit starts, high rpm bursts, and panic stops, all of which waste gasoline. (3) The Automobile Club of Southern California tests prove that hard acceleration uses as much as one-third more gas than easy acceleration. (4) Also remember that every time you use the brakes, you're using energy that was supplied by the engine. (5) This, in effect, wastes gas.*

1. What is the general topic of the paragraph? ____________________
2. In your own words, what is the main idea about this topic? (State your idea in a complete sentence.) ____________________

   ____
3. Is the main idea stated in a topic sentence? ______

   If so, what is the number of the sentence? ______

C. (1) One effective treatment for the sharp, crippling pain of migraine headaches has been biofeedback training. (2) This kind of headache is often set off by too much flow of blood to the brain. (3) Doctors teach patients to divert the extra blood flow to the hands. (4) An instrument that is very sensitive to temperature changes is attached to the patient's hand. (5) As more blood flows to the hand, the temperature rises. (6) The instrument emits higher and higher sounds. (7) Patients have learned to increase blood flow to the hands enough to raise the temperature ten

*Adapted from "20 Ways to Better Gas Mileage." John Fuchs," *Motor Trend Magazine* (Feb., 1974).

degrees in two minutes. (8) As this happens, the migraine is headed off. (9) At the Menninger Foundation in Kansas, researchers have helped 75 percent of the migraine patients they first treated with this method.*

1. What is the general topic of the paragraph? ______________________

2. In your own words, what is the main idea about this topic? (State your idea in a complete sentence.) ______________________

____

3. Is the main idea stated in a topic sentence? ______

If so, what is the number of the sentence? ______

D. (1) The oldest living thing on earth is now considered to be the bristle-cone pine tree. (2) Through carbon dating and patterns of tree-ring growth, scientists have established that some of these trees date from as long ago as 4500 B.C. (3) This means an incredible 6500 years of continuous life. (4) The few remaining bristle-cones are found in a narrow range of elevation and area, in the White Mountains of California just east of Bishop. (5) The dry cold air of this region has preserved these impressive old trees, which pre-date the pyramids of Egypt, Western civilization, and indeed all of written language and history. (6) The only danger to their existence is air pollution, which is spreading from California cities, and people's collecting habits. (7) Some bristle-cones have been cut down, or have had pieces removed to decorate a fire-place or wet bar.

1. What is the general topic of the paragraph? ______________________

2. In your own words, what is the main idea about this topic? (State your idea in a complete sentence.) ______________________

____

3. Is the main idea stated in a topic sentence? ______

If so, what is the number of the sentence? ______

E. (1) Self-hypnosis can lessen social fears such as excessive shyness, nervousness, awkwardness and even fear of flying. (2) It not only helps people shed fat, improve their eating habits and sleep more soundly. (3) It can also help cure more serious habits such as smoking, alcoholism and drug abuse. (4) Further, doctors have successfully used it as an anaesthesia for patients during dental work, childbirth, and certain operations where the patient must remain conscious. (5) Self-hypnosis is indeed a powerful tool that reminds us that mind and body are one.

*Adapted from "Biofeedback: Teaching Your Body to Heal Itself," John J. Fried, *Family Health* (Feb., 1974).

1. What is the general topic of the paragraph? ____________________
2. In your own words, what is the main idea about this topic? (State your idea in a complete sentence.) ____________________

____

3. Is the main idea stated in a topic sentence? ______

If so, what is the number of the sentence? ______

Check the answer key on the bottom of page 52.

WORDS IN CONTEXT

Without using your dictionary, try to determine the meaning of each word in **boldface** print. Choose the meaning below that best fits the context—the way it is used in the sentence.

Short Reading 2G

1. In the cases where the older person's mind really seems to decay, it is not necessarily a sign of decay due to old age or **senility.**
(a) excellent health **(b)** occasional forgetfulness **(c)** weakness in body and mind because of old age **(d)** giving up on life

Short Reading 2H

2. Many techniques, including **biofeedback,** hypnosis, and yoga, could be used to control tension.
(a) a machine hooked up to the body and feeding back information about physiological responses **(b)** a well-paying job **(c)** a method of transcending earthly concerns **(d)** a mild drug

Long Reading 2I

3. The carbon-monoxide intake reduces the blood oxygen level and impairs **hormone** production.
(a) a sexual attitude **(b)** related to the female reproductive system **(c)** a drug causing male characteristics in females **(d)** a chemical substance formed by one organ and carried to another that it affects

4. "If you're short of breath, tired, perhaps suffering from **vascular** disease complicated by smoking, then you're not going to feel much like engaging in sex.
(a) spots on the skin **(b)** excessive coughing **(c)** system of vessels for carrying blood **(d)** a condition caused by the white blood cells destroying the red

5. What sperm he did produce were sluggish—displaying low **motility.**
(a) intelligence **(b)** ability to reproduce **(c)** motion; movement **(d)** color quality

6. "There is some strong evidence that smoking mothers have a significantly greater number of unsuccessful pregnancies due to stillbirth and **neonatal** death."
(a) before birth **(b)** a newborn infant **(c)** after birth **(d)** false labor

Check your answers with the key on the bottom of the next page.

THEME FOR READING SELECTIONS: FEELING GOOD

The theme gives you a hint that the readings in this Lesson have something to do with your body—and your mind. The selections stress that a happy, healthy body goes along with a happy, healthy mind. The first article debunks the popular belief that senility has to accompany old age. The next reading comments on the power of the mind to control tension.

Imaginary Situation

Like most everyone else in the country, you've decided to join the quest for a sound mind in a sound body. You've picked up some popular magazines from the newsstand and decided to see what the current thinking is about the subject. As you read, you're looking for the main point of each article.

Exercise 2G—Short Reading

Try to read the following selection in one minute. (Remember to look for the topic sentence expressing the main idea.)

Research Debunks Old Myths About Mind's Decline

WPM

Many of us believe that a person's mind becomes less 10
active as he grows older. But this is not true, according to Dr. 23

Answer Key: Practice Paragraphs—Main Idea

A. **1.** my friend's pursuit of Total Beauty **2.** My girlfriend will try anything to become beautiful. **3.** Yes (1) [All the other sentences are examples illustrating the point made in (1).]

B. **1.** how to drive to save gas **2.** Economical driving means avoiding sudden stops and starts and racing the motor. **3.** Yes (1) and (2) [Either sentence by itself is too limited for a topic sentence.]

C. **1.** biofeedback training for migraines **2.** Biofeedback has been effective in treating migraine headaches. **3.** Yes (1) [Sentence (2) explains how migraine headaches work. Sentences (3) through (8) explain how biofeedback works. And sentence (9) gives statistics about the method's success.]

D. **1.** the bristle-cone pine tree **2.** These trees are the oldest living things—plant or animal—on earth. **3.** Yes (1) [This sentence is the only general, comprehensive sentence in the paragraph.]

E. **1.** advantages to self-hypnosis **2.** Self-hypnosis can be helpful in both physical and emotional problems. **3.** Yes (5) [All the other sentences are too limiting to be topic sentences.]

Answer Key: Words in Context

1. (c) **2.** (a) **3.** (d) **4.** (c) **5.** (c) **6.** (b)

Lissy F. Jarvik, professor of psychiatry at the University of Cali- 34
fornia, Los Angeles, and a board member of the New Center 44
for Aging at the Veterans Hospital. She has studied the mental 55
functioning of aging persons for several years. For example, 64
one of her studies concerns 136 pairs of identical twins, who 75
were first examined when they were already 60 years old. As 86
Dr. Jarvik continued the study of the twins into their 70s and 98
80s, their minds did not generally decline as was expected. 108

However, there was some decline in their psycho-motor 117
speed. This means that it took them longer to accomplish men- 128
tal tasks than it used to. But when speed was not a factor, they 141
lost very little intellectual ability over the years. In general, Dr. 152
Jarvik's studies have shown that there is no decline in knowl- 163
edge or reasoning ability. This is true not only into the 30s and 175
40s, but into the 60s and 70s as well. 184

As for learning new things, and ability to remember, 193
studies by Dr. Jarvik and others show that the old are equal to 206
the young. It is true that older people themselves often com- 217
plain that their memory is not as good as it once was. However, 229
much of what we call "loss of memory" is not that at all. There 243
usually was incomplete learning in the first place. For example, 253
the older person perhaps had trouble hearing, or poor vision, 263
or inattention, or was trying to learn the new thing at too fast a 277
pace. 278

In the cases where the older person's mind really seems 288
to decay, it is not necessarily a sign of decay due to old age or 303
"senility." Often it is simply a sign of a depressed emotional 314
state. This depression usually can be counteracted by counsel- 323
ling, therapy with a psychologist, or medications which fight 331
depression. 332

In American society, when an older person loses some- 341
thing, we tend to call him or her "senile." But notice that when 353
a younger person loses something, he does not blame it on se- 365
nility or loss of memory. He finds some other excuse! 374

Mark the number of words read (or the number to the right of the last line read). Then immediately answer the questions below without referring to the selection.

1. According to Dr. Jarvik's studies, middle-aged and older persons should expect to
(a) remember less. **(b)** reason better. **(c)** learn fewer new things. **(d)** lose little ability to remember, reason, or learn.

2. Both younger and older persons should realize that senility or mental decay due to aging is much less common than most of us believe. **T** **F**

3. A long-term study of 136 pairs of twins showed that the only factor which declined over the years was psycho-motor speed. **T** **F**

4. Usually, what appears to be depression is really senility. **T** **F**

Check your answers with the key on the bottom of page 56, and record your scores below and on the progress chart in the Appendix.

WORDS PER MINUTE ______

% COMPREHENSION ______

Bonus Question

The title expresses the main idea for the reading selection. **T** **F**

Note: The key to this extra question (and to those in following Short Readings) is on the bottom of page 56. These extra questions need not be included in the comprehension score.

Exercise 2H—Short Reading

Try to read the following selection in one minute. (Remember to look for the topic sentence expressing the main idea.)

Pain in the Neck Is All in Your Head

George Alexander

WPM

The busy executive who makes a phone call with his fists 11
clenched unconsciously and the secretary who types with her 20
knees pressed together tightly are suffering from the same 29
problem. They both have tension caused by too much use of 40
muscles not really involved with their tasks. 47

Speakers this weekend at the first meeting of the Ameri- 57
can Association for the Advancement of Tension Control kept 65
making the same point. The damaging effects of tension are 75
caused by the tensing of extra muscles for a long time. They 87
stressed the belief that tension starts with the brain's giving 97
commands to tense muscle bundles throughout the body. In 106
short, that pain in your neck is all in your head. 117

The speakers pointed out that people can create their 126
own headaches, backaches, high blood pressure, as well as 135
other ailments linked to tension. By the same token, they could 146
also be the agents of their own recovery. Many techniques— 156
including biofeedback, hypnosis, and yoga—could be used to 165
control tension. Most tension control techniques are based on 174
the belief that all behavior is learned and can be unlearned. 185

Dr. Edmund Jacobson, an eighty-six-year-old Chicago 194
physician, has an approach that involves simple exercises. At 203
first the patient uses only the big muscles in the arms and legs. 216
He learns to recognize the presence and the absence of tension 227
in those muscles. He then learns to concentrate on relaxing the 238
muscles until all the signs of tension are gone. Those who use 250
this method say they can get rid of tension even in the small 263
muscles around their eyes. They simply close their eyes for a 274
few minutes and relax the muscles at will. 282

One speaker, Charles Beach, a doctoral candidate at 290
Michigan State University, described tension control tech- 297
niques for athletes. He has worked for the past few years with 308
Los Angeles Dodger pitching star, Mike Marshall. Beach said 317
that an athlete needs some tension to compete well. Yet he 328
went on to make the point that the tensing of muscles not di- 341
rectly needed to hit or throw a baseball can keep an athlete 352
from playing well. Choking the bat can be one result of too 364
much muscular tension. 367

Beach discussed a tension control program that he and 376
Marshall ran. The high school athletes who completed the 385
program reported that while they might not perform any bet- 395
ter, they could block out crowd noises and get rid of butterflies 406
in their stomachs at crucial times. "So they didn't make herky- 417
jerky motions taking a foul shot in the last few seconds of 430
a basketball game," Beach points out. He further states that 440
herky-jerky motions are nearly always the result of too much 451
muscular tension. 452

Mark the number of words read (or the number to the right of the last line read). Then immediately answer the questions below without referring to the selection.

1. Tension can be controlled through
(a) strenuous exercise. **(b)** herky-jerky movements. **(c)** learning to find and then relax the tense muscles. **(d)** taking tranquilizers.

2. The speakers at the meeting suggest that tension can cause headaches, backaches, and high blood pressure. **T** **F**

3. Tense behavior is learned and can be unlearned. **T** **F**

4. Hypnosis is useless in controlling tension. **T** **F**

Check your answers with the key on the bottom of page 58, and record your scores below and on the progress chart in the Appendix.

WORDS PER MINUTE ______

% COMPREHENSION ______

Bonus Question

Is the second sentence or the last sentence the topic sentence for the second paragraph? ______

Exercise 21—Long Reading

LENGTH: 1332

Read the following selection as rapidly as you can but with good comprehension. (Remember to look for the sentence expressing the main idea.) Wait for a signal from your instructor before you begin.

Is Your Sex Life Going Up in Smoke?

Genell J. Subak-Sharpe

A large number of doctors are convinced that there is a link between smoking and sex. One of them is Alton Ochsner, a seventy-six-year-old senior consultant to the Ochsner Foundation Hospital in New Orleans. His views were twenty-four years ahead of the Surgeon General's report on the dangers of smoking. Dr. Ochsner described, on the basis of observing patients, a cause-and-effect relationship between heavy cigarette smoking and lung cancer. The same kind of clinical proof has convinced him that cigarette smoking can be dangerous to one's sexual health.

Ironically, he says, he is much more successful in convincing patients to stop smoking because of dangers to sexual health than because of more serious threats. "It has been estimated," Dr. Ochsner says, "that tobacco use kills about 360,000 people a year in this country alone. Yet people go right on smoking. But when I tell them that tobacco may have an adverse effect on their sexual activities, they suddenly take notice."

Dr. Ochsner likes to tell about a seventy-three-year-old man, a heavy smoker for forty-five years, who had a lung abcess removed. "I told him he had to stop smoking, so he did. Two months later, the lung had healed completely. Before he stopped smoking, he told me, he'd had sexual relations once every four to six months. Now it's three or four times a week."

More support comes from Joel Fort, M.D., director of San Francisco's Center for Solving Special Social and Health Problems. This center helps people both to overcome the cigarette habit and to deal with sexual problems. Dr. Fort automatically counsels smokers who complain of impotence to enroll in

Answer Key: Ex. 2G
1. (d) **2.** T **3.** T **4.** F (T)

the center's stop-smoking clinic. The overwhelming majority of men who do so, says Dr. Fort, report their sex lives markedly improved. He gives the same advice to women who complain of lack of interest in sex.

Dr. Fort thinks that smoking impairs sexual performance in two primary ways. (1) The carbon-monoxide intake reduces the blood oxygen level and impairs hormone production. (2) The nicotine intake shrinks the blood vessels. It is the swelling of the blood vessels that is the central mechanism of sexual excitement and erection.

Dr. Fort also cites secondary effects of heavy smoking. Lung capacity is reduced, cutting back on the ability to "last" during intercourse. Also, nicotine discolors the teeth and taints the breath, reducing the smoker's sexual attractiveness.

Only a few scientific studies of the relationship between smoking and sexual capabilities have been undertaken, however. Two Paris researchers, Dr. H. Cendron and J. Vallery-Masson, published a study of the effects of age, tobacco and other factors on male sexual activity. They took 70 men, 45 to 90 years old. The men were divided into two groups: 31 who smoked one or more packs a day, and 39 who either were nonsmokers or consumed fewer than five cigarettes a day. Slightly more than half the men had reported a decline in sexual activity between the ages of 25 and 40. "On this sample," the research team reported, "there is a significant difference between the smokers and non-smokers. Sexual activity between ages 25 and 40 decreased more often in the first group than in the second group."

Notes one physician: "If you're short of breath, tired, perhaps suffering from vascular disease complicated by smoking, then you're not going to feel much like engaging in sex. But if a patient stops smoking, increases his exercise and starts feeling more fit, his sexual interest and ability may improve too."

Such was the case with Ken Farrell. He was worried about a marked decline in his sexual capabilities. "I keep reading about guys in their 70s who are still going strong," he confided to his doctor. "And here I'm having trouble at 31!" He was smoking four packs a day when he finally consulted a doctor. The doctor found him underweight, but with nothing seriously wrong. "He advised me, though, to quit smoking, or at least to cut down," Farrell says. "About the same time I enrolled in an exercise program." In three months, Farrell reduced his smoking—to about ten cigarettes a day—and gained 15 pounds. He found himself much happier with both his health and his sex life.

Dr. Ochsner hopes that today's emphasis on sex will spur more scientific interest in studying the effects of smoking on sexual response. "The ironic thing," says Dr. Ochsner, "is that many men don't recognize they have a libido problem until after they quit smoking, and then they realize what they've been missing. It just seems sad to wait until you're 73 to make this discovery."

Also under consideration is the effects of smoking on fertility. One of the pioneer researchers in the field is Carl Schirren, M.D., a professor at Hamburg University, Germany. He studied fertility patterns in nearly 5000 men and reports that "no firm conclusions" can be drawn about smoking and male infertility. But he did observe "severe disturbances of sperm motility" in a group of men who smoked.

"A possible connection between their childlessness and the sperm damage by nicotine was made clear to these patients," Dr. Schirren reports. "And if they stopped smoking entirely, within six to ten weeks a considerable improvement in sperm motility resulted." He contends that "in every case of reduced male fertility, smoking should cease completely if children are desired."

Other studies tend to confirm this. For example, noted Australian biochemist Michael Briggs has found that heavy smoking does indeed lower testosterone (male sex hormone) production. Even more important, he found that hormone levels increase if smoking is stopped.

This happened in the case of Paul Conrad. He and his wife, Linda, had been married six years. Ever since their third anniversary Linda had gone from doctor to doctor in a vain attempt to discover why "we can't seem to have a baby." Finally, Paul agreed to be tested too. His examination turned up a normal level of the male hormone but a low sperm count. What sperm he did produce were sluggish—displaying "low motility." Then his doctor learned that Paul smoked three packs of cigarettes a day and had been a heavy smoker for 15 years. He advised the would-be father to stop smoking and return in three months for more tests.

Paul was doubtful, but he did kick the habit. When he was retested, there was marked improvement in sperm count and motility. Four months later, Linda was pregnant.

The evidence that women's smoking may affect ability to bear healthier children is more conclusive—and damning. Take Patricia Lansing, a chain smoker since high school. Her first pregnancy seemed normal, although her doctor did urge her to cut down from her four packs a day. Her baby was born dead, full-term yet more than two pounds lighter than normal nine-month babies. Patricia was understandably shattered.

Then she read a summary of a 1973 Surgeon General's

Answer Key: Ex. 2H
1. (c) **2.** T **3.** T **4.** F last

report, *The Health Consequences of Smoking*. One sentence jumped out at her: "There is some strong evidence that smoking mothers have a significantly greater number of unsuccessful pregnancies due to still-birth and neonatal death." "That statement was like a knife stabbing me," she remembers.

It would be almost impossible to prove that Patricia's smoking was responsible for her baby's death. But statistically, women who smoke run a far greater risk of a tragedy like Patricia's than do nonsmokers. Says the 1973 Surgeon General's report: "On the average, the smoker has nearly twice the risk of delivering a low-birth-weight infant as that of a nonsmoker." Such undersized infants run a higher risk of sickness and death than do larger babies.

On the brighter side is evidence gathered from a study of nearly 17,000 pregnancies in Britain. It suggests that women who give up smoking by the fourth month of pregnancy may avoid the risks to their babies. "The most damage from smoking comes in the second half of pregnancy," explains Joseph Warshaw, M.D., Director of the Yale University division of prenatal medicine. "I would advise any pregnant woman to stop smoking," he adds.

The potential harmful effects of smoking on fertility, childbirth, and sex life are worrisome. Again, data are skimpy, but many sex counselors and drug researchers are convinced, from personal observations, that a relationship exists.

TOTAL READING TIME ______

Immediately answer the questions below without referring to the selection.

1. Choose the answer that best completes the main idea. Although it has not been proven beyond any doubt,
- **(a)** smoking reduces the smoker's sexual attractiveness because it discolors the teeth and taints the breath.
- **(b)** some doctors believe that smoking can be damaging to one's sexual capacity, fertility, and ability to bear healthy children.
- **(c)** men are not sexually attracted to women who smoke.
- **(d)** smoking is the major factor in the decline of sexual performance.

2. Many patients seem more concerned about the effect smoking has on sexual health than on more serious health problems. **T F**

3. The 73-year-old man who stopped smoking had a decrease in his sexual performance. **T F**

4. The swelling of the blood vessels plays an important part in sexual performance. **T F**

5. There is little evidence to support the claim that a woman who smokes has less chance of bearing a healthy baby. **T** **F**

6. One solution for a man with the problem of sperm with "low motility" is to drink plenty of liquids. **T** **F**

7. Dr. Carl Schirren, M.D., is thoroughly convinced that smoking affects male fertility. **T** **F**

8. According to Dr. Warshaw, the most damage to babies from smoking mothers comes in the second half of pregnancy. **T** **F**

Check your answers with the key on the bottom of the page. Then turn to the Rate Chart in the Appendix to get your words per minute for this selection. Finally, record your scores below and on the progress chart in the Appendix.

WORDS PER MINUTE ______

% COMPREHENSION ______

Bonus Question

Which sentence in the first paragraph is the topic sentence for that paragraph and also is the main idea statement for the entire selection? ______________

Percentage Chart for Comprehension Check

Errors	0	1	2	3	4	5	6	7	8
% Right	100	88	75	63	50	38	25	13	0

Answer Key: Ex. 21
1. (b) **2.** T **3.** F **4.** T **5.** F **6.** F **7.** F **8.** T first or last

Lesson 3

Exercise 3A—Phrase Perception

key phrase					
1. to save gas	to have gas	to wave past	two saved gas	to give gas	to save gas
2. control pollution	central pollution	central pollution	controlled pollution	control pollution	controlled pullout
3. owning a car	owning cars	our own car	owning a car	owing a car	the owner's car
4. slow driving	slow driver	slow drivers	sloe gin	slow driving	slow drive
5. a seat belt	a neat belt	a seat below	a seat belt	seat belts	a near belt
6. car pool	car pooling	cat stool	car full	car pool	careful
7. pedal travel	petal travel	pedal travel	pedal traveled	better travel	pedal drag
8. careful driver	careful of driving	careful driver	carful of drivers	careful diver	scared of driving
9. radial tires	radial tires	radically tired	radial tire	radially tried	radical tire
10. make and model	make a model	make and mode	make and yodel	make and model	maker's model
11. a popular item	a populous item	a people's item	a popular item	a poplar stem	a popular mite
12. having overdrive	having overhang	having overdriven	have a hangover	having overdrive	having overdone
13. lower rpm	lower rim	lower rdm	lower rip	lower rpm	slower rpm
14. air filter	air flyer	air filter	fair filter	hair filter	air flight
15. natural resource	national resource	natural resources	nature's resource	natural resource	nocturnal resource
16. harmful emissions	harmful omissions	harmful emissaries	harmless emissions	armful of emissions	harmful emissions

17. wasting energy	wasteful energy washing energy	waste energy wasting energy	wasting energies
18. use the brakes	abuse the brakes use the brake	fuse the brakes using brakes	use the brakes
19. road tested	toad rested road tests	rod tested road tested	road testing
20. camping trip	camper truck camping trip	camping tent coming trip	camper rip-off

TIME ______

ERRORS ______

Exercise 3B—Phrase Perception

key phrase			
1. six swimming swans	swat six swans swim six seas	six sweet sins sick, sour swine	six swimming swans
2. this covered wagon	these costly wigs the wistful cat	this covered wagon those wiggling children	that wagging dog
3. the dripping faucet	the file cabinet the dripping faucet	the worst fault the faucet drips	the ripped garment
4. downfall of man	failure of men downfall of man	fall of women fallen down man	many funny clowns
5. a clean ashtray	a clean ashtray ashes and dust	clear an aisle a green rash	a betrayed clod
6. gangster movie	big motorcycle gang his padded shoulders	picture of mother moving the house	gangster movie
7. smokefilled lungs	lunge for more smokefilled lungs	dreadful smog smoked cigar	broken filling
8. polka-dot bikini	yellow dotted bikini polka band	polka-dot bikini skinny dotted bikini	dance the polka
9. down narrow streets	downed glass of water straight and narrow	marrow of bones down narrow streets	deft right turns
10. dance a jig	dance a jig a jagged edge	a rigged dance eat a fig	a fancy jig
11. in slow motion	in slow motion a big commotion	inside the track a solvent business	an insolent action
12. a crossword puzzle	never a cross word a crossword puzzle	a jigsaw puzzle a gross error	a puzzling word
13. handle with care	careful handling a careworn man	handle with care a dandy car	a hot handle
14. put to sleep	a sleazy slut do not weep	but not there see the hut	put to sleep
15. cook your goose	your cooked goose cook your goose	goose your crook work your geese	cupful of gin
16. pray for peace	four peaceful prayers for Pete's sake	pans of pears pray for peace	prey on people

17. win the war	war to win the winning war	win the war twin warriors	the won war
18. the lost letter	the lost letter the bitter dregs	the better lot the left leader	the rested girl
19. tread on me	thread my needle Fred and me	read this too tread on me	one dread night
20. rip it across	cross the rip rap the cross	trip it across plow the crop	rip it across

TIME ________

ERRORS ________

Exercise 3C—Word Comprehension

key word					
1. eliminate	relate	omit	evict	modify	enliven
2. function	misbehave	arrest	work	fold	nation
3. diminish	lighten	increase	polish	report	lessen
4. juvenile	young	gay	energetic	senile	delinquent
5. caress	hug	serene	lather	stroke	avoid
6. doubtless	final	sure	maybe	late	pure
7. portray	carry	hinder	picture	stretch	persist
8. tremor	soprano	treat	thief	quake	solitude
9. intent	ideal	addition	teepee	courage	purpose
10. versus	around	against	apart	along	before
11. sultry	sad	hot	ridiculous	heavy	cold
12. rehearsal	practice	morgue	auditorium	stage	realty
13. identify	intend	gather	recognize	plead	ignore
14. myth	mistake	tale	storm	radar	truth
15. nominate	elate	number	select	minimum	attain
16. debris	wind	abode	jewels	soil	rubbish
17. uncanny	useless	close	narrow	strange	ordinary
18. endorse	include	recommend	complete	need	contain
19. capsize	raise	reject	overturn	comment	shape
20. casualty	victim	origin	guilt	reduction	hope

TIME _______

ERRORS _______

Exercise 3D—Word Comprehension

key word					
1. rustic	rusty	rural	unusual	sophisticated	urban
2. gesture	joker	notice	movement	smile	stillness
3. scoundrel	villain	poet	search	lover	hero
4. obstacle	glass	attachment	nail	moment	barrier
5. singe	opera	burn	relish	mow	quench
6. wretched	frightening	joyous	miserable	crowded	alone
7. horde	crowd	dwelling	horn	solo	duty
8. divorce	abandon	weld	encourage	separate	harm
9. smudge	demolish	smear	confer	envy	survive
10. agile	aged	brittle	aisle	necessary	nimble
11. sullen	perky	sinister	sulky	native	smart
12. decade	ten	fifty	two	hundred	thousand
13. mortal	human	mild	wound	cruel	lengthy
14. adolescent	adult	lawyer	heroine	teenager	leader
15. accumulate	leave	realize	acquire	flatter	argue
16. transmit	lend	question	debate	relax	send
17. perturb	peal	please	disturb	terrify	gorge
18. relent	yield	furnish	lease	terminate	attack
19. pedestrian	writer	spectator	swimmer	walker	athlete
20. sentinel	politician	guard	soprano	doctor	representative

TIME ______

ERRORS ______

DIRECTIONS FOR PHRASE COMPREHENSION

These drills consist of a key phrase on the left, followed by five phrases on the right. Look at the key phrase and think of its meaning. Next quickly locate the phrase with similar meaning among the five on the right. Then cross it out, as in the following example:

key phrase

unusual story | ~~strange tale~~ | weird book | bad lie | common event | ugly day

Continue until you finish all twenty items. Look up and your instructor will indicate your time in seconds. Check your work with the answer key on page 70. Finally, write your time and number of errors at the bottom of the exercise.

Reread your errors to see if you have a pattern of poor perception or poor comprehension. For instance, do you consistently omit one important word in a phrase? Do you substitute look-alike words? Do you pay attention to only the first or the last word in a phrase? Try to correct your bad habit in the next exercise.

Exercise 3E—Phrase Comprehension

key phrase

1. going places | stationary life | moving train | packed suitcase | great people | traveling about
2. large painting | painted door | cold lard | soft pillow | big picture | polished car
3. sour fruit | celery stick | ripe fig | bitter lemon | stale bread | fresh flowers
4. engraved name | grave man | carved letters | entire story | smooth table | happy game
5. common mistake | constant pressure | misty weather | mental illness | ordinary error | unusual blunder

Answer Key: Ex. 3C
1. omit **2.** work **3.** lessen **4.** young **5.** stroke **6.** sure **7.** picture **8.** quake **9.** purpose **10.** against **11.** hot **12.** practice **13.** recognize **14.** tale **15.** select **16.** rubbish **17.** strange **18.** recommend **19.** overturn **20.** victim

Answer Key: Ex. 3D
1. rural **2.** movement **3.** villain **4.** barrier **5.** burn **6.** miserable **7.** crowd **8.** separate **9.** smear **10.** nimble **11.** sulky **12.** ten **13.** human **14.** teenager **15.** acquire **16.** send **17.** bother **18.** yield **19.** walker **20.** guard

6. torn pages	painful torment wet newspaper	soiled book ripped paper	worn chain
7. quick snooze	long sleep awful nightmare	frozen peas almost awake	short doze
8. quiet place	silent spot loud party	quick reply last resort	evil person
9. thick book	trick cigar short poems	fat volume big sticks	thin blood
10. earnest endeavor	earned wages deviled ham	nest egg hard task	serious attempt
11. to tumble	to raise up to fall	to run fast to jump	to halt
12. reverse order	revealing picture blank verse	additional pardon backward position	forward march
13. thorough review	careful re-examination rough times	through rivers critical remark	three views
14. nice compliment	simple complaint safe companion	pleasant praise obvious contrast	sharp insult
15. extra money	additional income silver and gold	exact examination counterfeit dollars	copper coins
16. to differ strongly	two different opinions to run backwards	too strange to wrestle angrily	to disagree forcefully
17. having a frolic	a sad occasion expensive folly	playing tricks engaging in merriment	foaming water
18. solve a problem	mend a tear find a solution	make a statement ask a question	inquire inside
19. total cost	more money crafty salesman	complete price bigger portion	cheap clothes
20. very appropriate	out in the cold full moon	recently shown doesn't fit situation	fits in most cases

TIME _______

ERRORS _______

HOW TO IMPROVE—PHRASE COMPREHENSION

These phrase-reading exercises add another building block to your reading skills. Perceptually, they give you more practice in widening your eye span. Intellectually, they require you to process rapidly an idea formed by several words. English is a phrasal language; reading by phrases is the last step before reading entire sentence units.

Search only for the phrase closest in meaning to the key phrase. Stop when you find it, and go on to the next item. As in the Phrase Perception exercises, focus only once per phrase, preferably on the dot above the phrase. Continue the sweeping eye movement and active search for meaning.

Notice that the phrases tend to get longer in later Lessons. Continue to perceive (see with understanding) each phrase at one glance, just as you perceived the single words and shorter phrases in earlier drills.

Exercise 3F—Phrase Comprehension

key phrase			
1. entire story	devious lie tired blood	complete tale realistic passage	inside story
2. unusual error	common mistake casual greeting	strange manner sure footing	weird blunder
3. being troubled	wrinkled face very worried	horror movies deny angrily	frightened look
4. obvious contrast	obscure thought plainly opposite	constant pressure vain attempt	clear similarity
5. according to plans	as arranged plain speaking	cordless instrument partial plate	haphazard action
6. horrible dream	dreamless sleep rapid transit	awakened early situation comedy	bad nightmare
7. brief encounter	countless millions lengthy day	short meeting unpleasant remark	new breed
8. vacuumed rug	vast holdings valiant deed	dirty floor clean carpet	firm cushion

Answer Key: Ex. 3E
1. traveling about **2.** big picture **3.** bitter lemon **4.** carved letters **5.** ordinary error **6.** ripped paper **7.** short doze **8.** silent spot **9.** fat volume **10.** serious attempt **11.** to fall **12.** backward position **13.** careful re-examination **14.** pleasant praise **15.** additional income **16.** to disagree forcefully **17.** engaging in merriment **18.** find a solution **19.** complete price **20.** fits in most cases

9. shorn head	shearing sheep close haircut	selfish child smoking gun	headless rider
10. desolate field	dissolved pill fellow traveler	lonely area crowded place	late friend
11. funny comedian	silent movie curtain call	runny nose blooming rose	comic actor
12. having courage	being brave small noise	feeling cowardly raving maniac	listening carefully
13. captured criminal	capsule summary enraptured fan	caught crook electric chair	law officer
14. seeming calm	easily excited appearing serene	open seam shallow water	callow youth
15. sorrowful expression	sad look expressive hands	mournful tale filled glass	full house
16. smelling trouble	smart trucker skinned nose	sniffing brandy expecting problems	sweet aroma
17. feeling satisfied	satisfaction guaranteed being content	fried pies silent house	uneasy peace
18. vast wasteland	broken mast wasted moment	endless emptiness welcome oasis	distant mirage
19. finished project	famished person famous star	left undone working hard	completed job
20. smooth sailing	easy to handle red sails	romantic swoon rough water	overturned boat

TIME ______

ERRORS ______

MORE PRACTICE PARAGRAPHS—MAIN IDEA

Read the following paragraphs. First, find the topic or subject being discussed. Second, find the writer's main idea about that topic. Remember that the main idea is not always stated clearly in one sentence.

A. (1) That cockroach you just stepped on with disgust is not just any old bug. (2) It is above all else a Survivor. (3) It has survived almost unchanged for millions of years and may just outlive the human race. (4) How does the cockroach manage? (5) For one thing, it adapts easily to changing conditions. (6) For another, it eats almost anything. (7) Also, it has few natural enemies; birds and mammals soon find out that eating a cockroach makes them sick. (8) In fact, eating a cockroach would probably make *me* sick.

1. What is the general topic of the paragraph? ______________________

2. In your own words, what is the main idea about this topic? (State your idea in a complete sentence.) ______________________

____

3. Is the main idea stated in a topic sentence? ______

If so, what is the number of the sentence? ______

B. (1) There was an increase of 12 million new jobs in the United States between 1960 and 1970. (2) Sixty-five percent of these new workers were women. (3) Forty-five percent of all adult American women today are working outside the home. (4) The majority of these women are in "sex-typed" jobs and in the low-paid jobs—the menial jobs—in business and industry. (5) Even more significant, they are often paid lower wages than men receive for the same jobs. (6) The median income of working women in 1969 was only 60 percent that of the men. (7) By 1972 it had fallen to 57.9 percent, and it is still falling. (8) Women still have not achieved equal pay for equal work, even though more women are working today than ever before.*

1. What is the general topic of the paragraph? ______________________

*Adapted from "21st-Century Woman—Free at Last?" *Los Angeles Times* (Sept. 15, 1974).

Answer Key: Ex. 3F
1. complete tale **2.** weird blunder **3.** very worried **4.** plainly opposite **5.** as arranged **6.** bad nightmare **7.** short meeting **8.** clean carpet **9.** close haircut **10.** lonely area **11.** comic actor **12.** being brave **13.** caught crook **14.** appearing serene **15.** sad look **16.** expecting problems **17.** being content **18.** endless emptiness **19.** completed job **20.** easy to handle

2. In your own words, what is the main idea about this topic? (State your idea in a complete sentence.) ______________________________

____

3. Is the main idea stated in a topic sentence? ______________

If so, what is the number of the sentence? ______

C. (1) The slightest mischance in my life makes me want to fling myself into the protection of someone else's bank account. (2) And yet I still speak of "our money" as clearly separated from "my money." (3) Occasionally, men become liberated and it is a dreadful shock. (4) "I'm not going to work this year; I need to think," announced a friend's husband. (5) She had spent seven years in his care and keeping and then, as she put it, "Finally I get my own business going and *he* wants to lie around all day." (6) Why not? (7) Women who say, "I like my freedom—I have my day organized and I can do what I like with my time," forget that men are entitled to some of that freedom. (8) They are also prisoners of the rigid structure of their roles and jobs.*

1. What is the general topic of the paragraph? ______________

2. In your own words, what is the main idea about this topic? (State your idea in a complete sentence.) ______________________________

____

3. Is the main idea stated in a topic sentence? ______

If so, what is the number of the sentence? ______

Check your answers with the key on the bottom of the next page.

*Adapted from "The Housewife's Moment of Truth," by Jane O'Reilly. *Ms.* Magazine, Spring 1972.

WORDS IN CONTEXT

Without using your dictionary, try to determine the meaning of each word in **boldface** print. Choose the meaning below that best fits the context—the way it is used in the sentence.

Short Reading 3G

1. There's a profound philosophy **embedded** deep within the sport [baseball].
   (a) stuck **(b)** hidden **(c)** seriously analyzed **(d)** on the surface
2. That feeling of freedom is enhanced by the sport's **pastoral** quality.
   (a) relating to country life **(b)** enthusiastic crowds **(c)** historical tradition **(d)** open door hiring policy
3. The games are played on fields of grass and dirt that **evoke** the countryside.
   (a) are similar to **(b)** are different from **(c)** call to mind **(d)** are near to

Check your answers with the key on the bottom of page 76.

THEME FOR READING SELECTIONS: SPORTS IN SOCIETY

The three selections in this Lesson are not simply about sports; they are about people's attitudes towards sports. The first reading, for example, tells of the author's special love for baseball. The second highlights Tim Gallwey's ideas about how your inner emotions affect your outer game. The last reading relates how Dick Gregory, famous comedian and political activist, used his mastery of long-distance running to gain status in a hostile white world.

Imaginary Situation

You are a fast-rising athlete. Your whole world is sports. You love to read anything about sports and sports figures. You want to convince your best friend, who has no interest in sports, that these athletic pursuits are

Answer Key: Practice Paragraphs—Main Idea

A. 1. the cockroach as a survivor **2.** The cockroach has several traits that have caused it to survive for a long time. **3.** Yes (2) [Sentence (1) is an introductory statement, and sentences (3) through (8) discuss its traits as a survivor.]

B. 1. women's pay scale versus men's **2.** Working women receive less pay than working men, even though the number of working women has increased. **3.** Yes (8) [Sentences (1) through (7) give statistics supporting the two contrasting points made in (8).]

C. 1. men's and women's liberation **2.** Men deserve freedom of choice as much as women do. **3.** No [Sentences (7) and (8) come close to stating the main point of the paragraph.]

worthwhile. The reading selections will give you enough information to convince that friend.

Exercise 3G—Short Reading

Try to read the following selection in one minute. Remember to find the topic and main idea, and connect the details to that topic.

Baseball on My Mind

Jacques Leslie

WPM

My father was a remote man. He came home from work 11
each day and silently ate dinner, while my mother did most of 23
the talking. I think one reason I still love baseball is that it is 37
one of the few things my father and I enjoyed together. He 49
liked to tell me about the days when, as a boy in Pittsburgh, he 63
sat in the bleachers and watched the immortal shortstop Hon- 73
us Wagner play. When I was little, my father and I played 84
catch. When I was older, he attended my Little League and 95
Pony League games. 98

The pleasure I took in baseball was instinctive. I liked 108
the feel of the perfectly sized ball in my hand. The enjoyment I 121
received from hitting the ball squarely was as deep as anything 132
I experienced for many years. Baseball was how I proved my- 143
self. I had had polio when I was four years old, and I still 156
walked with a limp years later. My success in baseball was my 168
way of showing that I could overcome. 175

My appreciation of baseball has expanded over the 183
years. There's a profound philosophy embedded deep within 191
the sport. Modern changes, such as the designated hitter rule, 201
which I despise, and the new characterless ball parks, have 211
erased some of baseball's history. These changes have harmed 220
the sport, but they haven't struck at its heart. Baseball's long 231
season rewards patience, determination, consistency—all the 238
old-fashioned virtues. 241

The game also has a unique, refreshing relationship to 250
time and space. Unlike other major sports in America, baseball 260
is played without a clock. The field isn't a rectangular grid, but 272
a broad area confined within two lines that extend into infinity. 283
It's as if we're free of time and space as long as the game lasts. 298
That feeling of freedom is enhanced by the sport's pastoral 308
quality: the stadiums are in the middle of cities, but the games 320
are played on fields of grass and dirt that evoke the country- 332
side.

More than any other American sport, baseball has a 341
sense of history. The hundreds of statistics that any fan knows 352

by heart deepen that feeling. So does the fact that the game has 365
been played, much the same way as it is now, for the last 378
hundred years. The wily manager, the seasoned veteran, the 387
feared slugger, the struggling utility man, the green rookie, 396
the crafty pitcher—these are all mythic figures who have been 407
with us as long as baseball has. We can go to a game today by 422
blurring our vision a tiny bit, imagine that Honus Wagner, and 433
not some modern equivalent, is making the diving play behind 443
second base. 445

Mark the number of words read (or the number to the right of the last line read). Then immediately answer the questions below without referring to the selection.

1. The main point of this selection is
 (a) baseball's status as the greatest American sport.
 (b) the author's love for baseball over the years.
 (c) the way baseball has changed over the years.
 (d) baseball's sense of history.

2. A common interest in baseball made the author feel closer to his father. **T** **F**

3. The author approves of the modern changes in baseball. **T** **F**

4. One reason the author likes baseball is the game's lack of restrictions on space and time. **T** **F**

Check your answers with the key on the bottom of page 78, and record your scores below and on the progress chart in the Appendix.

WORDS PER MINUTE ______

% COMPREHENSION ______

Bonus Question

Which sentence is the topic sentence in the last paragraph?______________

Exercise 3H—Short Reading

Try to read the following selection in one minute. Remember to find the topic and main idea, and relate the details to that topic.

Answer Key: Words in Context
1. (b) **2.** (a) **3.** (c)

Tim Gallwey's "Inner Game"

Jacques Leslie

WPM

One of the most exciting developments in sports in re- 10
cent years is the invention of the "inner game" by former ten- 21
nis pro Timothy Gallwey. In his books—*The Inner Game of Ten-* 32
nis, Inner Tennis: Playing the Game, and *Inner Skiing*—Gallwey 41
shows how sports can be learned much more easily than most 52
people believe. Using his methods, people who have never 61
played tennis can learn to play adequately in a few hours. The 73
"inner game" is also useful for advanced players. Even profes- 83
sionals such as six-time Wimbledon champion Billie Jean King 92
have found Gallwey's ideas valuable. People in other profes- 101
sions (music, acting, writing and other creative pursuits) have 109
benefited from Gallwey's ideas. 113

Gallwey believes that what prevents most people from 121
performing well is their lack of trust in themselves. He asks his 133
students to give up judging how well they play and to focus 145
only on what the activity feels like. The more they are able to 158
do this, the more they learn about what actually happens when 169
they play. Then their performance improves almost without 177
trying. 178

The most basic drill Gallwey uses in tennis is to ask stu- 190
dents to say out loud "hit" each time they hit the ball and 202
"bounce" each time the ball bounces. Students who do this for 213
a few minutes or longer usually find that the mental effort 224
prevents them from worrying about how well they are playing. 234
Thus, they become less nervous and play better. The reason 244
this works, Gallwey argues, is that the body naturally knows 254
how to play tennis, but the mind prevents the body from acting 266
naturally. The value of the "bounce-hit" drill is in occupying 277
the mind so that it doesn't have a chance to worry about how 290
the body is performing. 294

Gallwey avoids giving instructions like "Draw the racket 302
back when you start to swing," or "Toss the ball high on the 315
serve." He believes that instructions like these may actually 324
block learning because they increase students' tension and in- 333
terfere with concentration. Gallwey thinks that the body per- 341
forms best when it is left alone. It will naturally find a form that 354
is comfortable for it. 358

Gallwey's success indicates that his ideas have gained 366
much acceptance. *The Inner Game of Tennis* is the best selling 377
book ever written on tennis, and his other books also have 388
done well. Gallwey has demonstrated his ideas in a popular 398
series on public television. And he has given lectures through- 408
out the country. He often talks to business employees about 417
how to improve their work performance. American Tele- 425

phone and Telegraph, one of the largest corporations in the 434
world, was so impressed by Gallwey's ideas that all 1700 of its 446
executives are now being exposed to the "inner game." 455

Mark the number of words read (or the number to the right of the last line read). Then immediately answer the questions below without referring to the selection.

1. The most important point about Gallwey's "inner game" involves
   (a) a better method for playing tennis.
   (b) performing any activity naturally and without tension.
   (c) learning more effective strokes and racket grips.
   (d) learning to relax.

2. Gallwey believes sports are difficult to learn. **T** **F**

3. He advises students to stop judging their performance and to concentrate on how the activity feels. **T** **F**

4. Gallwey's ideas have not been widely accepted. **T** **F**

Check your answers with the key on the bottom of page 80, and record your scores below and on the progress chart in the Appendix.

WORDS PER MINUTE ______

% COMPREHENSION ______

Bonus Question

Does the second or third sentence in the first paragraph express the main idea for the whole selection? ______________________________

Exercise 3I—Long Reading

LENGTH: 1539

Read the following selection as rapidly as you can but with good comprehension. Again, look for the main idea and connect the details with it. Wait for a signal from your instructor before you begin reading.

Answer Key: Ex. 3G
1. (b) **2.** T **3.** F **4.** T (1st)

Track Star

Dick Gregory, with Robert Lipsyte

When I heard that the track team got to take showers every evening after practice, I decided to start training. Every day when school let out at three o'clock, I'd get into an old pair of sneakers and a T-shirt and gym shorts and run around the block. In the beginning, I'd just run for an hour, then go and take a hot shower. And then one day two girls walked by and one of them said, "What's he think he's doing?" And the other one said: "Oh, he must be training for the big races." I just kept running that day, around and around the block, until every time I hit the pavement pain shot up my leg and a needle went into my side, and I kept going around and around until I was numb and I didn't feel anything any more. Suddenly it was dark and the track team had all left. I could hardly walk home my feet hurt so much, but I couldn't wait until the next day to get out there again. Maybe I couldn't run as fast as the other guys, but I could run longer, longer than anybody in all of the city of St. Louis. And then everybody would know who I was.

I kept running all that fall and all that winter, sometimes through the snow, until everybody in school knew who I was, the guy who never took a rest from three o'clock until six o'clock. I don't think I ever would have finished high school without running. It was something that kept me going from day to day, a reason to get up in the morning, to sit through classes with the doctor's sons who knew all the answers and read books at home, to look forward to going a little faster and a little longer at three o'clock. When I ran, nobody would point at me and say I was poor or crazy. They'd just look at me with admiration and say: "He's training." I never got hungry while I was running even though we never ate breakfast at home and I didn't always have money for lunch. I never was cold or hot or ashamed of my clothes. I was proud of my body that kept going around and around and never had to take a rest.

When spring came, the coach called me over one day and asked me if I'd like to run on the track. I ran against the guys on the team, and they were faster than me, but I could keep going long after they were pooped out. Every so often the coach would walk by and tell me I was holding my arms wrong, or that my body was at the wrong angle, or my knees weren't coming up high enough. But I was on the inside now and I was getting a little faster every day. By the time school closed in June I was beating the boys on the track team. The coach told me to report for track first thing in September. There would be a locker for me and a uniform.

The following year, after school, I was out on the track

with my own uniform. The coach started spending a lot of time with me, teaching me how to start, how to pace myself, when to make that closing kick. I learned fast because I was hungry to learn. When the season opened, I was running in dual meets in the mile and the half-mile. I was doing well finishing third and second, and once in a while I'd win a little race.

I began to do even better at the track meets. Flagpole Gregory, they called me, Ironman Gregory. I could run all day. I had style. I wore argyle socks in the races and a handkerchief wrapped around my head. I had a little trick. When I came down the stretch I'd look up at the flagpole and make a little salute. Then I'd go into my closing kick and win going away. They thought I was very patriotic, that the flag gave me extra strength. Once in a meet against Vashon High, the other big Negro high school in St. Louis, some kids took the flag down figuring that would beat me. I never even knew it.

My first integrated meet was a cross-country run over at Wood River. It was the first time Negro and white ever competed against each other in the high schools of St. Louis, and things really began to open up for me.

It was wild. There were rumors and excitement and electricity in the air. We didn't know the white boys and they didn't know us. We'd never had a chance to love or hate each other on a man-to-man basis, to watch each other run, to see each other naked. There were Negro rumors that the white boys had special conditioning and food that gave them the strength to beat us in the long distances. There were white rumors that we needed only three runners at a track meet: one would win the 100 and the 220, the second would win both hurdles, and the third would win the half and the mile. Then the three regulars would borrow a Negro water boy and win the relays.

I was so nervous I was shaking when we came to the line. Coach St. James had given us a big buildup for weeks. He had made us learn strategy all over again, made us promise to lay off the grandstanding. No argyle socks, no saluting, no crossing the tape holding your buddy's hand, no waving at your girl friends. This was big time. If we won we'd get our names in the white newspapers the next day—we wouldn't have to wait until the *Argus,* the Negro newspaper, came out on Thursday.

The coach had told me that there was a little white boy in the race who had one of the best scholastic three-mile times in the country, and if I could beat him I could win the race. But

Answer Key: Ex. 3H
1. (b) **2.** F **3.** T **4.** F (2nd)

we had never run the course before. And we didn't even know which was the white boy to beat.

Bang.

I didn't break out too fast. Let the pack go on ahead, this is a long race. You could see right away how different it was, running against boys who had eaten better and taken better care of their bodies all their lives. They looked smooth, they ran smooth. I moved up into the pack, and then went on ahead. I didn't know any of these white boys, which were the early pace-setters, which were the ones saving themselves for a final sprint. So I decided to stay with the leaders. There was a little white boy way ahead of everyone else, running as easy as flowing water. He took the corners sharply, and never seemed to get scratched by the bushes along the course. I got scratched all the time. I decided he had to be the white boy to beat.

I moved up, past the leaders, and started to dog that white boy. He was running too fast for me, and when I tried to match his pace my breath got short and it felt like somebody was sewing up the left side of my stomach and there was broken glass inside my shoes. He kept running easy. I knew I could never outrun him. Have to trick this race, Greg.

About the two-mile mark, I came up alongside him and slapped him on the butt. "Nice going, baby," I said, and I fell back fast so he wouldn't hear me panting.

A little bit later I came up again and kicked him on the heel of his shoe. Not enough to break his stride or bother him or get myself disqualified. Just enough so I could say, "Excuse me, baby." Again I dropped back fast so he wouldn't hear my breath come out. That upset him, but he didn't break.

Not much time left now. Last chance. I came right up behind him and I held my breath. He felt me running right behind him and he heard my feet, but he never heard me breathe. There was a fire in my chest, and my mind got fuzzy, and when I tried to take a shallow breath my brain kept clicking to shut it off, but he was looking around him now and his eyes were wide and he was so scared he speeded up. I held my breath as long as I could, then I dropped back to where he couldn't hear me and I let it all out and got myself together again. He had speeded up too early, and when he tried to slow down and settle back into his pace his smooth stride was broken, and he was off. He was destroyed. He wasn't running his race any more; he was scared and his mind was all messed up.

I came up again and I knew I could pass him any time I wanted to, now. But I didn't know the course, and I didn't want to take the chance of making a wrong turn and getting disqualified. So I stayed a few yards behind him until the last 200 yards, a straight shot to the tape. I could see the officials and the band and the crowd and the photographers, and I passed him going away, and watched my knees all the way down the stretch, higher and higher, right through the tape. And then I got to see how Whitey treats his heroes.

First-class all the way. Had my picture on the front page of the Wood River paper, and on the sports pages of all the white St. Louis papers. Dick Gregory. No.1.

TOTAL READING TIME _______

Immediately answer the questions below without referring to the selection.

1. Choose the statement that best expresses the main idea.
   (a) Gregory wanted to join the track team so he could take showers every afternoon.
   (b) Gregory took pride in running well because it helped make up for his being poor, black, and unimportant.
   (c) Negroes are better athletes than whites.
   (d) If people try hard enough, they can succeed at anything.

2. Gregory started taking running seriously when he overheard a girl saying, "He must be training for the big races." **T F**

3. Gregory's salute to the flag during a race gave him the courage to win. **T F**

4. The cross-country run at Wood River was the first time Negro and white had competed against each other in the high schools of St. Louis. **T F**

5. Gregory used psychology in competing with the white boy. **T F**

6. Gregory lost in the Wood River cross country race. **T F**

7. Which of the following best indicates the poverty the author must have lived in:
   (a) That he wore a handkerchief on his head while running.
   (b) That he ran every day from 3 o'clock until 6 o'clock.
   (c) That he originally joined the track team because the team got to take showers.
   (d) That the rumors said that white boys had special treatment.

8. Whitey didn't treat Gregory as well as he did white heroes. **T F**

Check your answers with the key on the bottom of page 84. Then turn to the Rate Chart in the Appendix to get your words per minute for this selection. Finally, record your scores below and on the progress chart in the Appendix.

WORDS PER MINUTE _______

% COMPREHENSION _______

Bonus Question

Does the first or last sentence in the first paragraph best express the author's motives for running (thus expressing the main idea of the selection)? ______

Percentage Chart for Comprehension Check

Errors	0	1	2	3	4	5	6	7	8
% Right	100	88	75	63	50	38	25	13	0

Answer Key: Ex. 31
1. (b) **2.** T **3.** F **4.** T **5.** T **6.** F **7.** (c) **8.** F (last)

Lesson 4

Exercise 4A—Phrase Perception

key phrase			
1. with sticks	white strips will stack	while sick slight wit	with sticks
2. passing parks	parking cars barking dogs	passing parks raising sharks	tossing pills
3. since morning	mourning silks since morning	adorning fences more winces	marvelous sense
4. green shirt	green shirt short guess	clean skirt noon shift	great shift
5. below surface	scarred face blue face	surly blow below surface	low surf
6. less rapid	least rancid best raid	last race tree sap	less rapid
7. against walls	agate balls against walls	whole skin which grip	huge gains
8. through streams	though straight throw strikes	strict thought through streams	small throat
9. some money	sweet honey some money	soft moans sour mash	bear market
10. abstract idea	abstract idea icy arbitrator	trace house absolute victory	arbitrary solution
11. grocery cart	grammar school cancerous growth	gross error grown child	grocery cart
12. startling features	staring faces starring few	startling features feasible start	starting friction
13. by the fence	buy the fedora by the fence	abundant feast fly the plane	bright felon
14. burned house	brown mouse spurned host	high brow burned house	learned halls
15. calm mother	motheaten collar cowardly moment	calm mother mushy clams	cold monkey
16. past the door	past the door dour prediction	pass the flour packed luggage	passed test

17. extreme stealth	extremely wealthy expired singer	extra shirts stealing expenses	extreme stealth
18. broken nose	beautiful rose broken nose	broker's loan beautiful day	bronchial tube
19. annual return	anemic regent annual return	angle hair animal remains	real angle
20. over a hill	after the bill off the sill	over the clover over a hill	owe the bill

TIME ______

ERRORS ______

Exercise 4B — Phrase Perception

key phrase			
1. idealized girl	real whirl definite stir	whiter pearl great appeal	idealized girl
2. sailing the ship	nailing the strip sailing the ship	writing the script mending the rip	sifting the pail
3. executive's daughter	excellent draught effective dramatics	ebullient laughter executive's daughter	edible doughnut
4. across the street	the six acres after the scene	across the street accept the shift	acting the role
5. favorable report	favorable report fatal reversal	flavorful roll few rewards	favorite review
6. magnetic attraction	mechanical accuracy majestic aplomb	magnetic attraction many retractions	active magnet
7. lofty thought	tight logic legendary tale	tawdry location little tolerance	lofty thought
8. at the top	in a pot at the pole	rope a calf at the top	after the hop
9. chipped polish	chaste gown chipped polish	charity ball cheap pony	picked chicken
10. stolen passage	seamy paragraph secret patrol	stolen passage paternal scowl	second path
11. grocery cart	grocery cart gourmet wine	graduate school hollow gorge	groaning craft
12. jumped hurdle	bumped horse jammed door	honest judge jumped hurdle	hurt jockey
13. regarding him	retarding progress remarkably dim	reverting back relatively grim	regarding him
14. collection plate	late recollection callous patron	collection plate pale colonel	careful plot
15. running the race	ruining the rice patting the face	raising the roof reeling dance	running the race
16. serious drama	serious drama drastic solution	dramatic series deft insertion	frantic search

17. silver pen set	salt shaker the small sliver	pinned corsage the setting hen	silver pen set
18. eclipsed moon	limping loon eclipsed moon	escaped man eaten bone	ecstatic moan
19. to think of	to sink to two blinks	a thought of a mink coat	to think of
20. science fiction	scant favor science fiction	secret friction small fraction	fire screen

TIME _______

ERRORS _______

Exercise 4C—Word Comprehension

key word					
1. overcast	bound	dramatic	grateful	gloomy	sunny
2. plight	passport	height	beach	remainder	predicament
3. cutlery	portion	knives	cutlet	kitchen	vegetable
4. immune	eager	dangerous	protected	interior	tired
5. valet	servant	worth	peer	courage	enemy
6. liberal	empty	generous	off-beat	tight	closed
7. livid	purple	calm	bright	angry	diseased
8. particle	haircut	piece	flexible	edge	whole
9. client	reason	laughter	flexible	comrade	customer
10. efficient	elegant	competent	frustrated	sloppy	clean
11. prescribe	order	hint	receive	eject	erase
12. provision	expert	player	condition	eyesight	providence
13. exaggerate	delude	pronounce	overlook	honor	overstate
14. locality	helper	place	drama	native	house
15. pursue	shop	insure	lead	follow	halt
16. consistent	various	elastic	regular	proper	timid
17. jaunt	trip	illness	apron	length	humor
18. consequently	however	therefore	also	finally	further
19. mammoth	friendly	average	gigantic	loose	tiny
20. envelop	promote	mail	reserve	carry	surround

TIME _______

ERRORS _______

Exercise 4D—Word Comprehension

key word					
1. emotion	respect	movement	feeling	grief	science
2. cumbersome	false	awkward	straight	smooth	handsome
3. swivel	scrape	deceive	cure	satisfy	turn
4. deluge	storm	racket	stew	prophet	heatwave
5. defect	decoration	shack	parlor	flaw	perfection
6. taboo	sublime	public	forbidden	sexy	secret
7. inhabitant	gypsy	resident	human	nun	habit
8. treacherous	impure	social	glorious	educational	dangerous
9. embargo	treaty	sales	ban	shipment	addition
10. velocity	speed	truth	scorn	airplane	slowness
11. uproar	yell	animal	peace	disturbance	ladder
12. evident	alone	jealous	obscure	logical	obvious
13. tenement	mansion	apartment	trailer	garage	belief
14. research	survival	memory	investigation	question	posse
15. exquisite	expensive	beautiful	old	common	rough
16. maestro	beginner	assistant	writer	master	guide
17. involve	concern	reduce	evolve	enter	twist
18. merchandise	sale	luxury	business	profits	goods
19. cluster	solo	group	cowardice	party	row
20. reaction	cycle	cause	response	motion	option

TIME _______

ERRORS _______

DIRECTIONS FOR SENTENCE COMPREHENSION

These exercises have a key sentence that expresses a specific idea. Read this sentence carefully and think about its meaning. Ten sentences follow the key sentence. Read each one quickly and determine if the central thought is the same as (or similar to) the idea expressed in the key sentence. If it is basically the same, put a check in the right-hand column, as in the following example:

key sentence: It is not always wise to buy tires at "sale" prices.

1. Buying tires at special sales can be risky. ✓
2. Tires "on sale" are not guaranteed to be good buys. ✓
3. You should wait until a special sale before buying your tires. ______
4. Some people get good tire buys at sales, and some people get stuck with lemons. ✓

As soon as you finish all ten items, look up and your instructor will indicate your time in seconds.

Check your work against the answer key on page 94. Then write your time and number of errors at the bottom of the exercise.

Exercise 4E—Sentence Comprehension

key sentence: If anything can go wrong, it will. ("Murphy's Law")

1. You might as well prepare for the worst. ______
2. If there's a remote chance that something will go wrong, you can expect it to do so. ______
3. Things will go better if you "think positive." ______
4. God watches over saints and fools. ______
5. It is realistic to expect things to go wrong. ______
6. Unless something is absolutely fool-proof, trouble will occur. ______
7. If you plan very carefully, you will avoid failure. ______

Answer Key: Ex. 4C
1. gloomy **2.** predicament **3.** knives **4.** protected **5.** servant **6.** generous **7.** angry **8.** piece **9.** customer **10.** competent **11.** order **12.** condition **13.** overstate **14.** place **15.** follow **16.** regular **17.** trip **18.** therefore **19.** gigantic **20.** surround

Answer Key: Ex. 4D
1. feeling **2.** awkward **3.** turn **4.** storm **5.** flaw **6.** forbidden **7.** resident **8.** dangerous **9.** ban **10.** speed **11.** disturbance **12.** obvious **13.** apartment **14.** investigation **15.** beautiful **16.** master **17.** concern **18.** goods **19.** group **20.** response

8. With most things, there's a 50 – 50 chance that all will be well. ______
9. Difficulties will occur, whether we expect them to or not. ______
10. We have every reason to be optimistic about the future. ______

TIME ______

ERRORS ______

HOW TO IMPROVE—SENTENCE COMPREHENSION

The Sentence Comprehension exercises deal with larger units of meaning than the other drills. Therefore, you must read the key sentence carefully and think about it *before* deciding whether the sentences that follow are alike or different.

Read every word of the key sentence. Understand the whole sentence, not just a part of it. Notice whether the statement is broad and loose ("usually," "sometimes"), or limited ("always," "only"). Notice whether it is positive or negative.

Remember that the addition of one word can change the entire meaning. It is useful to *paraphrase* the key sentence—to put it mentally into your own words. Then you can recognize the same idea even when the sentence structure is different.

Exercise 4F—Sentence Comprehension

key sentence: Your story of the incident would be incredible if I had not witnessed it myself.

1. I cannot believe your story of what happened. ______
2. You are not telling the truth. ______
3. I would not believe you if I didn't know you well. ______
4. I would not believe you if I hadn't seen it myself. ______
5. You tend to have a low regard for the truth. ______
6. You and I really made up a good story. ______
7. In this case, seeing was believing. ______
8. I believe you because you have a good reputation. ______
9. It was a common incident which happens every day. ______
10. It's funny how the same incident can seem totally different to two different witnesses. ______

TIME ______

ERRORS ______

RETAINING DETAILS

If you're starting this section expecting to learn "How to Remember Everything You Read, In Two Easy Steps, With Our Magic Memory Formula"—sorry! There is no such formula. However, you should keep in mind some helpful hints. Some are based on research by psychologists and other learning experts on how we forget and remember. Other hints are based on plain logic and common sense.

The most important hint is *understand and remember the main idea before you look for the details.* For one thing, it's logical. When we locate a friend's apartment, we find the area and street, and then the building, before we look for the apartment number. To use another analogy (comparison), we need to see the forest before we examine each tree. In Lessons 2 and 3, you learned the importance of locating the *main idea* in any reading. Continue that habit, whether in this book or in other courses.

The second hint is *fit the details to the main idea!* Details don't add up to anything by themselves, even if they are understood and remembered perfectly. The human brain wants things to "add up." For example, try to retain the following details as they stand:

> "Group 4, walk 4 minutes, jog 6 minutes, walk 3 minutes, jog 6 minutes.
>
> Group 5, walk 4 minutes, jog 15 minutes. Group 6, walk 2 minutes, jog 17 minutes. Group 7, jog 19 minutes."

Look away from those sentences and try to "recite" the details. It's hard, unless you're a whiz at rote memory.

But suppose you had been reading a pamphlet about the physical fitness class at your local gym. One of the main ideas in the pamphlet is that the class is divided up on the basis of "fitness" into 10 groups, from group 1 (beginners) to group 10 (the physically fit). The lower-numbered groups walk more and jog less; the higher-numbered groups walk less and jog more. Now read the details again. "Recite" again. The exact numbers (4, 6, and so on) are not important. But you should retain more of the details, more meaningfully, because you now have a main idea or framework to unify them. The little trees are now grouped into a forest. The supporting details are now under the main idea umbrella.

A third hint is *notice and try to retain only those details that are necessary.* Don't overload the circuits unnecessarily! Many readers seem to retain easily minor facts and figures, or unimportant details, and nothing else. Why remember "$4,000 – $6,000 a year" from a paragraph, unless you also remember what it refers to? Why remember a photograph of a mouse terrifying a large cat, unless you also remember the purpose of that experiment. Think

Answer Key: Ex. 4E
2, 5, 6, 9 (perhaps 1)

Answer Key: Ex. 4F
4, 7

in terms of remembering the time span of a war rather than the exact date of a minor battle!

The fourth hint is *recognize the pattern of the details.* What shape can a framework of details or writings take? Perhaps, as many shapes as there are thoughts. But we do tend to communicate ideas through the use of certain recognizable patterns. If you, the listener or reader, can identify the pattern, you can remember the details more easily.

What are some common patterns for organizing detailed material? Terms vary, but a list of patterns usually includes the following: *description, space relationships, process, time sequence* (chronology), *example or illustration, classification, cause-and-effect, comparison and contrast, analogy* and *definition.*

Here's how to recognize these paragraph patterns:

Description. Details that fit this pattern tell who, what or how about the main idea. These details often describe the surface, or appearance, of someone or something:

My brother is a handsome fellow. His thick dark hair and dark green eyes give him the good looks of a movie star. To top it off, he has the firm, trim body of an athlete.

Space Relationship. Patterns may often overlap. These descriptive details, for example, may be organized according to a *space relationship.* They usually move in an order, such as left to right, up to down, north to south, or vice versa:

As I stood on the hilltop, my eye took in the signs of active life in the valley below. Down to the right was a schoolyard packed with young bodies at play. Directly below was a park where bands of old people were lawn-bowling. Off to the left I could see a group of joggers running along a well-worn path in single file.

Process. Sometimes descriptive details tell the steps in a *process.* Often this pattern will use words like *first, second, then, next:*

Changing a tire is a matter of four simple steps. First, jack up the side of the car where you want to change the tire. Second, twist off the lug nuts in the middle of the wheel. Next . . .

Time Sequence. Details are sometimes presented in the order they took place. This pattern is called *time sequence:*

The early years of Lisa's life were marked by wealth. She was born in 1955 to a family with vast landholdings in Montana. When she was just one year old, her grandmother died suddenly, willing her three city blocks in Manhattan. In 1958 still more riches graced her life when . . .

Example or Illustration. This pattern uses specific cases to move from the general (topic sentence) to the particular. In the following paragraph look for the three examples that support or explain the main idea:

Tom avoids doing his homework by "inventing" other work for himself. For example, he may suddenly decide his car just can't go without a washing another day. Or he might convince himself he has to sit down and pay all his bills before he cracks his history book. Or maybe all at once he feels he's getting too flabby and so hurries off to shoot some basketball. Meanwhile, he hasn't started on that ten-page term paper due tomorrow.

Classification. Paragraphs that separate details into categories or *classes* and then discuss each class fit this pattern. The students at your college, for instance, might be grouped—or *classified*—according to their religions, that is, Catholic, Protestant, Jew, Moslem, Buddhist. Or they might be classified by marital status, personality type, or study habits. But just *one* basis of classification is used at a time. A paragraph that classified students according to study habits might be organized like this:

Most of the students at our college fall into one of the following categories when it comes to study habits: the grind, the balancing artist and the "what, me worry?". The grind is at the books day and night, or so it seems. This student is the type who's likely to spend even spring break boning up in the library. The balancing artist, though, believes in the golden mean. This type of student may not get top grades but does get some pleasure. The balancing artist will work hard when necessary but knows when to forget it and go fishing. And then there's the "what, me worry?" kid who seldom passes up a party and just as seldom passes a test. This student's average life-span in college is about one semester.

Cause and Effect. This pattern starts with a cause (topic sentence) and gives its effects (supporting details). Or vice versa, it may give an effect or result (topic sentence) and then tell what caused it (supporting details). Which method does the following paragraph use?

When I was a young girl, I longed to be a doctor. Partly this was because I wanted to be like my favorite aunt who was a doctor. But this wish was also the result of all the many TV shows I watched about doctors and hospital drama. Partly too it was because I loved the image of myself as a heroine who could save people where all else had failed.

Comparison and Contrast. The details point out what it is that two or more subjects do or do not have in common. These paragraphs are often organized in one of two ways. The paragraph may present in turn each point of similarity or difference between subject A and subject B. Or it may discuss all aspects of Subject A, then all aspects of Subject B. These paragraphs will often have transition words like *but, however, on the other hand:*

Many high school graduates go straight on to college. Others go to work full-time, then decide later to start college. The graduate who goes off to a job always runs the risk of being unable to let go of that paycheck. It just may be too hard to live the lean life of a student again. However, once that person does return to college, she usually brings a maturity that's a big asset in the classroom. True, that student will be older than the others when she finally gets that college degree. On the other hand, this old-

er student more often knows from experience what kind of job best suits her. This student is less likely to end up in a make-do job after college.

Analogy. This is a form of extended comparison. It reasons that if two ideas, people, or events have certain things in common, they probably have certain other things in common too:

Learning to read well is like learning to improve in a sport. There are so many things to think of all at the same time. The inexperienced tennis player, for example, must remember to bend his knees; he must think of keeping his eye on the ball; he must remember to hold his wrist straight and follow through on his swing. The inexperienced reader also has to remember many things at once. He must try to read in phrases, not word by word. He must analyze new words, look for the main idea, note important details. And at the same time he must read faster and faster. Both the beginning reader and tennis player feel frustrated. But practice pays off for the tennis player; practice will pay off for the reader too and lead to higher and sharper skills. Reading well will become as natural as hitting a ball well.

Definition. A paragraph that defines an idea or event may use a combination of pattern. Note how the following paragraph also uses example to help define:

Aerobics (pronounced: a-er-ó biks) refers to a variety of exercises that stimulate heart and lung activity for a time period sufficiently long to produce beneficial changes in the body. Running, swimming, cycling, and jogging—these are typical aerobic exercises. There are many others. (Dr. Kenneth H. Cooper, The New Aerobics*)*

The patterns often combine or overlap. You can discover this for yourself if you try to think in any organized way about even a one-word topic such as "dogs." You will recognize this problem in looking for patterns in the reading exercises that follow this discussion.

Look for these common patterns in your other verbal activities—listening, talking, writing. You'll see them too in advertising, political speeches, course lectures, conversation with friends, even in your own thinking! They are simply logic patterns used by logical thinkers.

Again, to retain important details, you should:

1. Find the topic and the main idea.
2. Associate details with the main idea.
3. Remember only the important details.
4. Recognize the pattern by which the main idea is developed.

PRACTICE PARAGRAPHS—DETAILS

Read the following paragraphs and remember to grasp the topic and the main idea about the topic first, just as you did in Lessons 2 and 3. Then notice how the supporting details are organized.

A. (1) Although we were once a nation of farmers, today, farmers are becoming one of the smallest of our major occupational groups. (2) The reason for this major change is the change in farming technology. (3) In 1790 it took the surplus of nine farm families to support one city family. (4) Today, each farm family supports 20 city families. (5) In 1790 the rural (both farm and non-farm) residents made up 95 percent of our total population. (6) By 1920, when "farm" and "rural non-farm" were first separated in the census, farm people constituted only 30 percent of the population. (7) In 1970, they were only 5 percent of the total, and they are still decreasing.

1. In your own words, what is the main idea of the paragraph? (Write a complete sentence.) ______________________________

____

2. Is the main idea stated in a topic sentence? ______

If so, what is the number of the topic sentence? ______

3. The supporting details are organized in what type of pattern(s)? Check one or more:

contrast	______	example	______
cause and effect	______	time sequence	______
definition	______	classification	______

4. Briefly list the supporting details by their sentence numbers. Use chronological order (according to the dates).
(Parts of the answer are supplied to get you started.)
1) Sent. no. 3 and 5: 1790—9 farms to support one city family; 95 percent of nation are farmers

2) Sent. no.______: 1920—______________________________

3) Sent. no.______: ______—______________________________

B. (1) What's your girlfriend doing right now? (2) Or your sister? (3) Or your mother, for that matter? (4) Chances are good that she's got her nose deep in a type of book that tops the list of best-selling books week after week. (5) It's the historical romance, a kind of novel that's really more romance than it is history. (6) Full of danger and adventure, strong men and pretty women with lots of nerve and verve prance across every page. (7) And the things they put themselves through—all in the name of love. (8) Pirates! (9) Kidnapping! (10) Close Calls! (11) The Wild West! (12) Lover's Fights! (13) Passion! (14) Could it be that these books—so popular with women—tell us something important about what we've lost? (15) Are we tired of being such tame city-dwellers? (16) Do we long for the brave deed and bold kisses of a more romantic time gone by?

1. In your own words, what is the main idea of the paragraph? (Write a complete sentence.) ______________________________

____

2. Is the main idea stated in a topic sentence? ______

If so, what is the number of the topic sentence? ______

3. The supporting details are organized in what type of pattern(s)? Check one or more:

space relationship	______	comparison and contrast	______
definition	______	classification	______
time sequence	______	example	______

4. Briefly list at least six qualities of the historical romance.

1. ______________________________

2. ______________________________

3. ______________________________

4. ______________________________

5. ______________________________

6. ______________________________

C. (1) English is one of several dozen modern languages that are descended from the prehistoric parent language, Indo-European. (2) Written English, a Germanic language, can be described as having roughly three major historical phases. (3) The Anglo-Saxon (or Old English) period dates from around the fifth century A.D. to 1100 A.D.—from the arrival of the Angles, Saxons, and Jutes in Britain to the Norman-French invasion. (4) The Middle English period stretches through the Middle Ages, from around 1100 to 1500. (5) These centuries saw Anglo-Saxon modified by the influence of French and Latin. (6) The Modern English period, from 1500 to the present, has shown increasing influence of other modern languages and of ancient Greek and Latin. (7) However, the common vocabulary of English remains basically Germanic.

1. In your own words, what is the main idea of this paragraph? (Write a complete sentence.) ______________________________

____

2. Is the main idea stated in a topic sentence? ______

   If so, what is the number of the topic sentence? ______

3. The supporting details are organized in what type of pattern(s)? Choose one or more:

classification	______	time sequence	______
analogy	______	space relationship	______

4. Briefly, list the supporting details (three major historical phases and dates) by their sentence numbers. Use chronological order.

   1. Sent. no. 3: ______
   2. Sent. no. 4 and 5: ______
   3. Sent. no. 6: ______

D. (1) To condemn Suburbia has long been a literary cliché. . . . (2) I have yet to read a book in which the suburban life was pictured as the good life or the commuter as a sympathetic figure. (3) He is nearly as much a stock character as the old stage Irishman. (4) He is the man who "spends his life riding to and from his wife." (5) He is the eternal middle class man who knows all about Buicks and nothing about Picasso. (6) His sanctuary is the club locker room, and his ideas spring ready-made from the illiberal newspapers. (7) His wife plays politics at the P.T.A. and keeps up with the Joneses. (8) Or—if the scene is more gilded and less respectable—the commuter is the high-powered advertising executive with a station wagon and an eye for the ladies. (9) And his wife is a restless baggage, given to too many cocktails in the afternoon.*

1. In your own words, what is the main idea of the paragraph? (Write a complete sentence.) ______

   ______

2. Is the main idea stated in a topic sentence? ______

   If so, what is the number of the topic sentence? ______

3. The supporting details are organized in what type of pattern(s)? Check one or more:

space relationship	______	definition	______
example	______	time sequence	______

---

*From *Provence of the Heart* by Phyllis McGinley, 1949, The Viking Press, Inc.

4. List at least four literary clichés about a suburbanite.

____

____

____

____

E. (1) Dr. Gilbert Kliman, M.D., a child psychiatrist from White Plains, New York, is anxious to see preventive psychiatry viewed not as a narrow professional specialty, but as a general concern, like good nutrition, that can and should be practiced by everyone. (2) While it is true that most of us know we should eat a well-balanced diet, many of us continue to overindulge in favorite, but not soundly nutritious, foods or drinks. (3) Still, we try to lose weight, to guard ourselves against the temptations of gluttony. (4) We don't realize, though, that one should also have a well-balanced emotional routine, as well. (5) Too much of a feast of guilt, of self-disapproval, of anxiety, shows up just as unavoidably on the scales of unhappiness and impaired functioning. (6) We need to weigh ourselves in the emotional balance from time-to-time to check on whether we are mentally overweight. (7) And, if so, we need to see a professional to help us go on a mental health diet.*

1. In your own words, what is the main idea of this paragraph? (Write a complete sentence.) ____

____

2. Is the main idea stated in a topic sentence? ______

If so, what is the number of the topic sentence? ______

3. The supporting details are organized in what type of pattern(s)? Choose one or more:

contrast	______	analogy	______
definition	______	time sequence	______

---

*Adapted from "Can a Psychiatrist Help Normal People" by Don A. Sanche, *Today's Health*, (Jan., 1973).

4. In the blanks on the left, list the characteristics of a well-balanced diet. In the blanks on the right, list the characteristics of a well-balanced emotional routine.

______________________________	______________________________
______________________________	______________________________
______________________________	______________________________

Check the answer key on the bottom of page 104.

WORDS IN CONTEXT

Without using your dictionary, try to determine the meaning of each word in **boldface** print. Choose the meaning below that best fits the context—the way it is used in the sentence.

Short Reading 4G

1. This high degree of **sociability** may be essential for the development of language.
   (a) friendly interaction **(b)** intelligence **(c)** cooperation **(d)** energy
2. She **generalized** the word to all activities and all objects.
   (a) applied in a narrow sense **(b)** applied in a broader sense **(c)** made a mistake **(d)** forgot
3. Washoe did not make sentences from **random** groups of signs in sign language.
   (a) with a purpose **(b)** easy **(c)** difficult **(d)** chosen by chance or luck
4. Washoe's earliest combinations of words were **comparable to** the earliest combinations of children.
   (a) different than **(b)** similar to **(c)** bigger than **(d)** leading up to

Short Reading 4H

5. A white unicorn with a gold horn was quietly **cropping** the roses in the garden.
   (a) smelling **(b)** planting **(c)** cutting off **(d)** trampling
6. The unicorn is a **mythical** beast.
   (a) has two tongues **(b)** appears in tales and legends **(c)** enjoys music **(d)** likes to play pranks
7. She was very excited and there was a **gloat** in her eye.
   (a) disease **(b)** speck of dust **(c)** look of great satisfaction **(d)** sadness

Long Reading 4I

8. Several of this cursed brood leaped into the tree I stood under and began to discharge their **excrements** on my head.
   (a) baskets of fruit **(b)** weapons **(c)** angry words **(d)** bodily wastes
9. I never beheld in all my travels so disagreeable an animal, or one against which I naturally had so strong an **antipathy.**
   (a) hatred **(b)** curiosity **(c)** affection **(d)** irritation
10. They gently struck each other's right hoof before neighing several times by turns, and varying the sound, which seemed to be almost **articulate.**
    (a) able to be heard **(b)** artistic **(c)** having the power of speech **(d)** too talkative

11. I concluded that, if the inhabitants of this country possessed a **proportionate** degree of reason, they must be the wisest people upon earth.
(**a**) balanced relationship (**b**) sufficient (**c**) tremendous (**d**) small portion

12. I was soon to learn the meaning of that word to my everlasting **mortification.**
(**a**) grief (**b**) amusement (**c**) embarrassment (**d**) anger

Check the answer key on the bottom of page 106.

THEME FOR READING SELECTIONS: CREATURES, STRANGE AND COMMON

The selections in this Lesson are about animals, both real and unreal. But an article about animals is also an article about people. It's people who train them. It's people who study them. And, finally, it's people who write about them. The attitudes we people have toward animals, strange or common, are as varied as our attitudes toward our fellow humans. These selections start with an article about a "talking" chimpanzee. The next reading is a classic fable about a strange animal in a common place, told by James Thurber, a famous American humorist. The last article is an excerpt from *Gulliver's Travels* by Jonathan Swift. This writer of satire from the eighteenth century draws a picture of animals as reflections of mankind.

Answer Key: Practice Paragraphs – Details

A. **1.** There has been a decrease in the proportion of the American population who are farmers. **2.** Yes (1) [Sentence (2) gives the reason for the change, and sentences (3) through (7) give supporting statistics.] **3.** The major pattern is *contrast* (then and now). There are also *cause* and *effect* (technology caused decrease) and *time sequence*. **4.** (2) 6—farmers only 30 percent of nation (3) 4 and 7 today—1 farm supports 20 city families; only 5 percent of nation are farmers

B. **1.** A lot of women are reading historical romances for escape and adventure. **2.** Yes (5) [Sentences (1) through (3) catch your attention but do not introduce the topic. Sentence (4) presents the topic but does not sum it up. Sentence (5) defines the topic and prepares for the details that follow.] **3.** The paragraph *defines* the historical romance through *examples*. Sentences (14)—(16) show *comparison and contrast*. **4.** romance, adventure, danger, strong men, pretty women, pirates, kidnapping, close calls, the Wild West, lover's fights, passion, brave deeds, bold kisses

C. **1.** English, a Germanic language, has passed through three historical periods. **2.** Yes (2) [It mentions the "three historical phases" which are then described in sentences (3) through (7).] **3.** The patterns are *classification* (three phases) and *time* sequence (phrases listed in chronological order. **4.** (1) Anglo-Saxon, 400s to 1100 A.D. (2) Middle English, 1100 to 1500 A.D. (3) Modern English, 1500 to present

D. **1.** There are numerous negative literary clichés about suburban life. **2.** Yes (1) [Sentences (2) and (3) are expansions of sentence (1). Sentences (4) through (9) are a series of examples of literary cliches.] **3.** *Example* **4.** any example in sentences (4) through (9)

E. **1.** Dr. Kliman wants to see preventive psychiatry (like good nutrition) practiced by everyone. **2.** Yes (1) [This is the only general, comprehensive sentence in the paragraph.] **3.** The major pattern is *analogy*, an extended comparison between well-balanced physical and mental diets. A minor pattern is *contrast* (good dietary habits vs. bad dietary habits).

4.

well-balanced diet	*well-balanced emotional routine*
no overindulging in non-nutritious foods or drinks	no feasting on guilts, anxiety, etc. weigh on emotional balance regularly
guard against gluttony	get professional help for mental health diet

Imaginary Situation

At last! Tonight you have a date with that special someone you've had your eye on for months. You have just learned that he or she is wild about animals and likes nothing better than to discuss them in great, endless detail. You long to capture the heart and mind of your new friend. So read the following selections looking for details and examples you can use tonight to delight and amaze.

Exercise 4G – Short Reading

Try to read the following selection in one minute. Remember to find the topic and main idea. Relate the details to that topic.

A Chimp Learns a Language

Joyce Dudney Fleming

WPM

Washoe is a female chimpanzee who was born in the 10
wild. She was about a year old when her language training 21
began in June 1966. The Gardners [her trainers] chose a chim- 32
panzee instead of one of the other higher primates because of 42
the chimp's capacity for forming strong attachments to human 51
beings. They believe that this high degree of sociability may be 62
essential for the development of language. The language they 71
chose for Washoe was American Sign Language. 78

Her teachers taught her the sign for *more* in the context 89
of tickling, a romping, wrestling game Washoe played with 98
them. She generalized its use to all activities and all objects. 109
They taught her the sign for *open* using only three particular 120
doors in her house trailer. She transferred its use to all doors, 132
containers, drawers, the refrigerator and, finally, to water 140
faucets. They taught her the sign for *flower.* She used it for all 153
flowers and for a number of situations in which an odor was 165
prominent, such as opening a tobacco pouch or entering a 175
kitchen where food was cooking. So they gave her the sign for 187
smell. She can tell the difference between the two signs and 198
uses each appropriately. But the error she makes in odor 208
contexts is frequently *flower.* 212

In April 1967, less than a year after her training began, 223
she produced her first combination of signs, a kind of sentence. 234
Though no lessons on combinations had ever been given, her 244
teachers had signed to her in strings. As soon as Washoe had 256
learned eight or ten signs she started putting them together 266
in sets of two or three, much as small children learn to com- 279
bine words. She learned some of her combinations from her 288
teachers, but others she made up herself. For example, 297

Washoe invented *gimme tickle* to request tickling and *open food* 307
drink to ask that the refrigerator be opened. Her teachers had 318
always used the signs *cold box* for this appliance. 327
With just ten signs there is a large number of possible 338
two- and three-sign combinations. But Washoe did not make 346
sentences from random groups of signs. The ones she used 356
were usually the ones that made sense. The signs she used in 368
front of a locked door included *gimme key, open key, open key* 380
please, and *open key help hurry.* The Gardners analyzed Washoe's 390
two-sign combinations using a method developed for children. 398
They found that her earliest combinations were comparable to 407
the earliest combinations of children. 412

Mark the number of words read (or the number to the right of the last line read). Then immediately answer the questions below without referring to the selection.

1. Washoe's ability to learn language
- **(a)** did not exist.
- **(b)** was like that of a child at the same stage of development.
- **(c)** confused her trainers.
- **(d)** showed that her trainers were very talented.

2. A chimpanzee was chosen for the language experiment because a chimp gets along well with humans. **T F**

3. Washoe often used the sign for *flower* where the sign *odor* should have been used. **T F**

4. Washoe just mindlessly "aped" the signs her teachers had shown her. **T F**

Check your answers with the key on the bottom of page 108, and record your scores below and on the progress chart in the Appendix.

WORDS PER MINUTE ______

% COMPREHENSION ______

Bonus Question

Check the pattern that best describes the way in which the details are organized around the main idea:

Answer Key: Words in Context
1. (a) **2.** (b) **3.** (d) **4.** (b) **5.** (c) **6.** (b) **7.** (c) **8.** (d) **9.** (a)
10. (c) **11.** (a) **12.** (c)

space relationships ______ definition ______

example ______ cause-and-effect ______

time sequence ______

Exercise 4H — Short Reading

Read the following selection in one minute. Remember to look first for the main idea; then pay particular attention to the organization of the details.

The Unicorn in the Garden

James Thurber

WPM

Once upon a sunny morning a man who sat in a break- 12
fast nook looked up from his scrambled eggs to see a white 23
unicorn with a gold horn quietly cropping the roses in the gar- 35
den. The man went up to the bedroom where his wife was still 47
asleep and woke her. "There's a unicorn in the garden," he 58
said. "Eating roses." She opened one unfriendly eye and 67
looked at him. "The unicorn is a mythical beast," she said, and 79
turned her back on him. The man walked slowly downstairs 89
and out into the garden. The unicorn was still there; he was 101
now browsing among the tulips. "Here, unicorn," said the 110
man, and he pulled up a lily and gave it to him. The unicorn 124
ate it gravely. With a high heart, because there was a unicorn 136
in his garden, the man went upstairs and roused his wife 147
again. "The unicorn," he said, "ate a lily." His wife sat up 159
in bed and looked at him, coldly. "You are a booby," she 171
said, "and I am going to have you put in the booby-hatch." 183
The man, who had never liked the words "booby" and "booby- 194
hatch," and who liked them even less on a shining morning 205
when there was a unicorn in the garden, thought for a mo- 216
ment. "We'll see about that," he said. He walked over to the 228
door. "He has a golden horn in the middle of his forehead," he 241
told her. Then he went back to the garden to watch the uni- 253
corn; but the unicorn had gone away. The man sat down 264
among the roses and went to sleep. 271

As soon as the husband had gone out of the house, the 283
wife got up and dressed as fast as she could. She was very excit- 296
ed and there was a gloat in her eye. She telephoned the police 309
and she telephoned a psychiatrist; she told them to hurry to 320
her house and bring a strait-jacket. When the police and the 331
psychiatrist arrived they sat down in chairs and looked at her, 343

with great interest. "My husband," she said, "saw a unicorn this 353
morning." The police looked at the psychiatrist and the psychi- 362
atrist looked at the police. "He told me it ate a lily," she said. 376
The psychiatrist looked at the police and the police looked at the 388
psychiatrist. "He told me it had a golden horn in the middle of 401
its forehead," she said. At a solemn signal from the psychia- 411
trist, the police leaped from their chairs and seized the wife. 422
They had a hard time subduing her, for she put up a terrific 435
struggle, but they finally subdued her. Just as they got her into 447
the strait-jacket, the husband came back into the house. 456
"Did you tell your wife you saw a unicorn?" asked the 467
police. "Of course not," said the husband. "The unicorn is a 478
mythical beast." "That's all I wanted to know," said the psychi- 488
atrist. "Take her away. I'm sorry, sir, but your wife is as crazy 501
as a jay bird." So they took her away, cursing and screaming, 513
and shut her up in an institution. The husband lived happily 524
ever after. 526
Moral: Don't count your boobies until they are hatched. 535

Mark the number of words read (or the number to the right of the last line read). Then immediately answer the questions below without referring to the selection.

1. This story's main point is that
- **(a)** the unicorn is a mythical beast.
- **(b)** wives seldom believe their husband's tales.
- **(c)** people who see unicorns are crazy.
- **(d)** with a little wit, a person may be able to turn what looks like a bad situation to a good one.

2. The unicorn had a gold horn on its head. **T F**

3. The husband tried to stop the police from taking his wife to the booby-hatch. **T F**

4. Revenge is sweet. **T F**

Check your answers with the key on the bottom of page 110, and record your scores below and on the progress chart in the Appendix.

WORDS PER MINUTE ______

% COMPREHENSION ______

Answer Key: Ex. 4G
1. (b) **2.** T **3.** T **4.** F example, time sequence, cause-and-effect

Bonus Question

Check the pattern that best describes the way in which the details are organized around the main idea:

description	______	analogy	______
cause-and-effect	______	comparison and contrast	______
definition	______		

Exercise 4I — Long Reading

LENGTH: 1282

Read the following selection as rapidly as you can but with good comprehension. Pay particular attention to details. Wait for a signal from your instructor before you begin reading.

The Yahoos and the Houyhnhnms

Jonathan Swift

I was set ashore in a strange country and walked about to discover its inhabitants. I resolved to deliver myself to the first savages I should meet. I would purchase my life from them by some bracelets, glass rings, and other toys, which I had about me.

The land was divided by long rows of trees, not regularly planted, but naturally growing. There was plenty of grass and several fields of oats. I walked very carefully for fear of being surprised, or suddenly shot with an arrow from behind or on either side. I fell into a beaten road. There I saw many tracks of human feet, and some of cows, but most of horses.

At last I saw several animals in a field, and one or two of the same kind sitting in trees. Their shape was unusual and deformed, which a little upset me. So I lay down behind a thicket to observe them better.

Some of them, coming forward near the place where I lay, gave me an opportunity of examining them more carefully. Their heads and breasts were covered with a thick hair, some frizzled and others lank. They had beards like goats, and a long ridge of hair down their backs and the fore-parts of their legs and feet. The rest of their bodies were bare, so that I might see their brown buff-colored skins. They had no tails, nor any hair at all on their buttocks, except about the anus. This hair, I presume, helped them as they sat on the ground. This posture they used, as well as lying down, and often stood on their hind feet. They climbed high trees as nimbly as a squirrel, for they had strong extended claws before and behind, ending in sharp, hooked points. Several of this cursed brood leaped into the tree I stood under and began to discharge their excrements on my head. I escaped but was almost stifled with the filth, which fell about me on every side.

Upon the whole, I never beheld in all my travels so disagreeable an animal, or one against which I naturally had so strong an antipathy.

In the midst of this distress, I observed them all to run away all of a sudden as fast as they could. I ventured to leave the tree and go to the road, wondering what it was that could put them into this fright.

Looking to my left, I saw a horse walking softly in the field. This was the cause of my persecutors' flight. The horse started a little when he came near me, but soon recovering himself, looked full in my face with obvious wonder. He looked at my hands and feet, walking round me several times. I would have walked away, but he placed himself directly in the way. Yet he looked at me mildly, never offering the least violence.

We stood gazing at each other for some time. At last I took the boldness to reach my hand toward his neck, with the intention of stroking it. I used the common style and whistle of jockeys when they are going to handle a strange horse. But this animal seemed to receive my friendliness with contempt. He shook his head and bent his brows, softly raising up his right forefoot to remove my hand. Then he neighed three or four times, but so strangely that I almost began to think he was speaking to himself in some language of his own.

Then another horse came up, who applied himself to the first in a very formal manner. They gently struck each other's right hoof before neighing several times by turns, and varying the sound, which seemed to be almost articulate. They went some paces off, as if it were to confer together, walking side by side, backward and forward, like persons deliberating upon some important affair. But they often turned their eyes towards me, as if to watch that I might not escape. I was amazed to see such actions and behavior in brute beasts. I concluded that, if the inhabitants of this country possessed a proportionate degree of reason, they must be the wisest people upon earth.

The two horses neighed frequently towards each other, as if they were engaged in serious conversation. I could frequently distinguish the word *Yahoo,* which was repeated by each of them several times. I did not know what the word

Answer Key Ex. 4H
1. (d) **2.** T **3.** F **4.** T description, cause-and-effect

meant, yet while the two horses were busy in conversation, I tried to practice this word upon my tongue. And as soon as they were silent, I boldly pronounced *Yahoo* in a bold voice. I imitated, at the same time, as near as I could, the neighing of a horse. They were both visibly surprised at this. The gray horse repeated the same word twice, as if he meant to teach me the right accent. I spoke after him as well as I could, and found myself to improve every time.

Then the bay horse tried me with a second word, much harder to be pronounced. But I reduced it to English letters and spelled it *Houyhnhnm.* I did not succeed in this so well as the first word. But after two or three farther trials, I had better fortune, and they both appeared amazed at my ability.

The gray horse then took me to a long kind of building, made of timber stuck in the ground. I now began to be a little comforted. I took out some toys, which travellers usually carry for presents to the savage Indians of America and other parts, in hopes the people of the house would be thereby encouraged to receive me kindly.

As I waited, the horse neighed three or four times, and I waited to hear some answers in a human voice. But I heard no other response than the same dialect of horses, only one or two a little shriller than his. I began to think that this house must belong to some person of great note among them, because there appeared so much ceremony before I could gain admittance.

Finally, the gray horse led me into a room where I saw a very comely mare. She sat with a colt and foal, sitting on their haunches upon mats of straw, not unartfully made, and perfectly neat and clean. The mare rose from her mat, and coming up close, observed my hands and face. She then gave me a most contemptuous look. As she turned to the gray horse, I heard the word *Yahoo* often repeated between them. I was soon to learn the meaning of that word to my everlasting mortification.

The mare led me out into a kind of court, where there was another building at some distance from the house. Here I saw three of those detestable creatures whom I first met after my landing. They were all tied by the neck and fastened to a beam. The horse ordered the largest of these animals to be untied. The beast and I were brought close together and compared. The horse thereupon repeated several times the word *Yahoo.*

My horror and astonishment are not to be described, when I observed in this abominable animal a perfect human figure. The face of it indeed was flat and broad, the nose depressed, the lips large, and the mouth wide. The fore-feet of the Yahoo differed from my hands in nothing else but the length of the nails, the coarseness and brownness of the palms, and the hairiness on the backs. There was the same resemblance between our feet, which I knew very well, though the horse did not, because of my shoes and stockings.

TOTAL READING TIME ______

Immediately answer the questions below without referring to the selection.

1. Choose the statement that best expresses the main idea.
(a) The traveler hated the horses and loved the manlike beasts.
(b) He soon tamed both groups of animals.
(c) He hated the manlike beasts and respected the horses.
(d) He remained frightened of both groups of animals.

2. The first animals were afraid of the horses. **T** **F**

3. The first animals clawed viciously at the man. **T** **F**

4. The man was surprised to see
(a) the horses behaving like people. **(b)** such friendly horses.
(c) such fierce horses. **(d)** horses speaking good English.

5. The two horses seemed to be able to talk to each other. **T** **F**

6. The horse liked to have his neck stroked by the man. **T** **F**

7. The horses were called *Houyhnhnms* and the manlike beasts were called *Yahoos*. **T** **F**

8. The horses referred to the man as *Yahoo*. **T** **F**

Check your answers with the key on the bottom of page 114. Then turn to the Rate Chart in the Appendix to get your words per minute. Finally, record your scores below and on the progress chart in the Appendix.

WORDS PER MINUTE ______

% COMPREHENSION ______

Bonus Question

Describe in detail the manlike beast.

Percentage Chart for Comprehension Check

Errors	0	1	2	3	4	5	6	7	8
% Right	100	88	75	63	50	38	25	13	0

Answer Key: Ex. 41
1. (c) **2.** T **3.** F **4.** (a) **5.** T **6.** F **7.** T **8.** T Refer to paragraph 4

Lesson 5

Exercise 5A—Phrase Perception

key phrase			
1. broken doll	bristling dog brown bag	dill pickle broken doll	broken branch
2. off the horse	for the house of a pair	on the hat in his heart	off the horse
3. puzzled student	parched peanut dazzled prince	puzzled student dancing pair	partial payment
4. seeming concerned	redeeming plan seeming concerned	teeming crowd very careful	left behind
5. capital letter	become better summer castle	cold winter capital letter	strong fetters
6. having fallen	having fallen hot woolens	having stolen warm hearth	has fallen
7. cotton stockings	rotten boards criminal lawyer	cotton stockings card shark	rocking cradle
8. heated argument	hanging meat heartless accusation	mental illness heated argument	hated person
9. rich mechanic	pitch darkness rich mechanic	reached goal red mantle	repaired machine
10. into the rift	on the raft rapt attention	into the rift inner confusion	in a rage
11. shifting gears	lifting weights elevator shaft	mowing grass shifting gears	siphoning gas
12. foggy night	future right frozen food	faint light fierce fight	foggy night
13. polished silver	polite signal falling sliver	polished silver faint slip	relished supper
14. accurate solution	accurate solution solved mystery	ancient salute arched eyebrow	solvent arsenal
15. a short fable	a small stable a sharp fork	a smart farmer a low snort	a short fable
16. hostile driver	driven host hostile driver	hungry diner drinking hustler	horrible drivel

17. drawn dagger	cowed beggar dark driftwood	ragged dress drawn dagger	brown digger
18. crafty plaintiff	leaky raft crafty plaintiff	plain craft careful painter	carefully placed
19. too expensive	too expansive taken extra	too expensive too pensive	total expense
20. crooked picture	cracked pistol rookie pitcher	clean practice paid crank	crooked picture

TIME ______

ERRORS ______

Exercise 5B—Phrase Perception

key phrase			
1. either tray	leather strap weather vane	neither prays stray too far	either tray
2. off balance	a ballot off balance	one balloon for balance	balky child
3. typed page	paid time sage tycoon	thick rage typed page	tender age
4. having grown	having flown giving some	having grown raving mad	growing old
5. every night	every night average sight	very light real blight	even bright
6. good lunch	bad brunch much goodness	great crunch rushed goal	good lunch
7. dark secret	secrete oil sycamore bark	six sharks dark secret	drab secretary
8. stiff ruffle	straight ruff fine truffle	slick ruffian stiff ruffle	sick rogue
9. feeling hope	feeling hope smelling soap	jumping rope searing fire	feeling smooth
10. look under	loud thunder took over	look under good luck	wonder book
11. human voice	vocal man voiced thought	humane boy humus soil	human voice
12. bound feet	bound feet sweet broth	round foot bruised toes	loud fool
13. vast land	best band vast land	sand vat last wand	big load
14. many fees	any fees fine mane	more tea many fees	see many
15. calm rest	calm rest calla lily	best calf camel hump	red vest
16. mailed letter	better male nailed boards	mailed letter least maiden	little mall

17. catching balls	fetching dolls catching balls	latching doors falling latch	patching pants
18. ever after	every rafter awful evening	after events ever after	always even
19. of a sale	of a tale off the sill	sell off of a sale	off a rail
20. near nine	nearly mine dear man	near nine each wine	rear line

TIME ________

ERRORS ________

Exercise 5C—Word Comprehension

key word					
1. ornate	beautiful	plain	ugly	jewelry	elaborate
2. meditate	see	ponder	sleep	trance	figure
3. surly	certain	fearful	bad-tempered	tender	pleasant
4. extremity	utmost	permanent	simple	more	extra
5. spurn	aid	spoon	accept	reject	wound
6. aroma	perfume	odor	atmosphere	sight	circle
7. malicious	rowdy	gracious	murderous	spiteful	restful
8. superfluous	great	powerful	extra	quantity	necessary
9. compel	force	pay	shave	ask	argue
10. lust	broken	desire	bed	manners	bliss
11. idolize	degrade	godly	church	converse	worship
12. abate	push	adore	increase	subside	magical
13. aptitude	ability	test	skill	speed	habit
14. stifle	harden	smother	clarify	stiff	strike
15. delete	change	dilute	omit	add	replace
16. nimble	frantic	slow-moving	athletic	sorrowful	agile
17. formidable	middle-class	shape	selfish	impressive	formulated
18. lament	mourn	pass	celebrate	fail	glue
19. siesta	celebration	nap	party	picnic	diet
20. caper	walk	roll	dessert	cancer	prank

TIME ______

ERRORS ______

Exercise 5D—Word Comprehension

key word					
1. exterminate	bugs	destroy	harm	help	extra
2. pilfer	furnish	borrow	steal	fasten	give
3. deplore	disapprove	dig	depend	approve	differ
4. reprimand	compliment	frown	joke	scold	reply
5. vanquished	conquered	answered	recovered	dreamed	disappeared
6. redeem	read	recover	dress	shoot	modify
7. tedious	boring	calm	interesting	tender	work
8. anecdote	hymn	novel	story	annual	medicine
9. comply	defy	common	argue	agree	care
10. renown	recent	unknown	restful	foreign	famous
11. agitate	fast	agile	disturb	star	serve
12. insomnia	sleeplessness	sleep	sleepy	softly	sleepwalk
13. illegible	unwritten	unreadable	readable	uneducated	ignorant
14. replica	genuine	regain	graphic	copy	repent
15. dismantle	repair	destroy	disrupt	take back	take apart
16. ebb	tide	stamp	subside	push	enter
17. gist	point	just	story	question	gentle
18. sever	shoot	cut off	burn down	knife	stick
19. indelible	understood	permanent	invisible	erasable	distant
20. ecstasy	good	silly	joy	loss	moody

TIME _______

ERRORS _______

Exercise 5E — Phrase Comprehension

key phrase			
1. increase speed	go faster look ahead	go slower watch others	keep even
2. see the whole	look for mistakes perceive a unit	break it up notice spaces	think carefully
3. in the beginning	as a conclusion finally done	at the start like a fact	with certainty
4. absent a week	gone for good away a month	gone seven days in and out	sick at home
5. can't be true	is humorous very popular	seems incredible has been proved	very complicated
6. reliable person	can be counted on tells lies	is often late very rich	is irresponsible
7. beach excursion	becalmed boat chewing gum	dig for treasure trip to seashore	hunting shells
8. frequent disputes	seldom seen friendly parties	lecture often cordial chats	often argue
9. barren landscape	picturesque land fields and gardens	dull, empty scenery towering mountains	colorful painting
10. conceal evidence	assist the court cancel appointment	donate objects hide information	hint at truth
11. indulge in gossip	talk about people wait for news	adore turmoil hard of hearing	invent alibi
12. era of anxiety	cure for worry an achievement	period of stress look of dishonesty	time for bliss
13. baffle authorities	make experts wonder resent leaders	break the law file complaint	go to police

Answer Key: Ex. 5C
1. elaborate **2.** ponder **3.** bad-tempered **4.** utmost **5.** reject **6.** odor **7.** spiteful **8.** extra **9.** force **10.** desire **11.** worship **12.** subside **13.** ability **14.** smother **15.** omit **16.** agile **17.** impressive **18.** mourn **19.** nap **20.** prank

Answer Key: Ex. 5D
1. destroy **2.** steal **3.** disapprove **4.** scold **5.** conquered **6.** recover **7.** boring **8.** story **9.** agree **10.** famous **11.** disturb **12.** sleeplessness **13.** unreadable **14.** copy **15.** take apart **16.** subside **17.** point **18.** cut off **19.** permanent **20.** joy

14. an aerial feat	routine flight accomplishment in air	party on a plane airplane race	fear of heights
15. fearless retort	strong bottle quiet resort	timid speaker courageous reply	army attack
16. colossal blunder	great statue giant of a man	huge mistake family reunion	ear-splitting sound
17. arouse awe	become very angry drink and carry on	wake a group arrive late	inspire respect
18. customary residence	temporary home fashionable address	usual living quarters unusual habit	business office
19. feeling melancholy	liking foreign foods happy life-style	being sad touching melons	loving activity
20. probably sufficient	perhaps enough may be overdone	not enough variety looks bleak	too little

TIME _______

ERRORS _______

Exercise 5F — Phrase Comprehension

key phrase			
1. unclad sprinter	broken arm runner without clothes	under a bridge unpleasant clod	coughing a lot
2. delightful vision	poor eyesight pleasant sight	seeing too much vast wasteland	dirty eyeglasses
3. false compliment	true believer snarled traffic	throwing a ball artificial praise	filmed story
4. always on time	punctual every time small allowance	every minute counts semi-annual event	timely remark
5. wise selection	elected official smart choice	seldom wise foolish decision	messy paper
6. to review	all the way over the hill	look over has taken	to present
7. very happy	on his foot extremely glad	quite unexpected planning well	an attack
8. moving slowly	rapid movements roving alone	in slow motion bathtub ring	mothers together
9. cautious treatment	careful handling caught redhanded	broken leg careless trick	rented apartment
10. haughty manner	naughty girl oughtn't do	towering heights arrogant behavior	bashful boy
11. go down fast	fast ascent descend rapidly	distant relative going in circles	gone again
12. expensive material	hard exercise silver pen	cheap goods open window	high-priced cloth
13. weeping gentleman	weeded garden peeping Tom	crying man hysterical boy	seeping water
14. stopped vehicle	popped cork dented fender	tire chains truck stop	stalled car

Answer Key: Ex. 5E
1. go faster **2.** perceive a unit **3.** at the start **4.** gone seven days **5.** seems incredible **6.** can be counted on **7.** trip to seashore **8.** often argue **9.** dull, empty scenery **10.** hide information **11.** talk about people **12.** period of stress **13.** make experts wonder **14.** accomplishment in air **15.** courageous reply **16.** huge mistake **17.** inspire respect **18.** usual living quarters **19.** being sad **20.** perhaps enough

15. frantic wave	panicky gesture crying aloud	frank remark snappy salute	ranting and raving
16. snake in grass	a snail's pace serpent on lawn	rake the leaves slimy creature	picnic in woods
17. wounded knee	hurt leg bound and gagged	wind around lost and found	smooth kneecap
18. nervous laugh	tight nerve laugh alone	loud roar worried giggle	shy smile
19. clenched hand	strong fingers tight fist	polished nail close crates	handle lightly
20. remove completely	move restlessly return a part	disappear together do it twice	take away all

TIME ______

ERRORS ______

PRACTICE PARAGRAPHS—DETAILS

Directions: Continue to read, as in Lesson 4, for the topic and the main idea about the topic. Then notice how the supporting details are organized.

A. (1) Pay attention to your breathing. (2) How you breathe can tell you how relaxed you are. (3) When you are calm, your breathing is deep and steady. (4) It comes from the stomach, not the chest. (5) When you are nervous, excited or under stress, your breathing changes. (6) It becomes shallow and ragged, almost like panting. (7) It comes from the chest or throat. (8) Sometimes, when upset, you may even catch yourself holding your breath without knowing it. (9) Or you may exhale more quickly than you inhale. (10) Whenever you want to calm down, try to breathe to a rhythm. (11) Inhale to the count of three, exhale to the count of four. (12) Then get in the habit of checking your breathing from time to time to make sure you stay relaxed and at your best.

1. In your own words, what is the main idea of the paragraph? (Write a complete sentence.) ____________________

____

2. Is the main idea stated in a topic sentence? ______ If so, what is the number of the topic sentence? ______

3. The supporting details are organized in what type of pattern(s)?

____

4. Briefly describe your breathing in the following situations. (The first answer is supplied to get you started.)

1. When you are calm <u>deep and steady—from stomach</u>
2. When nervous ____________________
3. When upset ____________________
4. When you <u>want</u> to be calm ____________________

B. (1) Ping Pong, or Table Tennis as it is officially called, has had a shorter and more international history than many of our popular games. (2) Experts are not sure whether it was invented by New Englanders, the British in India, or the British in South Africa. (3) But all agree that ping pong made its appearance in the nineteenth century (the 1800s). (4) Parker Brothers, the American game and toy company, sold a game called "Indoor Tennis" in the 1890s. (5) But the British and Europeans,

Answer Key: Ex. 5F
1. runner without clothes **2.** pleasant sight **3.** artificial praise **4.** punctual every time **5.** smart choice **6.** look over **7.** extremely glad **8.** in slow motion **9.** careful handling **10.** arrogant behavior **11.** descend rapidly **12.** high-priced cloth **13.** crying man **14.** stalled car **15.** panicky gesture **16.** serpent on lawn **17.** hurt leg **18.** worried giggle **19.** tight fist **20.** take away all

not the Americans, were the world champions for half a century. (6) Then came the Great Paddle Breakthrough in the 1950s, when the Japanese designed the rubber paddle. (7) Since then, the Japanese and Chinese—do you remember "Ping Pong Diplomacy"?—have tended to dominate the championships.*

1. In your own words, what is the main idea of the paragraph? (Write a complete sentence.) ______________________________

____

2. Is the main idea stated in a topic sentence? ______ If so, what is the number of the topic sentence? ______

3. The supporting details are organized in what type of pattern(s)?

____

4. Briefly, list the supporting details by their sentence numbers. Use chronological order.

1. Sent. no. 2 and 3: ______________________________

____

2. Sent. no. 4: ______________________________

3. Sent. no. 5: ______________________________

4. Sent. no. 6: ______________________________

5. Sent. no. 7: ______________________________

C. (1) Before the rural revolution in America, thrift was an absolute value. (2) That means that frugality, the careful saving of money and produce, was seen as *good* in and of itself. (3) Thrift was a practical value in a "subsistence" economy in which each farm had to supply its own needs, and in which there was rarely enough of anything, including money. (4) But today's farm is part of the "market" economy, and thrift is now an outdated value. (5) It is pointless as an end in itself. (6) Like other Americans, the farm family saves only as a means to an end. (7) They will save on non-essentials only in order to buy a color television, a new car, or a house. (8) This value change, and many others, has accompanied the technological revolution in American agriculture.**

1. In your own words, what is the main idea of the paragraph? (Write a complete sentence.) ______________________________

____

---

*Adapted from "With a Ping and a Pong, Table Tennis Thrives Internationally," by George Beronius, *Los Angeles Times* (October 27, 1975).

**From "City vs. Country," in *Sociology* by Paul B. Horton and Chester L. Hunt.

2. Is the main idea stated in a topic sentence? ______

   If so, what is the number of the topic sentence? ______

3. The supporting details are organized in what type of pattern(s)?

   ____

4. Briefly, list the supporting details by their sentence numbers, in the order in which they are written.

   1. Thrift in the past

      a. Sent. 1, 2 and 3: ______________________

   2. Thrift today

      a. Sent. 4 and 5: ______________________

      b. Sent. 6 and 7: ______________________

Check your answers with the key on the bottom of page 130.

WORDS IN CONTEXT

Without using your dictionary, try to determine the meaning of each word in **boldface** print. Choose the meaning below that best fits the context—the way it is used in the sentence.

Short Reading 5G

1. Moaning quietly, with his head between his knees, **rheumy** eyes clamped tight, he sat limply until his turn came to be cleaned.
   (a) bright **(b)** watery and mucous-filled **(c)** fear-filled **(d)** half-blind

Short Reading 5H

2. I see a car turn off the highway and come **lumbering** across the ruts through the sage.
   (a) racing **(b)** sliding **(c)** moving slowly and awkwardly **(d)** moving expertly
3. Can you imagine people wanting to live this way? I for one am not going inside that **hovel.**
   (a) elegant mansion **(b)** wretched shack **(c)** haunted house **(d)** singles' apartment building
4. "We are here to deal with the noble leader of these people. . . ." "Deal with? Not me, not my job. They pay me to appraise, not **fraternize.**"
   (a) ignore **(b)** test **(c)** organize **(d)** socialize
5. "It would be very simple to go in and talk with him. . . ." "Inside in that **squalor?** Why, I'll just bet you anything that place is acrawl with black widows."
   (a) miserable filth **(b)** small dwelling **(c)** dense forest **(d)** abandoned nursery

Long Reading 5I

6. I couldn't afford to get my hopes up. I was ready to **capitulate** without a groan.
   (a) give in **(b)** go into business **(c)** feel happiness **(d)** feel hopeful
7. When Papa lectured, you listened. If anyone spoke up, it would be Mama, trying to **mediate.**
   (a) listen **(b)** make a fresh start **(c)** act quickly **(d)** help people reach an agreement
8. I had seen those photos of Mama when she lived in Spokane, twelve years old and her round face **blanched** with rice powder.
   (a) darkened **(b)** whitened **(c)** washed **(d)** covered

9. He stood there, hands on hips, glaring at me, and not at all satisfied with this **ultimatum.**
(a) beginning (b) process (c) final word or warning (d) crisis

10. In Papa's glare I sometimes detected a flicker of approval, as if my streak of independence, my refusal to be shaped by him, reflected his own **obstinance.**
(a) anger (b) stubbornness (c) humility (d) glee

Check your answers with the key on the bottom of page 132.

THEME FOR READING SELECTIONS: TRACING OUR ROOTS

People from many different lands and customs have contributed their work and ideas to make America as great as it is today. But the way has not been easy for these people as they adjusted to a new culture on this continent. Each group has had to struggle in its turn with the challenge of being different and the "outsiders." The first selection is from Alex Haley's *Roots,* the best-selling book (later made into a widely-watched television event). The excerpt gives the young slave boy Kunta's first reaction to America. The next reading is from the novel *One Flew Over the Cuckoo's Nest,* also made into a film. In it an Indian tells what it's like not to exist to the eyes and ears of others. The last selection presents a Japanese girl who struggles to be accepted in a modern American world that conflicts with traditional Japanese values.

Answer Key: Practice Paragraphs – Details

A. **1.** How relaxed or tense you are affects your breathing. **2.** Yes (2) [Note that all the details in the paragraph have to do with your manner of breathing. Sentence (1) presents the topic, *breathing;* but (2) is better as a topic sentence because it makes a statement about breathing—*that breathing can tell you how relaxed you are.*] **3.** *Cause and effect* is the best answer because the details explain how relaxation or tension *causes* different *effects* or results in your breathing. *Comparison* and *contrast, description,* and *process* are also present. **4.** (2) shallow and ragged, like panting (3) holding breath, or exhaling more rapidly (4) breathe to a rhythm

B. **1.** Ping pong has had a short and international history. **2.** Yes (1) [All the following sentences explain that short, international history.] **3.** The major pattern is *time sequence* with some *contrast* and *example.* **4.** (1) invented in the 1880s by Americans or British (2) Parker Brothers' "Indoor Tennis" in 1890s (3) first champions, British and Europeans (4) new rubber paddle, by Japanese (5) since 1950s, most champions Oriental

C. **1.** The value of *thrift* has changed among farm families, from being an end in itself to a means to an end. **2.** Yes (4) [Sentence (1) is incomplete as a topic sentence: it expresses only the "before." Sentence (8) is a concluding remark, giving the cause for change.] **3.** The major pattern is *comparison and contrast* (thrift then versus thrift now). Minor patterns are *definition* (what is thrift?) and *cause* and *effect* (why change in values came about?). **4.** (1) in old-type farming, thrift was necessary (2) in modern farming, thrift is outdated (3) modern farm families save only enough to buy large items

Imaginary Situation

All of us have been outsiders at some time in our lives, in some way. Even if we have not been strangers in another country, we still know what it feels like not to belong or to be a newcomer. Think back to some time in your life when you have felt different and like an outsider. Then read the following selections, noting the details. Compare these experiences with the details of your own experience.

Exercise 5G—Short Reading

Try to read the following selection in one minute. Again, look first for the main idea; then pay particular attention to the organization of the details.

from *Roots*

Alex Haley

WPM

Among the men who were still alive, Kunta was one of 11
the last who were able to climb down unassisted from their 22
shelf and up the steps to the deck. But then his wasting legs 35
began trembling and buckling under him. Finally he, too, had 45
to be half carried and half dragged to the deck. Moaning quiet- 57
ly, with his head between his knees, rheumy eyes clamped 66
tight, he sat limply until his turn came to be cleaned. The *tou-* 79
bob [white people] now used a large soapy sponge lest a hard- 90
bristled brush do further damage to the men's gouged and 99
bleeding backs. But Kunta was still better off than most, who 110
were able only to lie on their sides. It seemed as if they had 124
stopped breathing. . . . 126

Finally, Kunta could no longer even eat without help. 135
The draining shreds of muscle in his shoulders and elbows 145
refused to lift his hands enough for him to claw into the food 158
pan. Often now the feeding was done with the men up on 170
deck. One day Kunta's fingernails were scrabbling to get up 180
over the edges of the pan when the scarfaced toubob noticed it. 192
He barked an order at one of the lesser toubob, who proceed- 204
ed to force into Kunta's mouth a hollow tube and pour the 215
gruel through it. Gagging on the tube, Kunta gulped and slob- 226
bered the food down. Then he sprawled out on his belly. 236

The days were growing hotter. Even up on the deck 246
everyone was sweltering in the still air. But after a few more 258
days, Kunta began to feel a breath of cooling breeze. The big 270
cloths up on the tall poles started to snap again and soon were 283
billowing in the wind. The toubob up above were springing 293

about like monkeys. Soon the big canoe was cutting through 303
the water with froth curling at her bow. 311
The next morning, more toubob than usual came thud- 320
ding down through the hatch, and much earlier than ever be- 329
fore. With great excitement in their words and movements, 338
they rushed along the aisles, unchaining the men and hurried- 348
ly helping upward. Stumbling up through the hatch behind a 357
number who were ahead of him, Kunta blinked in the early- 368
morning light. Then he saw the other toubob and the women 378
and children standing at the rails. The toubob were all laugh- 389
ing, cheering, and gesturing wildly. Between the scabbed backs 397
of the other men, Kunta squinted and then saw. . . 406
Though still blurred in the distance, it was unmistakably 415
some piece of Allah's earth. These toubob really did have some 426
place to put their feet upon—the land of toubabo doo—which 438
the ancient forefathers said stretched from the sunrise to the 448
sunset. Kunta's whole body shook. The sweat came popping 457
out and glistened on his forehead. The voyage was over. He 468
had lived through it all. But his tears soon flooded the shore- 480
line into a gray, swimming mist, for Kunta knew that whatever 491
came next was going to be yet worse. 499

Mark the number of words read (or the number to the right of the last line read). Then immediately answer the questions below without referring to the selection.

1. The following is true of Kunta's condition on the boat:
(a) weak from pain and near starvation.
(b) happy to see land at last.
(c) ready to kill at any moment.
(d) ready to give up and die.

2. Kunta was in much worse condition than the other slaves. **T** **F**

3. The people in charge were called "toubob" by Kunta. **T** **F**

4. In spite of his condition, Kunta looked forward to the future in a new land. **T** **F**

Check your answers with the key on the bottom of page 134. Record your scores below and on the progress chart in the Appendix.

WORDS PER MINUTE ______

% COMPREHENSION ______

Answer Key: Words in Context
1. (b) **2.** (c) **3.** (b) **4.** (d) **5.** (a) **6.** (a) **7.** (d) **8.** (b) **9.** (c) **10.** (b)

Bonus Question

Check the pattern(s) that describe(s) the way in which the details are organized around the main idea.

classification ______ description ______

time sequence ______

Exercise 5H – Short Reading

Try to read the following selection in one minute. Pay particular attention to details.

from *One Flew Over the Cuckoo's Nest*

Ken Kesey

WPM

I lay in bed the night before the fishing trip and thought 12
it over, about my being deaf, about the years of not letting on I 26
heard what was said, and I wondered if I could ever act any 39
other way again. But I remembered one thing: it wasn't me 50
that started acting deaf; it was people that first started acting 61
like I was too dumb to hear or see or say anything at all. 75

Lying there in bed, I tried to think back when I first no- 87
ticed it. I think it was once when we were still living in the vil- 101
lage on the Columbia. It was summer 108

. . . and I'm about ten years old and I'm out in front of 120
the shack sprinkling salt on salmon for the racks behind the 131
house, when I see a car turn off the highway and come lumber- 144
ing across the ruts through the sage 150

The doors of the car open all at once and three people 162
get out. The first man stops and looks the village over. . . . 173

"Can you imagine people wanting to live this way? Tell 183
me, John, can you? I for one am not going inside that hovel," 196
the fat guy says. 200

"That hovel," John says through his mustache, "is 208
where the Chief lives, Brickenridge, the man we are here to 219
deal with, the noble leader of these people." 227

"Deal with? Not me, not my job. They pay me to ap- 238
praise, not fraternize." 241

This gets a laugh out of John. 248

"It would be very simple to go in and talk with him." 260

"Inside in that squalor? Why, I'll just bet you anything 270
that place is acrawl with black widows. They say these 'dobe 281
shacks always house a regular civilization in the walls between 291
the sods. And *hot,* lord-a-mercy, I hope to tell you. I'll wager it's 304

a regular oven in there. Look, look how overdone little Hia- 314
watha is here. Ho. Burnt to a fair turn, he is." 325
What he said makes me madder the more I think about 336
it. He and John go ahead talking about our house and village 349
and property and what they are worth, and I get the notion 361
they're talking about these things around me because they 371
don't know I speak English. They are probably from the East 381
someplace, where people don't know anything about Indians 390
but what they see in the movies. I think how ashamed they're 402
going to be when they find out I know what they are saying. 413
I let them say another thing or two about the heat and 425
the house; then I stand up and tell the fat man, in my very best 440
schoolbook language, that our sod house is likely to be cooler 451
than any one of the houses in town, *lots* cooler! . . . 461
And I'm just about to go and tell them, how, if they'll 473
come on in, I'll go get Papa, when I see that they don't look like 488
they'd heard me talk at all. . . . Not a one of the three acts like 502
they heard a thing I said; in fact, they're all looking off from 415
me like they'd as soon I wasn't there at all. 525

Mark the number of words read (or the number to the right of the last line read). Answer the questions below without referring to the selection.

1. The narrator said he started acting deaf because
   (a) people expected too much from him.
   (b) other people first started acting like he was too dumb to hear or say anything.
   (c) he was insulted by the fat man who visited his Indian village.
   (d) the roar of the waterfall near his village had ruined his hearing.

2. The fat man thought the chief's house would be cool. **T F**

3. At the time of this story the narrator spoke no English. **T F**

4. The visitors were embarrassed when they realized the Indian boy had heard what they were saying. **T F**

Check your answers with the key on the bottom of page 136. Record your scores below and on the progress chart in the Appendix.

WORDS PER MINUTE ______

% COMPREHENSION ______

Answer Key Ex. 5G
1. (a) **2.** F **3.** T **4.** F time sequence; description

Bonus Question

Check the pattern(s) that best describe(s) the way in which the details are organized around the main idea.

description	______	cause-and-effect	______
analogy	______	space relationships	______

Exercise 51—Long Reading

LENGTH: 1265

Read the following selection as rapidly as you can but with good comprehension. Pay particular attention to details. Wait for a signal from your instructor before you begin reading.

Carnival Queen

Jeanne Wakatsuki Houston and James Houston

By the spring of that year, when it came time to elect the annual carnival queen from the graduating seniors, my homeroom chose me. I was among fifteen girls nominated to walk out for inspection by the assembled student body on voting day.

I knew I couldn't beat the other contestants at their own game, that is, look like a bobbysoxer. Yet neither could I look too Japanese-y. I decided to go exotic, with a flower-print sarong, black hair loose and a hibiscus flower behind my ear. When I walked barefooted out onto the varnished gymnasium floor, between the filled bleachers, the howls and whistles from the boys were double what had greeted any of the other girls. It sounded like some winning basket had just been made in the game against our oldest rivals.

It was pretty clear what the outcome would be, but ballots still had to be cast and counted. The next afternoon I was standing outside my Spanish class when Leonard Rodriguez, who sat next to me, came hurrying down the hall with a revolutionary's fire in his eye. He helped out each day in the administration office. He had just overheard some teachers and a couple of secretaries counting up the votes.

"They're trying to stuff the ballot box," he whispered loudly. "They're fudging on the tally. They're afraid to have a Japanese girl be queen. They've never had one before. They're afraid of what some of the parents will say."

He was pleased he had caught them, and more pleased

to be telling this to me, as if some long-held suspicion of conspiracy had finally been confirmed. I shared it with him. Whether this was true or not, I was prepared to believe that teachers would stuff the ballot box to keep me from being queen. For that reason I couldn't afford to get my hopes up.

I said, "So what?"

He leaned toward me eagerly, with final proof. "They want Lois Carson to be queen. I heard them say so."

If applause were any measure, Lois Carson wasn't even in the running. She was too slim and elegant for beauty contests. But her father had contributed a lot to the school. He was on the board of trustees. She was blond, blue-eyed. I was ready to capitulate without a groan.

"If she doesn't make carnival queen this year," Leonard went on smugly, "she'll never be queen of anything anywhere else for the rest of her life."

"Let her have it then, if she wants it so much."

"No! We can't do that! *You* can't do that!"

I could do that very easily. I wasn't going to be caught caring about this, or needing it, the way I had needed the majorette position. I already sensed, though I couldn't have said why, that I would lose either way, no matter how it turned out. My face was indifferent.

"How can I stop them from fudging," I said, "if that's what they want to do?"

He hesitated. He looked around. He set his brown face. My champion. "You can't," he said. "But I can."

He turned and hurried away toward the office. The next morning he told me he had gone in there and "raised holy hell," threatened to break this news to the student body and make the whole thing more trouble than it would ever be worth. An hour later the announcement came over the intercom that I had been chosen. I didn't believe it. I couldn't let myself believe it. But, for the classmates who had nominated me, I had to look overjoyed. I glanced across at Leonard and he winked, shouting and whooping now with all the others.

At home that evening, when I brought this news, no one whooped. Papa was furious. I had not told them I was running for queen. There was no use mentioning it until I had something to mention. He asked me what I had worn at the tryouts. I told him.

"No wonder those *hakajin* [Caucasian] boys vote for you!" he shouted. "It is just like those majorette clothes you wear in the street. Showing off your body. Is that the kind of queen you want to be?"

Answer Key: Ex. 5H
1. (b) **2.** F **3.** F **4.** F description, cause-and-effect

I didn't say anything. When Papa lectured, you listened. If anyone spoke up it would be Mama, trying to mediate.

"Ko," she said now, "these things are important to Jeannie. She is. . ."

"Important? I'll tell you what is important. Modesty is important. A graceful body is important. You don't show your legs all the time. You don't walk around like this."

He did an imitation of a girl's walk, with shoulders straight, an assertive stride, and lips pulled back in a baboon's grin. I started to laugh.

"Don't laugh! This is not funny. You become this kind of woman and what Japanese boy is going to marry you? Tell me that. You put on tight clothes and walk around like Jean Harlow and the *hakajin* boys make you the queen. And pretty soon you end up marrying a *hakajin* boy. . ."

He broke off. He could think of no worse end result. He began to stomp back and forth across the floor, while Mama looked at me cautiously, with a glance that said, "Be patient, wait him out. After he has spoken his piece, you and I can talk sensibly."

He saw this and turned on her. "Hey! How come your daughter is seventeen years old and if you put a sack over her face you couldn't tell she was Japanese from anybody else on the street?"

"Ko," Mama said quietly. "Jeannie's in high school now. Next year she's going to college. She's learning other things. . ."

"Listen to me. It's not too late for her to learn Japanese ways of movement. The Buddhist church in San Jose gives odori [Japanese dance] class twice a week. Jeannie, I want you to phone the teacher and tell her you are going to start taking lessons. Mama has kimonos you can wear. She can show you things too. She used to know all the dances. We have pictures somewhere. Mama, what happened to all those pictures?"

I had seen them, photos of Mama when she lived in Spokane, twelve years old and her round face blanched with rice powder.

"Papa," I complained.

"Don't make faces. You want to be the carnival queen? I tell you what. I'll make a deal with you. You can be the queen if you start odori lessons at the Buddhist church as soon as school is out."

He stood there, hands on hips, glaring at me, and not at all satisfied with this ultimatum. It was far too late for odori classes to have any effect on me and Papa knew this. But he owed it to himself to make one more show of resistance. When I signed up, a few weeks later, I lasted about ten lessons. The teacher herself sent me away. I smiled too much and couldn't break the habit. Like a majorette before the ever-shifting sidewalk crowd, I smiled during performances, and in Japanese dancing that is equivalent to a concert violinist walking onstage in a bathing suit.

Papa didn't mention my queenship again. He just glared at me from time to time, with great distaste, as if I had betrayed him. Yet in that glare I sometimes detected a flicker of approval, as if this streak of independence, this refusal to be shaped by him, reflected his own obstinance. At least, these glances seemed to say, she has inherited *that.*

TOTAL READING TIME ______

Immediately answer the questions below without referring to the selection.

1. Choose the statement that best expresses the main idea.
- **(a)** Jeannie's papa thinks she smiles too much.
- **(b)** The school staff was afraid to have a carnival queen who was Japanese.
- **(c)** While Jeannie struggles for acceptance at school, her papa fears she is becoming more American than Japanese.
- **(d)** Jeannie is excited about being chosen queen.

2. Jeannie's becoming queen was a sign of her acceptance. **T F**

3. Jeannie wore a long white gown during the contest for queen. **T F**

4. Leonard Rodriguez kept the contest honest. **T F**

5. Jeannie's father wanted her to marry a *hakajin* boy. **T F**

6. Jeannie's mother quietly took her side. **T F**

7. Jeannie's papa was secretly proud of her independence. **T F**

8. Jeannie became a very good odori dancer. **T F**

Check your answers with the key on the bottom of page 140. Then turn to the Rate Chart in the Appendix to get your words per minute for this selection. Finally, record your scores below and on the progress chart in the Appendix.

WORDS PER MINUTE ______

% COMPREHENSION ______

Bonus Questions

Fill in the blanks with answers to the following questions about details. Check your answers by referring to the paragraph indicated by the number in parentheses.

1. Give a piece of information about Lois Carson, who almost was named queen.

____

____(8)

2. Give an example of what Jeannie's papa would consider proper behavior for a young Japanese woman. ____

____(17–26)

Percentage Chart for Comprehension Check

Errors	0	1	2	3	4	5	6	7	8
% Right	100	88	75	63	50	38	25	13	0

Answer Key: Ex. 51
1. (c) **2.** T **3.** F **4.** T **5.** F **6.** T **7.** T **8.** F **(1)** slim, elegant, blond, blue-eyed, father on the board of trustees **(2)** modest clothing, graceful body, non-assertive walk, unsmiling face, knowledge of Japanese ways of movement, as taught in odori classes, marriage to a Japanese boy

Lesson 6

Exercise 6A—Phrase Perception

key phrase			
1. coffee and cream	cream and coffee	cream in coffee	scream in rage
	Mrs. Olsen's cat	coffee and cream	
2. sweep the room	wipe the broom	sweep the room	root for home team
	weep and wail	sweeten the drink	
3. sweet and low	lowdown sweat	sweet answers	sweet and low
	low and sweet	an allowed sweet	
4. four foul fingers	fold five fingers	four fragile forks	finger in fire
	four foul fingers	four fat fowls	
5. leaves of grass	leaves of grass	leave the grass	mow the lawn
	weave the cloth	believe in me	
6. ten tender tales	one bending trail	trapped by the tail	tell ten tales
	tenderly tell Ted	ten tender tales	
7. row the boat	hoe the tow	row the boat	sow the oats
	toe the line	blow the whistle	
8. awake at dawn	away in a manger	the rooster crows	dig here again
	awake at dawn	await the clown	
9. tear in eye	eye the tear	the torn curtain	in near future
	an awful eyesore	tear in eye	
10. a pretty picture	frame the picture	picture the pretty	a pretty picture
	a ready word	a big package	
11. a sharp retort	a short harp	a shorn sheep	a tart reply
	a sharp retort	a shaggy dog	
12. giving haggard looks	looking very haggard	haggling over price	living in huts
	reading good books	giving haggard looks	
13. sit on the stool	spit in the pool	sitting on the fence	sit on the stool
	put down the fool	see over the sty	
14. hop up high	a high-up hop	hop up high	pop-up box
	turn on light	sigh too loud	
15. hold on tight	hold on tight	fold a towel	much too bold
	onto one door	tied up tight	
16. hide in here	hear his tirade	abide with me	turn the tide
	hide in here	hard-hearted Hannah	

17.	tea and sympathy	see my symphony peas and beans	tease the child tea and sympathy	sea and surf
18.	take another path	rake the other yard another path taken	take another bath the other path	take another path
19.	rest in peace	the best place full of peace	rest in peace trust in me	a peaceful guest
20.	jump over the sticks	overcome the ticks jump onto the back	put three lumps in jump over the sticks	pull over the stump

TIME _______

ERRORS _______

Exercise 6B—Phrase Perception

key phrase	Choices		
1. dirty kitchen sink	dirt in kitchen sink sink, dear Kit	sink in dirt, Kit dirt on chin	dirty kitchen sink
2. in the garden alone	alone in the garden in the garden alone	in the lone garden in the garbage bag	work in garden alone
3. this hunting trophy	they hunt trophies these hunting trophies	this hunting trophy trophies for hunting	hunt this trophy
4. sing the unsung hero	sing the unsung hero the hero swings high	the unsung hero sings a single hero swinging	sing a song, Hero
5. prophet of doom	prop up the room prophet of doom	a doomed prophet prophecy of doom	prophesy doom
6. rose by another name	name my other rose the other rose's name	rose has another name roll by another day	rose by another name
7. the worm turns	the turned worm the warm churn	turn the worm the worn turf	the worm turns
8. talk to your plants	plant one more kiss talking about plans	talk to plants talk to your plants	walk to your plants
9. heaven only knows	know only heaven only heavenly knowledge	heaven only knows know heaven alone	known in heaven
10. a goose-feather pillow	a feather pillow goose-feather pillows	feather the pillow a goose-feather pillow	a good pillow
11. gather ye rosebuds	ye rosebuds gathered ye gathered rosebuds	gather ye rosebuds gather your rosebuds	rosebuds get gathered
12. make hay in sunshine	make hay in sun more hay in sunshine	hayride in sunshine hay in sunshine	make hay in sunshine
13. one more record crop	more one-record crops more than one record	count one more record one record to count	one more record crop
14. wrinkled red raincoat	red wrinkled raincoat crumpled red raincoat	wring the raincoat wrinkled red raincoat	red raincoat was wrinkled
15. magnificent obsession	magnificent obsessions obsessed with magnificence	magnificent obsession magnificent session	magnified object
16. policeman's whistle	the policeman's whistle policeman's whim	policemen's whistle policemen whistle	policeman's whistle
17. gun of the murderer	gum of the murderer gun of the murderers	gun for the murdered gun of the murderer	grab for the murderer
18. jail for the guilty	jail the four guilty jail for the guilty	pail for the guilty for the jailed guilty	wail for his guilt

19. tools of the thief	tools of the thief pool of the thief	tell the thief off tool of the train	of the thief's tools
20. the judge's white hair	white-haired judge whiten his hair	judge the hare the judge's white hair	the judge's hair

TIME ________

ERRORS ________

Exercise 6C—Word Comprehension

key word					
1. articulate	talkative	artistic	fluent	amputate	particular
2. obstinate	shy	stubborn	block	opportunity	obstacle
3. arid	dry	fertile	wet	green-filled	acid
4. abhor	approve	horrible	attitude	detest	horde
5. wary	wasteful	careless	postponed	tired	cautious
6. extravagant	cheap	moderate	excessive	priceless	harsh
7. abolition	termination	government	slavery	partition	amendment
8. secrete	treat	hide	send	uncover	hasty
9. sham	master	real	wrap	pretend	shake
10. valiant	soldier	villain	cowardly	pretentious	brave
11. astound	preview	suspect	surprise	astral	gift
12. deceased	body	dead	coffin	decent	alive
13. imply	suggest	infer	regulate	hinder	refer
14. destitute	future	humble	hollow	poor	rich
15. wane	decline	waste	increase	stubborn	hag
16. mute	talkative	silent	loud	hard	moon
17. famished	satisfied	overcome	uneasy	family	starved
18. trivial	large	cruel	petty	generous	trial
19. obscure	open	clear	obstacle	vague	cautious
20. sublime	ordinary	noble	king	subtle	entire

TIME _______

ERRORS _______

Exercise 6D—Word Comprehension

key word					
1. encore	once	repeat	song	play	entire
2. insignia	emblem	signature	name	cross	failure
3. tantrum	dull	taste	fit	tease	trick
4. rove	raise	stay	fall	drive	wander
5. fabulous	rich	story	wonderful	gorgeous	fatal
6. apprehend	capture	criminal	burglarize	chase	escape
7. forego	force	give up	win	give in	take
8. concede	insist	go before	give in	defy	fortune
9. cleave	trim	knife	dirty	split	clean
10. astound	send	tough	confound	expect	surprise
11. expire	die	expand	breathe in	spirit	live
12. adversary	contest	opponent	partner	enemy	friend
13. captivate	seduce	cough	charm	jail	beg
14. smite	shoot	fight	caress	small	strike
15. amputate	break	sew on	risk	cut off	hold out
16. apprentice	scholar	carpenter	learner	appreciate	veteran
17. strategy	sanity	trap	tip	plan	tournament
18. commanding	petty	important	masterful	treatment	previous
19. tangible	touching	concrete	torn	gentle	target
20. homage	halfway	houseful	return	restful	honor

TIME ________

ERRORS ________

Exercise 6E—Sentence Comprehension

key sentence: Reading for ideas instead of words will increase reading rate.

1. Reading rate is increased by reacting to ideas, not single words. ______
2. It is more difficult to grasp ideas than to merely recognize words. ______
3. How well one understands ideas in reading material is often related to how well one understands the vocabulary used in the material. ______
4. Ideas are more important than isolated words. ______
5. In increasing speed, reading word for word is not as effective as reading for ideas. ______
6. A poor vocabulary often means a slower reading rate. ______
7. It is easier to read faster when reading interesting material. ______
8. One can read faster when one stops reading word for word and starts reading for ideas. ______
9. Wordy sentence structure sometimes obscures the meaning of a reading passage. ______
10. The rate of understanding ideas can be dependent on the rate of reading. ______

TIME ______

ERRORS ______

Answer Key: Ex. 6C
1. fluent **2.** stubborn **3.** dry **4.** detest **5.** cautious **6.** excessive **7.** termination **8.** hide **9.** pretend **10.** brave **11.** surprise **12.** dead **13.** suggest **14.** poor **15.** decline **16.** silent **17.** starved **18.** petty **19.** vague **20.** noble

Answer Key: Ex. 6D
1. repeat **2.** emblem **3.** fit **4.** wander **5.** wonderful **6.** capture **7.** give up **8.** give in **9.** split **10.** surprise **11.** die **12.** opponent **13.** charm **14.** strike **15.** cut off **16.** learner **17.** plan **18.** masterful **19.** concrete **20.** honor

Exercise 6F — Sentence Comprehension

key sentence: Our life is frittered away by detail. (by Henry David Thoreau)

1. We should not spend our valuable time regretting past mistakes. ______
2. We waste our lives, little by little, attending to small, unimportant tasks. ______
3. Our breakfast tables are enriched by the sight of corn fritters. ______
4. A man who spends his time wisely achieves more. ______
5. Many people spend hours looking for better ways to occupy their time. ______
6. Insignificant matters take up so much of our time that our lives seem to go by without meaning. ______
7. One should pay more attention to important problems and ignore unimportant matters. ______
8. Our ambitions are frustrated by the interference of petty employers. ______
9. Advance planning saves much wasted time. ______
10. The days of our lives seem needlessly spent in taking care of minor details. ______

TIME ______

ERRORS ______

SCANNING FOR SPECIFIC ANSWERS

What is the reading skill called "scanning"? It might be defined as selective skipping. *When you scan print, you are looking for one thing in particular.* You have a specific question or word or number in mind, and you run through the material at high speed until you find the answer. Then you stop, fixate, and read only what you need.

Scanning can be the simple task of finding the exact word or number—as in our perception drills. Or it can be more difficult, as when the wording of your information may be different from the wording of your question. The different kinds of scanning often overlap. The important point is that *you recognize what you are looking for.*

The scanning rates suggested by many experts may be frightening. They speak of 2,000 wpm and up. Actually, you have already practiced scanning many times, at 2,000 wpm and much more. In fact, a words-per-minute rate is rather meaningless in scanning, because you are selecting so little and ignoring so much. Keep in mind, however, that you are rapidly processing even the material you choose not really to *read.*

When you scan you begin, as in all reading, with a purpose. Here are some of the simplest reasons to use your scanning ability:

1. finding a name in the phone book, a word in the dictionary, "Cleaners" in the yellow pages, or page 51 in this book;
2. locating a certain street or town on a map;
3. looking for news of a specific athlete, meeting, or auto accident in the newspaper;
4. finding the subject, author or title you want in the library's card catalog or on the shelf;
5. using office skills such as filing, billing, and checking for errors;
6. locating information in a book index or table of contents;
7. looking for a specific item as you do in the number, letter, word, or phrase perception drills in this book.

The following scanning tasks require some translation of your ideas, some flexibility of where to look. But they still assume that you have a specific question and will know when you find the answer:

1. looking in the movie ads or TV guides for "any good show" (you may, in the process rule out all westerns, porno films, etc.);
2. looking in the classified newspaper ads for rentals, furniture, etc., that are available in your area or in your price range;

Answer Key: Ex. 6E
1, 5, 8

Answer Key: Ex. 6F
2, 6, 10

3. finding how many buses or planes travel between two cities, and when;
4. using a reference guide or a book index for information, say, on "Women's Lib"—it may be listed under "Sex Discrimination," "Employment," "Equal Rights," etc.;
5. looking for answers to multiple-choice questions;
6. looking for similar words, phrases, and sentences in the comprehension exercises in this book.

When you scan, you zero in on specific answers like a hawk swooping down on a mouse. The image is not extreme if you have ever done a research paper or worked in a busy office. You do need good perception, a clear idea of what you're looking for, and the discipline to ignore everything else. The following exercises should help you become faster and more accurate in your scanning ability.

Exercise 6G — Scanning

Scan the opposite page for answers to the following questions.

You have decided to enroll in a community college. So you scan the college catalog to familiarize yourself with the requirements.

STARTING TIME ______

1. Under what circumstance could you get a "W" grade? ______________________

2. If you withdraw from a regular course during the twelfth week because you are not passing, might you get a "U" grade? ______________________

3. The last day to change your class program is found in the semester schedule of classes and what other places? ______________________

4. Where do you file to withdraw from one or all of your classes? ______________________

5. If a class has a number beginning with 90 – 99, what kind of class is it? ______________________

FINISHING TIME ______

Check your answers with the key on the bottom of page 154, and record your scores below.

TOTAL SCANNING TIME ______

NUMBER OF ERRORS ______

Exercise 6G — Scanning

COLLEGE REGULATIONS

It is important that every student gives careful attention to his educational objectives and the program of studies before he registers. Deadline date for change of program, refund of A.S. Membership, etc., are indicated in each semester's schedule of classes and in the Student Handbook.*

ATTENDANCE AND STUDENT REQUEST TO WITHDRAW FROM A CLASS

Since attendance is considered necessary for normal progress in a class, the student is expected to be in class regularly and on time.

First Ten Weeks: A student may withdraw from a single class or from all classes during the first ten weeks without penalty. Proper forms for withdrawal are available in the Counseling Office.

After Ten Weeks: A student may withdraw from a single class or from all classes by filing proper forms available in the Counseling Office. A grade check will be made with the instructor. If the student was passing the course at the time of his last attendance, he will receive a "W" grade. If he was failing, he may be given a "U" (unsatisfactory withdrawal) grade.

Exceptions. This policy does not apply to "classes for adults" numbered 90 – 99. All students who withdraw will be given "W" grades in these classes.

ATTENDANCE AND INSTRUCTOR REQUEST TO DROP A STUDENT

A student may be dropped from a class when, in the instructor's judgment, the number of absences has become excessive. Such judgment should be based exclusively on the student's prospect for successfully completing the course. When a student is dropped from class, he will receive a "W" grade, except under the following conditions: If the last attendance occurs after the 10th week and if the student was doing failing work, the instructor may assign a "U" grade. *Exception:* This policy does not apply to classes numbered 9000 – 9999. All students who withdraw will be given "W" grades in these classes. Failure to follow these procedures by discontinuing attendance in class may result in "U" (unsatisfactory withdrawal) grades and possible disqualification from college.

*(From Santa Monica College General Catalog, 1974 – 76)

Exercise 6H – Scanning

Scan the opposite page for answers to the following questions.

You consider drafting as a possible career. Again, scan the college catalog for requirements.

STARTING TIME ______

1. If you are not interested in the Associate in Arts Degree, what are the other three general academic goals that you might pursue in preparing for employment? ______

______

2. How many units would you need for an Occupational Certificate? ______

______

3. For an A.A. degree in Drafting Technology, how many units must you take in the major? ______
4. How many courses are available for "selection" in the major? ______

______

5. Where do you find a page listing the General Education courses? ______

______

FINISHING TIME ______

Check your answers with the key on the bottom of page 156, and record your scores below.

TOTAL SCANNING TIME ______

NUMBER OF ERRORS ______

Answer Key: Ex. 6G
1. If you withdraw or are dropped from a class after 10 weeks and are passing at the time of your last attendance **2.** yes **3.** Student Handbook **4.** Counseling Office **5.** "classes for adults"

Exercise 6H – Scanning

MAJOR IN DRAFTING TECHNOLOGY

Employment in the field and an Associate in Arts Degree in Drafting Technology are the primary purposes of this major.*

A. ASSOCIATE IN ARTS DEGREE – 60 UNITS

1. The major consists of 20 units including:
   Drafting Technology 3, Advanced Drafting, and other courses selected from:
   Drafting Technology 2, Fundamentals
   Drafting Technology 35AB, Advanced Drafting and Layout
   Electronic Engineering Technology 5, Computer Fundamentals
   Manufacturing Engineering Technology 1, Machine Processes
   Manufacturing Engineering Technology 2, Metal Joining
   Manufacturing Engineering Technology 3, Metal Casting
   Manufacturing Engineering Technology 7, Welding Processes
   Manufacturing Engineering Technology 10, Numerical Controls
   Manufacturing Engineering Technology 11AB, Tool Design
   Manufacturing Engineering Technology 14, Numerical Controls
2. The required General Education courses are included in the Santa Monica College graduation requirements listed on a page following this section on majors.

B. OCCUPATIONAL CERTIFICATE

A Certificate in Drafting Technology or Tool Design may be earned by completing 20 units with a C or better grade point average. Courses are to be selected from those listed above for the major.

C. VOCATIONAL DIPLOMA

A Vocational Diploma is awarded to students who complete 40 units or more in Drafting Technology with a C grade point average. Courses are those listed in the major and other courses in the Metal Trades. Units may be counted toward the Associate in Arts Degree as well as this diploma.

D. TRANSFER

1. *Drafting and Design, California State University at Fresno*
   Art 11, 12; Construction Technology 5, 6, 7, 8, 9
   Drafting, California Polytechnic State University at San Luis Obispo
   Chemistry 1; General Engineering 7; Electricity 40 or 40X; Electronic Engineering Technology 12, 13, or 13X; Mathematics 2, 7, 8; Manufacturing Engineering Technology 1, 10; Physics 6, 7
   California State University at San Jose
   The Technical and Architectural option in the Industrial Studies major is also a study area related to the Santa Monica Drafting major.
2. General Education
   The California State University and Colleges General Education pattern is listed on a page following this section on majors.

*(From Santa Monica College General Catalog, 1974–76)

Exercise 6I—Scanning

Scan the opposite page for answers to the following questions.

You try to decide which English course to take by scanning the schedule of classes.

STARTING TIME ______

1. You can't take World Literature or English Literature I and II without first taking what course? ______
2. If you want to take Harrell's Monday class, English 48, will it conflict with Chodos' English 4? ______
3. If you are given a grade of C in English 1, can you then enroll in Dodge's Advanced Composition class? ______
4. Is English 98 a college-level course? ______
5. Is there a class in Creative Writing on Monday evenings? ______

FINISHING TIME ______

Check your answers with the key on the bottom of page 158, and record your scores below.

TOTAL SCANNING TIME ______

NUMBER OF ERRORS ______

Answer Key: Ex. 6H
1. Occupational Certificate, Vocational Diploma, or Transfer **2.** 20 **3.** 20 **4.** 10 **5.** following this section on majors

Exercise 6I—Scanning

Section Number	Time	Room	Instructor	
ENGL 30 BEGINNING CREATIVE WRITING				**3 UNITS**
1318	9:30–11 TT	LA 124	Casty A H	
1319	11 MWF	LA 136	Casty A H	
5354	**7–10 WED**	**SMHSH213**	**Bilson B T**	
1320	9–12 SAT	LA 231	Ellman D M	
ENGL 31 ADVANCED COMPOSITION				**3 UNITS**
Prereq- Engl 1 With Grade B				
1321	8–9:30 TT	SA 10	Dodge R H	
ENGL 46 POWER READING				**3 UNITS**
Prereq- Group C—Engl Placement Test				
Offered Only On A Credit-No Credit Basis.				
One Hour Per Week Required in the Learning Center				
1322	8 MWF	SA 12	Dye A G	
1323	9 MWF	SA 12	Dye A G	
1324	12–1:30 TT	SA 12	Saintleon S K	
1325	1:30–3 TT	SA 12	Saintleon S K	
1326	3–4:30 TT	SA 12	George P C	
5355	**7–10 TUES**	**SA 12**	**Hearn W G**	
5356	**7–10 WED**	**SA 12**	**George P C**	
5357	**7–10 THURS**	**SA 12**	**Hearn W G**	
ENGL 47 ADVANCED POWER READING				**3 UNITS**
Prereq- Group B—Engl Placement Test				
One Hour Per Week Required in the Learning Center				
1327	9:30–11 TT	SA 12	Dye A G	
ENGL 48 POWER AND SPEED READING				**3 UNITS**
Prereq- Engl 1 or B in Engl 21 or 47				
One Hour Per Week Required in the Learning Center				
1328	11 MWF	SA 12	Dye A G	
1329	12 MWF	SA 12	Dye A G	
5358	**7–10 MON**	**SA 12**	**Harrell W M**	
1330	9–12 SAT	SA 12	Harrell W M	
ENGL 98 CORRECT USAGE				**0 UNITS**
For Completion of High School Requirements.				
9808	**7–10 MON**	**SMHST215**	**Harris J K**	
9809	**7–10 WED**	**SMHST215**	**Harris J K**	
		ENGLISH LITERATURE		
ENGL 4 WORLD LITERATURE II				**3 UNITS**
Prereq- Engl 1				
1331	12 MWF	LA 236	Marsh J E	
5359	**7–10 MON**	**SC 274**	**Chodos J W**	
ENGL 5 ENGLISH LITERATURE I				**3 UNITS**
Prereq- Engl 1				
1332	9 MWF	LA 231	Doten D G	
1333	9:30–11 TT	LA 231	Marrant D E	
5360	**7–10 WED**	**LA 231**	**Doten D G**	
ENGL 6 ENGLISH LITERATURE II				**3 UNITS**
Prereq- Engl 1				
1334	12 MWF	LA 231	Theiss N L	
5361	**7–10 TUES**	**LA 220**	**Dodge R H**	

Master Numbers over 5000 in Bold Type indicate Evening Sessions

(From Santa Monica College Schedule of Classes, Spring 1975)

Exercise 6J — Scanning

Scan the opposite page for answers to the following questions.

You learn to use the dictionary in your English class — by scanning for answers.

STARTING TIME ______

1. What is the population of Gettysburg, Pennsylvania? ______
2. From what language did we borrow the word *ghetto?* (Look in the square brackets.) ______
3. What are the two ways of spelling the noun plural of GI? ______
4. What is the feminine noun form of the word *giant?* ______
5. How many meanings are listed for the simple verb *get?* ______

Check your answers with the key on the bottom of page 160, and record your scores below.

TOTAL SCANNING TIME ______

NUMBER OF ERRORS ______

Answer Key: Ex. 6I
1. Engl 1 **2.** Yes **3.** No **4.** No **5.** No

Exercise 6J—Scanning

get / giant 302

get (gĕt) *v.* **got, got** or **gotten, getting. 1.** To obtain or acquire. **2.** To procure; secure. **3.** To go after; fetch. **4.** To make contact with by or as if by radio or telephone. **5.** To earn: *get a reward.* **6.** To receive: *get a present.* **7.** To buy. **8.** To catch; contract: *get chicken pox.* **9.** To reach by calculation: *If you add them, you'll get 1,000.* **10.** To have obtained or received and now have: *I've got a large collection of books.* **11.** To understand: *Do you get his point?* **12.** *Informal.* To register, as by eye or ear: *I didn't get your name.* **13.** To cause to become or to be in a specific condition: *He can't get the hook loose.* **14.** To cause to move, come, or go: *Get that dog out of here!* **15.** To bring or take: *I'll get him in here.* **16.** To prevail upon: *I'll get my friend to agree.* **17.** To capture: *The police got him.* **18.** *Slang.* To reciprocate by causing harm: *I'll get you for that remark.* **19.** *Informal.* To strike or hit: *That blow got him on the chin.* **20.** *Slang.* To puzzle: *Her attitude gets me.* **21.** To have the obligation: *I have got to go.* **22.** To become or grow. —Used as a linking verb: *I got well again.* **23.** To arrive: *When will we get to New York?* **24.** To betake oneself: *Get out!* **25.** *Informal.* To start: *Get going!* —**get across.** To make or be understandable or clear: *Am I getting this across to you?* —**get ahead.** To be successful. —**get along. 1.** To be mutually congenial. **2.** To manage with reasonable success. **3.** To advance in years. —**get around. 1.** To avoid doing or encountering; circumvent. **2.** *Informal.* To convince or gain the favor of by flattering or cajoling. —**get at. 1.** To determine; ascertain: *I'm trying to get at his point.* **2.** To reach: *It's under the desk and I can't get at it.* **3.** To lead up to or arrive at, as a conclusion or meaning: *Do you understand what I'm getting at?* —**get away with.** *Informal.* To be successful in avoiding retribution or the discovery of something done. —**get back at.** *Informal.* To retaliate or have revenge against. —**get by.** To manage; survive: *We'll get by.* —**get down to.** To concentrate on. —**get in. 1.** To enter or be allowed to enter. **2.** To arrive. —**get it. 1.** To comprehend; understand. **2.** *Informal.* To be punished or scolded. —**get nowhere.** To make no progress; have no success. —**get off. 1.** To get down from or out of. **2.** To leave; depart. **3.** To write and send, as a letter. —**get on. 1.** To climb up onto or into; enter. **2.** To get along. **3.** To advance: *He's getting on in years.* —**get out of. 1.** To derive or draw: *He gets out of it what he can.* **2.** To avoid or get around. —**get over.** To recover from (a sorrow, illness, etc.). —**get there.** *Informal.* To attain one's goal. —**get through to. 1.** To make contact with. **2.** To make understandable to. —**get to. 1.** To be able to: *I hope I get to go.* **2.** To reach: *We never got to that point.* **3.** *Informal.* To happen to start: *Then we got to remembering good times.* [< ON *geta.*] —**get'a•ble, get'ta•ble** *adj.*

get•a•way (gĕt'ə-wā') *n.* **1.** An act or instance of escaping. **2.** A start, as of a race. —*adj.* Used for escape: *a getaway car.*

get-to•geth•er (gĕt'tə-gĕth'ər) *n.* An informal social gathering.

Get•tys•burg (gĕt'ĭz-bûrg). A town in S Pennsylvania, the site of a major Civil War battle. Pop. 8,000.

get-up (gĕt'ŭp') *n.* An outfit or costume, esp. one remarkable in some way.

GeV *Phys.* Giga (10^9) electron volts.

gew•gaw (gyōō'gô') *n.* A trinket; bauble. [?]

gey•ser (gī'zər) *n.* A natural hot spring that intermittently ejects a column of water and steam. [< ON *geysa,* to gush.]

Gha•na (gä'nə). A republic in W Africa. Pop. 7,600,000. Cap. Accra. —**Gha•na'ian, Gha'ni•an** (gə-nā'ən) *adj.* & *n.*

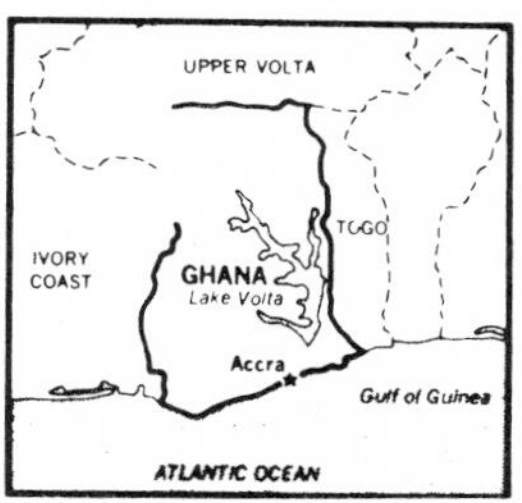

Ghana

ghast•ly (găst'lē, gäst'-) *adj.* **-lier, -liest. 1.** Terrifying; dreadful. **2.** Deathly pale. **3.** Extremely unpleasant. [< OE *gāst,* soul, ghost.]

gher•kin (gûr'kĭn) *n.* A small cucumber, esp. one used for pickling. [Du *agurkje.*]

ghet•to (gĕt'ō) *n., pl.* **-tos** or **-toes.** A section of a city to which an ethnic or economically depressed minority group is restricted, as by poverty or social pressure. [It.]

ghost (gōst) *n.* **1.** The disembodied spirit of a dead person, supposed to haunt living persons or former habitats. **2.** A slight trace or vestige. **3.** A faint secondary photographic or television image. —**give up the ghost.** To die. [< OE *gāst.* See **gheis-.**] —**ghost'ly** *adj.*

ghost•writ•er (gōst'rī'tər) *n.* A person who writes for another who is credited with authorship. —**ghost'write'** *v.*

ghoul (gōōl) *n.* **1.** An evil spirit supposed to plunder graves and feed on corpses. **2.** A grave robber. [Ar *ghūl.*] —**ghoul'ish** *adj.*

GHQ general headquarters.

gi gill[2].

GI (jē'ī') *n., pl.* **GIs** or **GI's.** An enlisted man in the U.S. armed forces. —*adj.* **1.** Pertaining to or characteristic of a GI or U.S. military procedures. **2.** Issued by an official U.S. military supply department.

GI Government Issue.

gi•ant (jī'ənt) *n.* **1.** A legendary manlike being of enormous size and strength. **2.** One of unusually great size or importance. —*adj.* Gigantic; huge. [< L *gigās (gigant-).*] —**gi'ant•ess** *fem.n.*

ă pat/ā ate/âr care/ä bar/b bib/ch chew/d deed/ĕ pet/ē be/f fit/g gag/h hat/hw what/
ĭ pit/ī pie/îr pier/j judge/k kick/l lid, fatal/m mum/n no, sudden/ng sing/ŏ pot/ō go/

(From the American Heritage Dictionary, paperback edition. New York: Dell Publishing Company, Inc., 1973)

WORDS IN CONTEXT

Without using your dictionary, try to determine the meaning of each word in **boldface** print. Choose the meaning below that best fits the context—the way it is used in the sentence.

Long Reading 6K

1. Research by **neurologists** indicates there is a real physical difference between short-term memory and long-term memory.
   (a) expert in study habits **(b)** instructor in a memory course **(c)** specialist in problems of the nervous system **(d)** one who studies horoscopes
2. Use your imagination to help you remember what you learned. With a little effort, you can feel your way into an **amoeba!** After all, amoebas do, and they're not very smart.
   (a) single-celled organism **(b)** small closed area **(c)** altered state of consciousness **(d)** a germ

Long Reading 6L

3. Do **isometrics** or static stretching, while you sit or stand in one place.
   (a) exercising in a cool area **(b)** exercising to a metric beat **(c)** mental exercises **(d)** tensing and relaxing muscles at regular intervals

Check your answers with the key on the bottom of page 162.

THEME FOR READING SELECTIONS: STUDY SKILLS

The two Long Readings in this Lesson will be useful for any student. The first offers useful tips on preparing for a test. The second tells you how to take a test . . . and pass!

Imaginary Situation

You are a college student who didn't do well last semester because you panicked on tests. You plan to overcome this problem and have found two highly recommended articles that assure you of success. Read with a positive attitude, then picture yourself putting into practice what you learn.

Answer Key: Ex. 6J
1. 8,000 **2.** It. (abbreviation for Italian) **3.** GIs or GI's **4.** giantess **5.** 25

Exercise 6K — Long Reading LENGTH: 1241

Read the following selection as rapidly as you can for general idea. Wait for a signal from your instructor before you begin reading. (Scanning exercise follows with separate timing.)

I. How to Prepare for a Test*

Anne Dye

Does that title mean there's going to be a part II? Yes it does. And if that question already occurred to you, you know one trick about passing tests: you read every word carefully, especially in headings and directions.

Why two parts? Because there are two main reasons why a person fails a test. One, he/she/it (no sexism here) doesn't know the material. Two, he/she/it knows the material but doesn't know how to take a test. And pass it. These are two very different reasons, and often two very different persons. Which type are you?

If you're the first type, you fail tests because you don't know the material — maybe it's time you admitted it. Some time, you'll have to stop blaming the test, the course, the instructor's personality, the weather, your daily cycle, your life cycle, your job, your horoscope, your mother/father/children, your love life/lack of a love life — and admit that you flunked the test because you didn't know the stuff. There is, after all, some truth in the old saying: "If all else fails, *study!*"

1. *So let's assume you decide to study* — to learn the material before taking the test. When do you start? Contrary to popular belief, not — unless you absolutely have to — the night before the test. *You start to study the day you register for the class.* Ask yourself and other people questions like: What is the field like? What's the instructor like? Your best hopes (and fears) will be confirmed the first class meeting.

Start studying the course outline, the instructor, the outside reading list. Get the right mental set for success in *this* course. Never mind what worked back in high school, or with Dr. X. What is important *here?* (You can't memorize everything, you know.) Is it library research? Reading the textbook on your own? Attendance, lectures, note-taking? Details and rote memory? Or Sweeping Generalities and Purple Prose correctly spelled? (Good writers do well in these courses.) What will be covered, in how much time? Will you have to give up some of your 50 hours a week at the market? Or some skiing

*Based on an article written at the request of a Santa Monica College publication, *The Corsair,* Feb. 1975.

weekends? Or your husband? Or your year-old twins? Don't forget, a good education requires some sacrifice!

In any case, the course will be full of hints on how to pass the tests, from Day One on.

You can ignore the hints by sleeping in the back row, cutting class and getting your input from another student (beware of known nerds, here). You can cram the night before if you have a photographic memory and excellent mental health. But then if you freeze up and flunk, don't complain. Because in the School Game, sub-game "Passing a Test" (apologies to Dr. Eric Berne), a sensible person starts playing from the very beginning.

2. Besides deciding to study, *you can learn to take better lecture and reading notes. One ploy you can use is to take all notes in your own words.* It's hard, because you not only have to listen and read, you have to *think*. But it's good, because it makes all that new knowledge your very own, not someone else's. And it avoids the unpleasant shock of suddenly having to think on the test, for the very first time in the course.

Another ploy you can use (Notice the neat transition? What was the first ploy? Don't look back!), *take your lecture or reading notes on one side of the page only.* That leaves the other side free for questions, technical terms, summaries by the instructor, summaries by you, phone numbers, grocery lists, and similar highlights. If you don't like that idea, then try leaving the last few lines of every notepage blank—for the same things. If you can immediately do a little outline or sentence summary at the bottom of every page, that's good. Reviewing those summaries for a test is a lot easier than wading through pages and pages of run-on notes, doodles, etc.

3. Last (another transition!), you may have a *memory problem.* "I learn it at the time, but I just can't recall it later." Well, join the club. Except for a few braggarts, we all have memory problems.

One Helpful Hint comes from the psychologists, who say we have two kinds of memory. "Short-term memory" is a matter of minutes or hours, perhaps a day; "long-term memory" is, well, longer. Research by neurologists indicates there is a real physical difference between the two. Short-term is what you use without much effort, during a lecture or while cramming for next hour's test. *Long-term is what you need to really learn anything from a course,* especially from Day One to Finals. How to convert? Literally, you keep plugging—plugging the short-term information into the long-term circuits of the brain.

Answer Key: Words in Context
1. (c) **2.** (a) **3.** (d)

You go over the new information *in small pieces,* and *often.* No big indigestible review, just quickies—for example, just after a lecture, or at the end of the week. And not once, but several times. The forgetting curve is steepest just after learning something, so the sooner you review, the better.

Don't make a big thing of reviewing, or you won't ever do it. An efficient student will glance over his notes just before class, or just after. You can look up from your reading and gaze into space. Remember, put that small unit of information *in your own words;* re-reading or re-underlining impresses no one, especially not your own mind.

Other ideas for remembering: you can make a diagram or outline or picture of what you learned, on paper or in your head. Visualize how it fits together. If it doesn't fit, ask your instructor. He/she/it does have office hours, you know. Draw circles, maps, pyramids, time lines—put the facts in, in their right order. Make the big ideas big, the small details small. Use your imagination. For history, I used to find out how the costumes and houses looked in a certain period, then memorize the events like a movie. Instant Hollywood! Or you can place yourself at Gettysburg, or at Socrates' school, or Rising With the Middle Class, or standing in a Depression Breadline. People did, you know. It may be harder to make yourself into a "paramecium," or to smile "enigmatically" (for vocabulary study). But with a little effort, you can feel your way into an amoeba! After all, amoebas do, and they're not very smart. The point is "education" literally means to "lead you out." Let it. You might even end up enjoying the course, not to mention passing the test.

Or did you think that taking a course is simply a way to pass a test? Pshaw! Knowledge is Life! More important, it is Money! What if that first day on your desk job you are asked to dissect a cat? "But Mr. Plimpton, I forgot that as soon as I turned in my lab book," Only too late you gaze around the giant office and see the rows of lab trainees busily dissecting cats and filing the parts in the proper desk drawers. Only too late, you realize that what you learned—and forgot—may come in handy on a later job. Of course, Mr. Plimpton may then say, "You're fired! May I marry you?" But don't count on it.

Now, quiz yourself. (Remember the principle of immediate review!) What three major pieces of advice were presented in "How to Prepare for a Test"?

TOTAL TIME ______

Answer the question below without referring to the selection.

1. Of the following rules for preparing for a test, three are major points in the article and one is a supporting detail. Which one is the minor detail?
   (a) You must first decide to study—beginning the first day of class.
   (b) Take better notes.
   (c) Read the course outline carefully.
   (d) To remember better, study with imagination and review briefly but often.

Answer the *scanning* questions below by referring to the selection.

STARTING TIME ______

2. Should you use study methods that have worked for you before? ______

3. Does the writer feel that cramming the night before a test is always a bad idea?

4. At what point after learning do we forget the most? ______

5. What individuals have "memory problems"? ______

6. Knowledge is Life, but more important, it often is ______

7. Why is it hard to "take all lecture notes and reading notes in your own words"?

8. In taking notes, what two places can you leave blank for summarizing? ______

FINISHING TIME ______

SCANNING TIME ______

Check your answers with the key on the bottom of page 166. Then turn to the Rate Chart in the Appendix to find your words per minute for this selection. Finally, record your wpm score below and on the progress chart in the Appendix.

WORDS PER MINUTE ______

% COMPREHENSION ______

Percentage Chart for Comprehension Check

Errors	0	1	2	3	4	5	6	7	8
% Right	100	88	75	63	50	38	25	13	0

Exercise 6L—Long Reading

LENGTH: 1525

Read the following selection as rapidly as you can for general idea. Wait for a signal from your instructor before you begin reading. (Scanning exercise follows with separate timing.)

II. How to Take a Test—And Pass

Anne Dye

Let's assume that you have really prepared for the test, by studying.* If so, you can forget about those books that tell you "How to Pass a Test Without Really Knowing Anything." You know, tips like "In a multiple choice test, eight times out of ten the instructor will place the correct choice in the number three slot." Rules like that are hard to memorize. They also make education sound like Las Vegas or Santa Anita Race Track.

You are a serious student and you believe that knowledge is life, wisdom, freedom—even money. ("Even money"? We're back at the track!) Naturally some tips about test-making and test-taking are useful, as you'll see later. But you should put most of your energy into learning the material, not the rackets.

1. In *preparing* for a test, the most important factor is you—your will, your decisions, your priorities. In *taking* a test, the most important factor is again you—your mental set, your self-confidence. We all know people who "test out" near the top of their abilities, while others with the IQ of Einstein get F's or drop out of school. Which type are you? If you're the first type, bless you and skip to section II before I stir up anxieties you never thought you had. If you're the second type, read on.

Know then that some anxiety or tension is common when we're being examined or judged. It may even be necessary, for a top performance. Even great actors and musicians usually admit to tension before a performance. "Exam," "test," "criticism," "performance"—these words alone can cause a little rise in the heart beat. But there is a difference between

*(See "How to Prepare for a Test," pp. 161.)

some tension, and too much. If you are too tense, you can't perform as well as you are able. You may even look like an idiot on a test.

You can do several things to handle your anxiety if it becomes too great.

First, you can practice a lot. Take all the tests you can, everywhere—timed, untimed, objective, essay. This way, if you fail a test, it's just part of the practice, right? *Second,* know yourself. Does your mind work best after cramming all night? After five hours of double features the night before? After lots of sleep, followed by a bracing yogurt breakfast? Does it help you to meditate? Pray a lot? Scream at the family? Listen to yourself, follow your own advice, and ignore annoyances at test time, even if they be friends and loved ones. Better not try extra coffee or pills, unless you're used to them.

But you might try some common remedies, if yours aren't working well. For example, do your last reviewing of material before sleep. Latest research indicates that short-term memory is converted into long-term memory during REM (Rapid Eye Movement) sleep. Remember to remember the *main points*—details are usually recalled without much effort. Some overlearning is good. But too much overlearning, plus lack of sleep and perfectionism, can lead to the opposite result. You can forget everything you ever knew, including your name.

We also know that oxygen and the brain and exercise are all interrelated. Don't neglect exercise during the school year, and especially not during test periods. Learn the actor's trick of relaxing with deep yawns, the yoga trick of short energetic breathing. Try the settling art of centering—"I am me, and no test can wipe me out." Do isometric or static stretching, while you sit or stand in one place.

Take care of Number One—you.

2. The test—*previewing.* Days and even weeks before, find out all you can about it. An instructor who is fair and organized will answer such questions as: How much will be covered? How should I study for it? How much will it count toward my course grade? What type of test will it be?

The type of test does affect the professional student's type of review. For example, *objective* or *short-answer* tests require a no-nonsense command of facts, dates, terms, details. Look over study guides on rote memory, if you need shortcuts. An *essay* test requires a good overall view of the material. You

Answer Key: Ex. 6K
1. c **2.** No (or Not necessarily) **3.** No **4.** just after learning something **5.** all of us **6.** money **7.** because you have to *think* **8.** other side of page or last few lines at bottom of page

also need a clear mind on exam day for organizing and writing well. An *open-book* exam sounds easy until you learn that the testing period is so short that you haven't time to "open the book," much less to read in it. A *take-home* test expects you to have been an intelligent active learner all semester. It's like a research paper without the library references. If the instructor decides to give you all a break and announces it will be a "*creative, imaginative*" exam—watch out. You'll need all your physical and mental health to be instantly creative in response to his questions.

3. The test—*zero hour.* You are now that ideal test-taker—semi-relaxed, semi-tense, healthy, rested, self-confident, intelligent, full of knowledge, and creative. Or are you? For a moment, are you shot down by the sight of all those tests being passed out? What about those two students who finished theirs before you even read yours? If this is the case, now is the time to *practice a little testmanship.* It's the fine art of taking a test. We all know it exists, because we've seen the best students in a class fail. And we've seen some pretty dull people get A's—not once, but many times.

What are some reasonable *test-taking tips?*

a.) Listen to and follow oral directions by the instructor, who may be saying, "Answer only the first ten questions. I changed my mind about the second ten."

b.) Survey the test quickly, beginning to end, before starting. Ask any legal questions of the instructor. You have a right to readable copy and clear directions. Again, a fair and organized instructor will explain things like: How will the test be scored? How much time is allowed? Are errors or guessing counted against the total score? But he or she will not be kind about questions that have already been answered orally or on the test.

c.) Read all directions three or four times. If you're allowed to write on the test itself, mark all the key words in the directions or topic choices. Rephrase the directions. Translate them into your own words. "Select one of these three topics" means dump two of them, concentrate on the one you know best. "Check the correct answer(s)" means that one *or more* answers may be correct. "Topic one will count as half of your grade" means that you can treat topics two and three as minor. You should give them each only one-quarter of your time.

This is a good time to use your knowledge of the instructor's personality. What kind of replies does he or she want? Should you repeat his or her pet theories word for word? Or should you be "creative" and personal? Will a differing opinion be accepted if you include enough "proof"? (A sticky question.) Does he or she enjoy trick questions and hair-splitting definitions? Or should you avoid reading too much into every little word? Professional students become expert at this kind of thing.

d.) Budget your time. Use your watch or the wall clock. Far from increasing your tension, it should help you pace yourself. You can also set reasonable goals. In forty minutes, no instructor expects you to write an M.A. thesis on Plath's poetry. Nor can you describe in detail all the factors in a child's early environment. But you are expected to follow directions, finish the test, and divide your time as the test indicates.

For example, if you have sixty minutes for forty items, try to be at or near the half-way mark (item twenty) in thirty minutes. Besides this obvious kind of arithmetic, plan to have time for a short preparation and ending period.

As another example of time-planning, take the one-hour essay or theme on one topic. You should divide your hour as follows: ten–fifteen minutes for reading the topics, choosing one, and jotting down an outline for it. Forty minutes for writing. Five minutes for proof-reading. A forty-minute writing period is not mind-blowing. It means you should write four or five well-organized paragraphs.

Planning your test time means that 1) you will answer all the questions that you do know, and 2) if a written exam, your answer will appear organized and checked over. The former will please you, and the latter will astound and delight your instructor. It's better to discuss broadly the "four main causes of the Civil War" than to write six pages about Cause No. 1, and then run out of time.

Five minutes spent on proof-reading at the end of a test is worth 15 minutes madly plunging up to the wire. You may find that you skipped items that you knew well, spelled Plato as Pluto or the famous Monkey Trial as the Monkey Trail. Most instructors don't mind corrections as long as they are neat and legible.

4. *After the test.* Advance to the nearest lavatory mirror. Gaze steadily at your ravaged face. Repeat firmly ten times, "I did the best I could. I'm OK." Then go and sit in the sun.

TOTAL TIME ______

Answer the question below without referring to the selection.

1. Of the following rules for passing a test, four are major points in the article and one is a supporting detail. Which one is the minor detail?
(a) Keep yourself in good shape, mentally and physically.
(b) Gear your study method to the type of test.
(c) Use "testmanship" during the test.
(d) Check your spelling before handing in the test.

Answer the *scanning* questions below by looking for the answers in the selection. Scan as quickly as you can.

STARTING TIME ______

2. What trick do actors use to relax? ______
3. If you have exactly one hour for an essay test or theme, about how much time should you budget for planning? ______
4. What is the one most important factor in taking a test? ______
5. What is the first of several things you can do if your test anxiety is "always too high"? ______
6. If you find errors on your test, should you copy the test over, or make corrections on it? ______
7. What are the four sensible test-taking tips in part 3? ______
8. How much time should you allow at the end of the test for proofreading? ______

FINISHING TIME ______

SCANNING TIME ______

Check your answers with the key on the bottom of the next page. Then turn to the Rate Chart in the Appendix to find your words per minute for this selection. Finally, record your wpm score below and on the progress chart in the Appendix.

WORDS PER MINUTE ______

% COMPREHENSION ______

Percentage Chart for Comprehension Check

Errors	0	1	2	3	4	5	6	7	8
% Right	100	88	75	63	50	38	25	13	0

Answer Key: Ex. 6L
1. d **2.** yawning **3.** 10–15 minutes **4.** you **5.** practice a lot **6.** make corrections on it **7.** (1) Listen to oral directions; (2) Survey the test; (3) Read all directions 3–4 times; (4) Budget your time **8.** 5 minutes

Lesson 7

Exercise 7A—Phrase Perception

key phrase			
1. a big mouth	an ugly mule	a birch tree	a big mouth
	an apple pie	a bagpipe	
2. to commence	to comprehend	to come here	too common
	topple over	to commence	
3. a sweet child	a swell cat	a crafty swindle	a black phone
	a sweet child	a swinging chair	
4. in a circle	inner circle	in a circle	on the clock
	in a moment	into the breach	
5. the valley below	below the rail	the vast lot	the valley below
	the vain girl	the soft blow	
6. bright metal	bright metal	right pedal	night patrol
	fright wig	brilliant man	
7. pack a lunch	poke a bunch	punch a back	pack a lunch
	back for brunch	snack for lunch	
8. the center ring	the ringing bell	the cantering horse	the round cell
	the central rat	the center ring	
9. long road	right load	long road	large reed
	last ride	lost ring	
10. the white rose	the wheat roll	the long wait	the white rose
	the lost whale	the wilted rose	
11. a good life	a great rifle	a dog's life	a loud ghoul
	a dull file	a good life	
12. five fingers	four ringers	live stingers	five fingers
	fine singers	foul swingers	
13. vanity fair	valiant four	vanity fair	vain fear
	first failure	meager fare	
14. make sad	bad rake	make mad	fake size
	make sad	mild man	
15. rather thin	rather thin	neither tin	rather tan
	fine lather	gather men	
16. to be prompt	to see beans	to be fast	to be prompt
	to be parched	to prompt him	

17. really famished	really finished realty office	very varnished really famished	real family
18. to remain home	the remainder to remain home	the real hustle to hold meetings	to sail away
19. given a box	given a fox giving rocks	liven a room leaving a boss	given a box
20. insert something	omit something invert sums	serve things serve strangers	insert something

TIME ________

ERRORS ________

Exercise 7B—Phrase Perception

key phrase			
1. beneath contempt	benign content beneath contempt	corrupt benefactor burst canteloupe	bent cantilever
2. written orders	white orbs bright border	light odor written orders	bitten partner
3. catching fish	scratching dishes hatching lists	catching fish patching pants	matching wish
4. around ten	arid land tender arms	round fin arrow straight	around ten
5. near distraction	fear distortion near distraction	traction gears dear mistake	need affection
6. in the dark	in the dark into the park	on a lark inner spark	in a shark
7. typed letter	typical setter torn fetters	typed letter tasty fritter	better types
8. having been right	being half bright hastening the sight	have frightened behaving nightly	having been right
9. neither vase	either face whether asked	vast bother neither vase	nether regions
10. every airline	very aimless even alignment	every airline alien aviator	level airfield
11. thrifty husband	thrice hustled thrifty husband	shifty human hurting throat	mighty hungry
12. sounding the alarm	rounding the addition founding the island	pounding the album selling the alcohol	sounding the alarm
13. frustrated teacher	frustrated teacher fuddled talker	fraternity brother frowning fugitive	frumpish dresser
14. tea for three	two for tea for two trees	for the tease forced travel	tea for three
15. knitted sweater	keepsake sword knitted sweater	swift kite nightly swindle	knifed swine
16. running fawn	ruining fast rutted furrow	rural lawn running fawn	routine feast

17. losing the pen	losing the pen posting the rule	loading the wren hosing the den	penning the letter
18. take the plunge	lunge at cake play the flute	rake the plume bake the pie	take the plunge
19. of another planet	her mother's plant of another planet	the onerous plot off the other	to smother ants
20. frantic searcher	loud screamer frozen dinner	fast runner frantic searcher	funny antics

TIME ________

ERRORS ________

Exercise 7C—Word Comprehension

key word					
1. oblivious	conscious	obvious	memorable	unaware	carefree
2. skirmish	ticklish	fight	wiggly	peace	agreement
3. tolerable	welcome	complete	unbearable	lasting	acceptable
4. segregate	melt	integrate	separate	multiply	unite
5. eccentric	odd	electric	common	radical	metric
6. appalling	calming	horrifying	fruitful	colorful	appealing
7. ultimate	chief	close	threaten	pretend	final
8. ire	tax	grief	rare	anger	gaiety
9. compile	gather	erect	finish	divide	scatter
10. dormant	weak	forgetful	sleeping	active	awake
11. panorama	view	world-wide	outdoors	movie	bandage
12. silhouette	shade	details	dance	outline	painting
13. strata	rate	society	levels	data	union
14. ensemble	part	group	role	cue	stage
15. inquisitive	cruel	passive	relieved	curious	arrogant
16. designate	draw	elect	appoint	find	poll
17. flail	beat	pass	delicate	incomplete	hug
18. evaluate	lower	assess	overlook	imitate	raise
19. deficient	subtraction	define	failing	complete	lacking
20. incision	choice	wound	mark	cut	flaw

TIME ______

ERRORS ______

Exercise 7D — Word Comprehension

key word					
1. diverse	rare	different	divide	poetry	alike
2. annihilate	analyze	construct	anniversary	destroy	elate
3. furtive	quick	candid	sneaky	forthright	active
4. allay	relieve	together	recline	aggravate	friend
5. enhance	flatter	inhabit	dance	worsen	improve
6. mediocre	middle	ordinary	medicine	spectacular	terrible
7. crucial	special	crude	important	weak	little
8. naive	native	dumb	sophisticated	young	innocent
9. genteel	well-bred	soft	gentle	intelligent	coarse
10. accessible	closed	excessive	available	sensible	convenient
11. mire	mirror	lawn	code	mud	water
12. chronic	chord	constant	timely	wrinkled	brief
13. diligent	lazy	toil	difficult	different	hard-working
14. immature	unripe	imitate	manure	old	developing
15. despondent	writer	disciple	depressed	happy	bland
16. bedlam	quiet	bedpan	illness	confusion	tired
17. demure	decent	shy	immoral	extrovert	mature
18. droll	amusing	troll	mournful	dramatic	rude
19. discretion	gossip	abandon	belief	talk	judgment
20. convalesce	confine	merge	recuperate	shake	convenient

TIME _______

ERRORS _______

Exercise 7E—Phrase Comprehension

key phrase			
1. endorsing someone	acquired holiday a compatible act	giving approval to letting them in	red sails in sunset
2. making a living	by hook or crook in the future	something unknown a prearranged meeting	earning income
3. a pile of debris	a stack of wastes knotted together	a nursery for children frenzied killer	cruel judge
4. denied the privilege	overly dressed barred opportunity	to find difficult might lead again	is equal to
5. a loving caress	a good human an affectionate hug	highly concentrated pleasant & cheerful	tea for two
6. his greatest error	perhaps others do be considered	locked in the barn night and day	his biggest mistake
7. deluged by gifts	off the side pursuing action	glutted with presents set it up	never alone
8. an array of food	a variety of edibles many hot dogs	lovely tablecloth be sure to	let do
9. measles shot	for the aged the needs of	to set free make wise	an inoculation
10. a lofty human	the story of passive action	large monster a noble person	in every way
11. be flustered	to make different be confused	bright luster hang onto	chair backs
12. wretched behavior	empty out to recreate	awful conduct as fast as	experience pain

Answer Key: Ex. 7C
1. unaware **2.** fight **3.** acceptable **4.** separate **5.** odd **6.** horrifying **7.** final **8.** anger **9.** gather **10.** sleeping **11.** view **12.** outline **13.** levels **14.** group **15.** curious **16.** appoint **17.** beat **18.** assess **19.** lacking **20.** cut

Answer Key: Ex. 7D
1. different **2.** destroy **3.** sneaky **4.** relieve **5.** improve **6.** ordinary **7.** important **8.** innocent **9.** well-bred **10.** available **11.** mud **12.** constant **13.** hard-working **14.** unripe **15.** depressed **16.** confusion **17.** shy **18.** amusing **19.** judgment **20.** recuperate

13.	a probing mind	a searching intelligence our purpose	run for your life silly thoughts	body & soul
14.	perturbing episode	in low esteem conclude by saying	a great outcry utter chaos	unsettling experience
15.	a happy jaunt	pleasant & cheerful a gay journey	in some places happens often	more later
16.	raging controversy	arena in which heaven help her	a motive for a serious conflict	most crucial
17.	guilty culprit	the offender are found to	display kindness crime doesn't pay	bravery & faith
18.	anticipated wedding	running for office noodle pudding	foreseen marriage expectant mother	one day
19.	hectic party	in all events solemn heretic	hallowed grounds closed meeting	wild get-together
20.	extinct creature	succinct answer vanished dinosaur	down the hatch lock the door	large animal

TIME ________

ERRORS ________

Exercise 7F — Phrase Comprehension

key phrase			
1. harboring guilts	free parking good potato salad	feelings of remorse a rainy day	a safe port
2. a positive answer	to reply yes unsure of oneself	a double negative let it be	a light statement
3. to quench thirst	to squeeze hard to spill beer	widespread rumor satisfy need for drink	rain water
4. to happen biannually	late blooming flower a careless driver	a year of accidents two floor mats	twice-a-year event
5. a supplementary note	a friendly letter additional statement	flexible bones arthritic fingers	vagabond lover
6. accumulating wealth	losing one's money gathering grapes	becoming rich a covered table	birds flying south
7. potentially explosive	might blow up blind justice	the fertile land a weighty matter	a wet firecracker
8. an array of flowers	ring around the rosy a plague on you	an army of soldiers a nice arrangement	abundance of flora
9. a soft caress	a sweet smile a light stroke	a rough touch a sour note	the right handle
10. a biographical novel	a scientific lecture improving writing	book about someone else a new approach	the study of bugs
11. survival of the fittest	tight-fitting sweater a painful death	a certain victory endurance of the best	gasping for breath
12. a haughty manner	a high position a foolish act	a good etiquette a shaky situation	snobbish behavior
13. inquisitive glance	facial masque traveling salesman	questioning look gumdrop machine	poker face
14. unexpected betrayal	southern exposure a funny trick	surprise treachery strange explanation	unlocked gate
15. uncanny power	a strong dog extraordinary ability	not often right under great stress	a penthouse suite

Answer Key: Ex. 7E
1. giving approval to **2.** earning income **3.** a stack of wastes **4.** barred opportunity **5.** an affectionate hug **6.** his biggest mistake **7.** glutted with presents **8.** a variety of edibles **9.** an inoculation **10.** a noble person **11.** be confused **12.** awful conduct **13.** a searching intelligence **14.** unsettling experience **15.** a gay journey **16.** a serious conflict **17.** the offender **18.** foreseen marriage **19.** wild get-together **20.** vanished dinosaur

16. toeing the line	behaving properly tying shoelaces	a sore foot lining up pins	parallel bars
17. a loud uproar	a roaring lion into the breach	a noisy disturbance a lost art	out with a bang
18. boost the morale	a booster shot a dark cellar	a moral dilemma raising the flag	uplift mental condition
19. eating with relish	a clean radish a gourmet cook	a good appetite seasoning the food	a picky eater
20. horrid disease	case of measles prescription medicine	under the sickbed a bad odor	disgusting illness

TIME ________

ERRORS ________

SQ3R—HOW THE PROS STUDY-READ

1. **S**urvey
2. **Q**uestion
3. **R**ead
4. **R**ecite
5. **R**eview

The two readings in this Lesson are different from others in this book in that they are to be "studied," not read to build speed. They were chosen to give you practice in a proven method of studying a textbook: *SQ3R*.

Most untrained students begin a reading assignment in a textbook "cold." By that we mean they begin reading the first word of the unit and continue passively, until they reach the last word. They read without system, without questioning, without much interest. Result: they often end without any idea of what they have read. So they re-read, or they go back and—again passively—mark nearly everything. (We have all seen these "yellow pages"; almost every line has been highlighted.) And still they can't recite the content in any organized way. Usually they complain, "I just can't get into this subject." Or, "I study but I can't remember any of it."

If this sounds like you, then try the SQ3R method. It forces you to study actively, to test yourself, to "recite" the material immediately in your own words. Why recite? Because you haven't learned anything unless you can tell it to yourself, or to others, in your own words.

Before you begin study-reading, set your goals. Select a study unit that you know you can *read and absorb* in the time available. A unit should be any clearly marked section of your book, such as one chapter or the pages between two large headings. You must allow time to "recite," or test yourself, in this study period.

Now for SQ3R itself. Learn the steps, and practice them on the two reading in this Lesson. Much of what you have already learned in "Finding the Main Idea" and "Retaining Details" will be useful in this study technique. Remember that you will be a pro—a professional student—only if you learn to use the method with your other course work. Naturally, you should use common sense in adapting it to fit various fields and kinds of textbooks.

Step 1. S = Survey

This step will bring to light the topic and main ideas. Some experts call this first step pre-reading, preview, or overview. Whatever you call it, it means to read selectively and aggressively. It makes you think. It arouses

Answer Key: Ex. 7F
1. feelings of remorse **2.** to reply yes **3.** satisfy need for drink **4.** twice-a-year event **5.** additional statement **6.** becoming rich **7.** might blow up **8.** abundance of flora **9.** a light stroke **10.** book about someone else **11.** endurance of the best **12.** snobbish behavior **13.** a questioning look **14.** surprise treachery **15.** extraordinary ability **16.** behaving properly **17.** a noisy disturbance **18.** uplift mental condition **19.** a good appetite **20.** disgusting illness

your mind and makes it receptive. The idea is to "start with the large" before you "fill in the small."

Now survey the unit to be studied: Consider carefully the title or chapter heading, the author, illustrations, subheadings, and any system of print or numbering used by the author. Next read the introduction or first paragraph. Then read the first one or two sentences of every following section or paragraph. (Remember these first sentences usually contain the topic sentences.) Finally, read the summary or last paragraph.

Then stop to digest the information. As a result, in 70 to 90 percent of most informative prose you will get an idea of the general content. You will know the author's topic, main idea, and important supporting ideas. You should also have picked up some idea of the author's organization. Do you also know many details? If you do, you were not selective enough. Don't read details until later.

Step 2. Q = Question

This step enables you to approach the actual reading with an inquiring mind. It forces you to become involved with the subject, even though you may have no interest in it.

Ask yourself questions about your survey: What does the title or topic mean? How many subdivisions are there? How do these develop the writer's main idea? How much of this do I know already? How does this knowledge fit into the course? Into my life? At the very least, turn the title and subheadings themselves into questions. For really effective studying, you can write these down as the first stage of a rough outline. But leave room between each question for important notes you will fill in later.

Step 3. R = Read

Read through the entire study unit, from the title or section heading to the end. As you read, relate the main ideas to the supporting details. Allow what you know about the author's organization or framework to aid you. Check important ideas as you read, but do not stop to underline or take notes. This will interrupt your train of thought. Save your underlining and notetaking for the next steps.

Step 4. R = Recite

Recite what you have read to firmly implant the most important ideas in your memory. *How* you recite depends on the subject matter, your needs, and your study abilities. (Let's hope you don't leave this step until you are asked to recite on a final exam.)

At least, go over what you have read mentally: that is, recite to yourself. A more effective way is to tell someone else. This forces you to clarify yourself even more. You may also recite by taking a quiz immediately—as you do in this book when you answer the comprehension questions. The most effective way, however, of reciting is to take notes. You might fill in the outline you began in Step 2. Show by indenting or diagramming the difference between "umbrella" or general ideas and the supporting details. At this point write down the ideas *in your own words,* without looking at the textbook.

Step 5. R = Review

Review by skimming quickly through the study unit again. Look for any important material you may have remembered wrong or forgotten entirely. Change or add to your outline. Stress what the author seems to stress. Since by now you really know what is important and what isn't, this is the time to underline or mark in your text or notes. Mark sparingly, no more than once per paragraph (and often less).

When you try the SQ3R method on the two reading selections in this Lesson, follow the directions exactly, even if they seem slow and awkward at first. You need to be aggressive, intelligent, and directed in this hardest reading task of all—study reading.

WORDS IN CONTEXT

Without using your dictionary, try to determine the meaning of each word in **boldface** print. Choose the definition that best fits the context—the way it is used in the sentence(s).

Long Reading 7G

1. The calf has been **gestating** in the female for the last 13 months.
   (a) reducing **(b)** developing **(c)** moving **(d)** stagnating

Long Reading 7H

2. It was a flashflood of super-**colossal** size.
   (a) frightening **(b)** insignificant **(c)** gigantic **(d)** colorful
3. The giant effects of violent **erosion** may have resulted from a great flood.
   (a) a natural wearing-down of the earth **(b)** an earthquake below the sea **(c)** the process whereby green plants make food **(d)** volcanic build-up
4. An earth **satellite** took a photo of the Scablands.
   (a) camera **(b)** something orbiting the earth **(c)** something under the surface of the earth **(d)** photographer who specializes in geology
5. Were the erosion features of Mars **scoured** simultaneously by a single outburst, as in Washington?
   (a) developed **(b)** looked at **(c)** scrubbed out **(d)** angered

Check your answers with the key on the bottom of the next page.

THEME FOR READING SELECTIONS: THE SCIENCES

The root of the word *science* means *to know*. The word still carries that original idea of seeking for knowledge. It implies a curiosity in the world around us and a desire to know and understand. For thousands of years humans have been curious about the whale, the largest animal that has ever lived. The first science article in this lesson presents the California grey whale and describes the cycle of its migration and impressive reproduction. The second selection, a look at the formation of the Scablands of Washington, appeals to our fascination with the earth's development.

Imaginary Situation

Assume you are preparing to take exams in your science classes. Your grasp of these subjects has just started to improve. Now you're eager to score high on the test to assure yourself of a good grade. Your best friend, who did well in the course last semester, lets you in on her secret. The SQ3R method always works for her, and it will for you too!

APPLY THE SQ3R METHOD TO THE NEXT LONG READING

Step 1. S = Survey

Survey the title, author's name, and subheadings. Then copy them in the space below, as if you were beginning an outline. Skip a couple of lines between each subheading.

Next, read the first and last sentences following each subheading. Now think over the main points and the organization of the article.

Answer Key: Words in Context
1. (b) **2.** (c) **3.** (a) **4.** (b) **5.** (c)

Step 2. Q = Question

Ask yourself how the eight subheadings explain the topic of the article. Formulate at least one question for each subheading—a question you think will be answered in the reading selection. Write the question(s) indented underneath the appropriate subheading in the lines above.

Step 3. R = Read

Now go back to the reading selection and read as directed.

Exercise 7G—Long Reading

LENGTH: 757

Study-read the following selection carefully, using the SQ3R method. Wait for a signal from your instructor before you begin reading.

The Migration of the California Grey Whale

Thomas O'Neil

An Introduction

One of nature's greatest achievements is the California grey whale. At birth a grey whale calf weighs 2,000 pounds and is fourteen feet long. Every day the calf consumes fifty gallons of the mother's milk and gains fifty pounds of weight. At maturity this whale will weigh 80,000 pounds, be fifty feet long and eat several tons of food each day. The California grey whale spends most of its sixty-year life span on the road.

An Arctic Summer

Every year thousands of grey whales make the longest migration of any animal, traveling 7,000 miles each way between the Arctic and Baja, California. The grey whales spend the long summer days in their Arctic feeding grounds in the Bering Sea between Alaska and Russia. Unlike a fish, the whale is warm-blooded and must therefore maintain a relatively high internal body temperature. In the cold Arctic waters the grey whale is protected by an outer layer of blubber which averages six inches in thickness. Other whales such as the Greenland Night whale have been found with a two-foot thick layer of blubber covering their bodies.

Feeding Habits

During these summer months in the Arctic the grey whales fatten themselves by consuming enormous quantities of small shrimplike animals called amphipods. Recent observations of a young grey whale, Gigi II, held in captivity at Sea World in San Diego during 1971 and 1972, suggest that the grey whale feeds by sweeping its enormous head over the bottom. The amphipods on which it feeds are either stirred off the bottom or leap off the bottom to escape. These animals and the surrounding water are sucked into the whale's mouth. As the water is expelled from the mouth, it passes through coarse baleen fibers. The small animals are trapped and swallowed.

The Move South

In October as the days get shorter and ice begins to form over the Arctic feeding grounds, the California grey whale begins its long journey south to the warm waters of Baja, California. During this three month long trip the whales traveling in groups stay close to the shore of North America, swimming both day and night and averaging about 100 miles per day.

Skyhopping

Occasionally the whale will take a look around above the water or "skyhop." Either by beating its tail flukes rapidly or by resting its tail on the bottom, the whale pushes its upper eight to ten feet of body out of the water and takes a look around. At other times the whale will leap its fifty-foot body almost clear of the water, creating a huge splash as it re-enters the water. This "breaching" may be to dislodge whale lice or barnacles or possibly part of a courtship display.

Mating

During the trip south the grey whales that are sexually mature, at least three years old, and not pregnant already, form mating groups. These groups are composed of three whales, two males and a female. The dominant male couples with the female while the second male is kept busy positioning the two whales on their sides facing each other and keeping them together during the sex act. This is no small job, since each whale can be fifty feet long and weigh forty tons.

At the Breeding Grounds

During December and January the grey whales arrive at the warm lagoons along the coast of Baja, California. The whales swim miles inland along narrow shallow channels. These channels are the breeding grounds of the California grey whale. The calf has been gestating in the pregnant female for the last thirteen months, that is, since her last journey south. The expectant cow is aided in the birth of the calf by another female that acts as a midwife. At birth the calf sinks toward the sea floor. Being a mammal the whale must breathe at the surface. The midwife guides the baby whale to the surface for its first gulp of air. The calf then finds its mother's nipples and rich whale milk is forced into its mouth. During the next two months the calf will grow twenty feet and double its weight.

The Voyage Back

In March the whales begin their long journey north to the Arctic. The newly-pregnant females leave first, followed by the males and immature females. The last to leave the warm waters of Baja are the females and their calves. The whales arrive at their Arctic feeding ground in June. Many scientists believe that during this entire eight month long, 14,000 mile journey, the California grey whale does not feed at all!

TOTAL READING TIME ______

Step 4. R = Recite

Immediately answer the questions below without referring to the selection.

1. Choose the statement that best expresses the main idea.
   (a) A whale calf weighs 2,000 pounds at birth and is 14 feet long.
   (b) The migration cycle of the California grey whale is directly related to its breeding cycle.
   (c) The California grey whale leaves its Arctic feeding grounds when they begin to ice over.
   (d) The newly-born whale is assisted to the surface of the water by a whale "midwife."

2. The grey whales make a shorter migration than most creatures that migrate. T F

3. A layer of blubber approximately six inches thick protects the whale in Arctic waters. T F

4. The whale feeds on small shrimplike animals called amphipods. T F

5. The whale probably "skyhops" in order to increase the circulation of its blood. T F

6. A mating group consists of two females and one male. T F

7. The warm lagoons along the coast of Baja, California are more appropriate for breeding than the Arctic waters. T F

8. Many scientists think the whale does not feed from the time it leaves Arctic waters until it returns. T F

Now try to answer your own questions that you wrote in Step 2. Fill in your outline with any additional details you think are important.

Step 5. R = Review

Check your answers with the key on the bottom of page 192. If any were wrong, review the article to find the correct answers.

Turn to the Rate Chart in the Appendix to get your words per minute for this selection. Finally, record your scores below and on the progress chart in the Appendix.

WORDS PER MINUTE ______

% COMPREHENSION ______

Bonus Questions (Scanning)

1. How many miles does the California grey whale migrate on a one-way trip between the Arctic and Baja California? ______

2. For how many months does a baby whale gestate in the cow's stomach? ______

______

Percentage Chart for Comprehension Check

Errors	0	1	2	3	4	5	6	7	8
% Right	100	88	75	63	50	38	25	13	0

APPLY THE SQ3R METHOD TO THE NEXT LONG READING

Step 1. S = Survey

Survey the title, author's name, and subheadings. Then copy them in the space below, as if you were beginning an outline. Skip a couple of lines between each subheading. Make a separate outline for each major division.

Part I

____

____

____

____

____

____

____

____

____

Part II

____

____

____

____

____

____

____

____

____

____

Next, read the first and last sentences following each subheading. Now think over the main points and the organization of the article.

Step 2. Q = Question

Ask yourself how the subheadings explain the topic of each Section. Formulate at least one question for each subheading—a question you think will be answered in the reading selection. Write the question(s) indented underneath the appropriate subheading in the lines above.

Step 3. R = Read

Now go back to the reading selection and read as directed.

Exercise 7H—Long Reading

LENGTH: 1202

Study-read the following selection carefully, using the SQ3R method. Wait for a signal from your instructor before you begin reading.

The Day the Dam Burst

Dietrick E. Thomsen

What do eastern Washington and northern Mars have in common? Evidence of super-colossal flooding!

Introduction

Geology used to be a narrow science. While physicists and chemists were proposing laws that applied to distant stars as well as to our planet earth, geologists studied only the rocks and soil of the earth. Now geology is branching out. Space probes and manned space visits have brought the moon and other planets within reach. As a result, scientists are beginning to study the geology of these other planets.

Geologists are finding that there are both similarities and differences between the earth and the other planets. Not only do they compare planets, but they also use the history of one planet to help explain the history of another. One example of this new process is the comparison now being made between a unique feature of the earth's geology, the so-called "Channeled Scablands" of eastern Washington, and certain features of the planet Mars. On Mars these prominent features are called "valles."

Answer Key: Ex. 7G
1. (b) **2.** F **3.** T **4.** T **5.** F **6.** F **7.** T **8.** T **(1)** 7,000 miles **(2)** thirteen months

The "Channeled Scablands" of Washington

The Scablands occupy about 15,000 square miles of the state. They are a region of bare black rock cut up with channels, rock basins, and old cascade ledges. The land shows giant ripple marks and ragged buttes. Immense gravel bars are present.

In the early 1920s, J. Harlen Bretz, a geologist at the University of Chicago, gave the Scablands their name. He suggested that their unusual appearance—which looks like the giant effects of violent erosion—resulted from a stupendous flood that occurred about 20,000 years ago. In the years since Bretz made his suggestion, there was much argument over it. Not all scientists agreed with his theory. But now, a photo taken by an earth satellite has confirmed the flow patterns he thought existed in the Scablands. The photo is such good testimony that U. S. Geological Survey has put out a press release and a pamphlet for the public to read, which takes Bretz' explanation for granted.

The Spokane Flood

Of course, the flood occurred long before there was a city of Spokane, or a Washington state. However, it is usually called "The Spokane Flood." It was possibly the greatest flood the world has ever seen. It did not rise slowly from the rain-soaked earth, as did the Biblical deluge that floated Noah's Ark. Rather, it was a flashflood of supercolossal size. In just two days it drained an ancient lake that covered 3,000 square miles of what is now Montana.

What caused the giant prehistoric flood?

Before the flood, the Scablands had been a basin or valley with a floor of rock. The basin is tipped or tilted, running from high in the northeast to low in the southwest. It slopes at the rate of about twenty-five feet per mile.

About 100,000 years ago, during one of the glacial periods, the continental ice sheet extended solidly to a point just north of the Scablands basin. Tongues of ice reached out from the sheet into valleys south of the main ice front. They dammed up rivers and made glacial lakes. The biggest and most important ice dam blocked the Clark Fork River until it made the ancient lake in Montana. The lake is called "Lake Missoula" because the site of the present-day town would have been 950 feet under its waters.

The water rose and rose behind this large ice dam until the surface came to 4,125 feet above sea level, or a depth of 2,000 feet at the dam. This is twice the maximum depth of Lake Superior. The ancient lake contained an estimated 500 cubic miles of water, or about half the volume of present-day Lake Michigan. Finally the water reached the top of the ice dam and began to flow over it. Running water erodes ice very quickly. So once the water had cut a sizable channel in the ice, the dam suddenly gave way.

The water burst out in a gigantic surge. The maximum rate of flow is estimated at 9.5 cubic miles per hour. This is ten times the combined flow of all the present-day rivers of the world! The water went past at sixty times the rate of the Amazon river. The water rushed in several stupendous streams across the great basin, now called the Scablands. It created the giant erosion features that are seen there—huge ripples, rock pools, dry waterfalls. The flood probably came across the basin in a series of surges. The crest, or greatest depth, may have lasted at most for a day or two at most points. On its way to the ocean, the water made a couple of temporary lakes as it caused rivers to back up. Then it finally reached the sea.

Did any humans see this fantastic flood?

So far, the earliest traces of man in the region go back only to 10,000 years ago, or 8,000 B.C. This is many thousands of years after the flood. But 8,000 B.C. is by no means the earliest date for humans on the North American continent. So it is still possible that human beings did witness the flood. If they did, they would have had to be lucky enough to be standing on the safety of a mountain top in the Bitterroot range.

Similar Flooding on Mars?

Events similar to the Spokane Flood are now proposed to have taken place on Mars. In an issue of *Icarus,* two scientists, Victor R. Baker of the University of Texas and Daniel J. Milton of the U.S. Geological Survey, argue this point. They feel that gigantic floods occurred in the history of the Martian "valles" called Kasei, Ares, Tiu, Simud, and Mangala.

Their reasoning is based on photos of the Martian channels taken by Mariner 9 from orbit around Mars. These photos look very similar to the ones of the Scablands by earth satellites. The scientists agree that some of the Martian features, when looked at separately, could be the result of wind erosion. But taken together, the photos look strangely like the Scablands.

If glacial damming and river water caused the Washington flood, what caused the erosion marks on Mars? There is little or no water on Mars now. But that does not necessarily mean that there never was any water. Nor does it mean that there had to be a Martian atmosphere in which it rained for thousands or millions of years. The water could have come from the inside of the planet, just as the earth's water originally did, and it could have lasted on the surface only a short time. The "valles" in question all run generally north from the equator.

Two questions remain to be answered. Were the valles scoured simultaneously by a single outburst, as in Washington? Or was flooding in any single channel a single or repeated event?

Baker and Milton answer the question this way. "Scabland-type erosion takes place when very deep swift water acts upon closely jointed bedrock. If the comparison to the Channeled Scablands is correct, we can also describe what happened on Mars. Floods involving water discharges of millions of cubic meters per second, but perhaps lasting no more than a few days, have occurred on Mars."

TOTAL READING TIME ______

Step 4. R = Recite

Immediately answer the questions below without referring to the selection.

1. Choose the statement that best expresses the main idea.
   (a) No one knows what caused the gigantic erosion on Mars and in Washington state.
   (b) Scientists have proved beyond a doubt that the "valles" on Mars were caused by gigantic flooding.
   (c) Satellite photos of both the Scablands and Mars indicate that both areas may have had massive floods in the past.
   (d) Human beings may have watched the "Spokane Flood" that created the Scablands.

2. We know more at the present about the ancient flood in Washington than we do about the seemingly flooded area on Mars. **T F**

3. Through space exploration, geologists are able to study the geology of other planets as well as that of the earth. **T F**

4. The Scablands are unique; it is the only area of its kind on earth. **T F**

5. Both Washington and Mars show evidence of erosion caused by solid ice. **T F**

6. The "Spokane Flood" occurred about one million years ago. **T F**

7. We have found traces of man in the Spokane region dating from 8,000 B.C. This proves that
   (a) man first arrived there at that date.
   (b) the region was heavily populated.
   (c) the first "Americans" were Indians.
   (d) humans were living there 10,000 years ago.

8. The scientists Baker and Milton insist that no flooding could have occurred on Mars. T F

Now try to answer your own questions that you wrote in Step 2. Fill in your outline with any additional details you think are important.

Step 5. R = Review

Check your answers with the key on the bottom of page 198. If any were wrong, review the article to find the correct answers. Turn to the Rate Chart in the Appendix to get your words per minute for this selection. Finally, record your scores below and on the progress chart in the Appendix.

WORDS PER MINUTE ______

% COMPREHENSION ______

Bonus Questions (Scanning)

1. What is one reason that scientists study the history of a planet?

____

2. Approximately how deep was the water just before the ice dam broke?

____

Percentage Chart for Comprehension Check

Errors	0	1	2	3	4	5	6	7	8
% Right	100	88	75	63	50	38	25	13	0

TRY THE SQ3R METHOD ON YOUR OWN TEXTBOOK

Title of text: ______________________________

Author: ______________________________

Learning Unit (chapter, heading, number of pages): ______________________________

____

Section, chapter, or heading under which the learning unit falls (copy from table of contents): ______________________________

Step 1. S = Survey

Survey the titles, headings, subheadings of the unit. Copy the subheadings in the space below, as if you were beginning an outline. Skip a couple of lines between each subheading.

____

____

____

____

____

____

____

____

____

____

____

____

____

____

____

Next, read all of the first paragraph, the beginnings of the following paragraphs, and all of the last paragraph. Now think over the main points and the organization of the unit.

Step 2. Q = Question

What questions does the Survey raise in your mind? Jot them down (indented) underneath the appropriate subheadings in the lines above.

Step 3. R = Read

Read to answer the questions raised above, from beginning to end of the unit. Try to connect the main ideas to the supporting details as you read. Check important ideas as you read, but do not stop to underline.

Step 4. R = Recite

Now try to answer your own questions that you wrote in Step 2. Fill in your outline with any additional details you think are important. Use your own words: this requires you to organize your thoughts.

Step 5. R = Review

Review by repeating the Survey. Also, skim through any important material. Review your outline and make changes or additions. Finally, mark or underline important points in your notes.

Answer Key: Ex. 7H
1. c **2.** T **3.** T **4.** T **5.** T **6.** F **7.** d **8.** F (1) to help explain the history of another (2) 2,000 feet

Lesson 8

Exercise 8A—Phrase Perception (Variation)

Note: The key phrase may be repeated more than once. See key on bottom of next page for number of repetitions.

key phrase

key phrase			
1. shoes and socks	socks and shoes shoes and socks	shoes and socks shoes and stockings	shoe the horse
2. red schoolhouse	read schoolbook red pooltables	red schoolhouse red poolhouse	red schoolhouse
3. sit quietly there	sit there quietly sit quietly there	sit quietly here sit quietly there	sit quite quietly
4. a good purpose	a good purpose a purple hood	a purple food a good papoose	a hidden purpose
5. fly away now	fly away now fly away now	now fly away fly away now	fly that way
6. fields and streams	field that hit shields and strings	streams and fields fields and streams	fields and streams
7. big soft pillow	soften big pillow bag some pills	big soft pillow pigpen has fallen	dig soft ridges
8. the quick defeat	the quiet defeat the quick defeat	the quick defeat the deaf queen	the queer defect
9. isolate the town	the brown insole isolate the gown	the round isobar isolate the town	isolate the town
10. eat with relish	the reddish seat eat with relish	beat with relish a real feat	eat the radish
11. caught in a maze	caught in a maze bought a matzo ball	caught in a haze caught with a mate	caught in a maze
12. this superb dinner	this super dinner this superb dinner	this inner stupor this superb dinner	this winning suburb
13. a conscious effort	a consecrated fort a conservative effort	a formed conscience a conscious effort	a conscious effort
14. strike the knave	stroke the slave strike the grave	strike the knave strike the knave	the grave knack
15. those precious few	these precise few these precious few	these precocious few those precious few	these few luscious

16. reverse the trend	reverse the trend revive the trend	review the trick reverse the trend	the reversed trend
17. the mangled body	mangle the body the mantle board	the mangled body the mangled body	the tangled web
18. that gentle person	fat genteel person that gentle person	that genuine person that gentle son	that gentle person
19. figure the fraction	figure the fraction figure the fraction	the figured fraction figure the faction	puncture the fragment
20. throughout infinity	through infinity though finite	throughly infirm throughout infinity	throughout infinity

TIME _______

ERRORS _______

Exercise 8B—Phrase Perception (Variation)

Note: The key phrase may be repeated more than once.

key phrase			
1. an open book	an open door an optional book	open a book an open book	an open book
2. be always gay	be almost gay be always gay	be always gay being always gay	be another guy
3. pitch the tent now	pitch the tent now stitch the rip now	pinch the red cow pitch the tent now	watch the rent grow
4. reading fiction	creating friction reading fiction	working fractions meeting factions	reading non-fiction
5. built like a brick	like a built brick built like a brick	built like a bat build like a brick	built like a brick
6. very bruised ego	very bruised ego various broken eggs	very broken ego very bruised ego	very bruised skin
7. lovely green lamp	lovely green ramp love sample dreams	lovely green lamp lovely green lamps	lovely damp stream
8. navy blue suit	navy blue blouse navy blue suit	blue-suited navy sweet blue knave	navy blue suit
9. twice seen film	twice seen film twice seen film	twice seen film twice seen film	wind the filmstrip
10. catch the ball fast	catch the ball fast snatch ball fast	catch the ball fast pitch the ball fast	watch the ball fall
11. cover the bed	cover the bad the covered bed	cover the beds cover the bed	cover the bed
12. estimate damage	estimate the profit estimate damage	estimate the damage estimated damage	estimate the damages
13. good baked potato	bake good potatoes good baked potato	good raked yard good baked potato	baked potatoes
14. snakes in a pen	snakes in a pen snails in a pail	snake in a pen snakes in a pen	snakes in a bin

Answer Key: Ex. 8A
Key phrase repeated once in items: 4, 7, 10, 15 Repeated three times: 5 Others repeated twice

15. twist and shake	twisted and shaken twist and shake	twist a snake shake and twist	twist and shake
16. pick a pretty posy	pick a pretty pose pick pertinent point	pick a pretty posy pick a pretty posy	pick a pretty posy
17. turn page slowly	slowly turn page burn pack slowly	turn cheek slowly turn page slowly	turn page slowly
18. hunt with hounds	hunt for pound hunt with hound	hunt with hounds hunt without hound	hunt with hounds
19. a shattered pot	a shattered pot a shattered part	shatter the pot a shattered pot	a flattened pot
20. the first circle	the first circus the burst crate	the fast circuit the first circle	the first circle

TIME ________

ERRORS ________

Exercise 8C—Word Comprehension

key word					
1. curtail	wound	stop	pretend	mask	increase
2. secluded	isolated	bent	relieved	observed	busy
3. malady	female	health	song	illness	germ
4. adept	change	awaken	skilled	fighter	awkward
5. frugal	lavish	stingy	dance	nightly	economical
6. elongate	lengthen	elaborate	hurdle	longitude	shorten
7. sear	buy	vision	scorch	rowdy	raw
8. listless	enthusiastic	inactive	snail	hearing	gay
9. ravenous	convalescent	mealtime	wisdom	hungry	gracious
10. invoke	humor	send	ask	entail	notice
11. bolster	support	market	survey	elderly	underline
12. slothful	retiring	energetic	fatigue	permanent	lazy
13. futile	necessary	useless	future	significant	hoard
14. esteem	respect	dishonor	team	status	unit
15. saturate	soak	seated	elevate	moisten	dry
16. lateral	ladder	money	sideways	final	upwards
17. rift	marine	break	bridge	urgent	primary
18. boisterous	timid	dynamic	beehive	noisy	silence
19. feign	fine	motivate	faint	groan	pretend
20. cryptic	cynical	secret	affectionate	open	clear

TIME ________

ERRORS ________

Answer Key: Ex. 8B
Repeated once: 4,7 Repeated three times: 5 Repeated four times: 9 Others repeated twice

Exercise 8D—Word Comprehension

key word					
1. plausible	false	incredible	believable	praise	garment
2. eradicate	revolt	erase	radiate	permanent	avoid
3. pulverize	fight	make	caress	crush	cut
4. chagrin	shock	smile	cousin	poise	embarrassment
5. disintegrate	mix	decay	grow	bore	interest
6. anonymous	unknown	everyone	nonsense	name	signed
7. apex	bottom	side	peak	cleanser	choose
8. turbulent	cheerful	hurried	engine	agitated	calm
9. indisposed	placed	rejected	healthy	decided	ill
10. intensity	tenderness	strength	friendship	weakness	intention
11. mutation	change	pretense	maintain	station	remainder
12. cull	honor	yell	get	select	average
13. ardor	work	grapes	passion	open	lifeless
14. putrid	beautiful	rotten	sweet	odor	sour
15. revoke	realize	give	vocal	repeal	reveal
16. grotesque	bizarre	huge	ordinary	clumsy	artistic
17. deity	human	god	statue	daily	belief
18. clientele	patients	lawyers	customers	relatives	animals
19. eloquent	pronounce	tongue-tied	bilingual	stumble	well-expressed
20. component	group	combine	friend	part	division

TIME ________

ERRORS ________

Exercise 8E—Sentence Comprehension

key sentence: A majority of the women in the United States who work do so because of real economic need, not because they want more spending money for luxuries.

1. Although it is generally believed that most American women work for extra money, the majority work out of financial need. ______
2. Too many American women neglect their homes and work for luxuries their husbands cannot buy them. ______
3. Many women work to send their children to college. ______
4. Since 1940, the number of mothers who work has increased about nine times. ______
5. Because of rising inflation, economic needs dictate that more women work now than ever before. ______
6. The majority of American women spend over half their wages for luxuries. ______
7. A woman's place is in the home, not in the office or factory. ______
8. Most wages earned by women are spent for household needs, whereas wages earned by men are spent for larger monthly bills. ______
9. Statistics prove that more working women than working men give to charities. ______
10. The main reason that most women in America work is a need for money to buy necessities, not to buy extra items. ______

TIME ______

ERRORS ______

Answer Key: Ex. 8C
1. stop **2.** isolated **3.** illness **4.** skilled **5.** economical **6.** lengthen **7.** scorch **8.** inactive **9.** hungry **10.** ask **11.** support **12.** lazy **13.** useless **14.** respect **15.** soak **16.** sideways **17.** break **18.** noisy **19.** pretend **20.** secret

Answer Key: Ex. 8D
1. believable **2.** erase **3.** crush **4.** embarrassment **5.** decay **6.** unknown **7.** peak **8.** agitated **9.** ill **10.** strength **11.** change **12.** select **13.** passion **14.** rotten **15.** repeal **16.** huge **17.** god **18.** customers **19.** well-expressed **20.** part

Exercise 8F—Sentence Comprehension

key sentence: Both heredity and environment influence students' academic successes.

1. Where students live has more influence on them than who their parents are. ______
2. Genetic characteristics and living conditions are both factors influencing students' success in school. ______
3. Atmospheric conditions affect students' ability to study. ______
4. Students' parentage is more important than environment in scholastic progress. ______
5. Students' progress in school is affected by environment and heredity. ______
6. Making good grades is a result of a highly cultural background. ______
7. Students' surroundings while growing up and the qualities inherited from their parents affect how well they do in school. ______
8. Students have difficulty with their homework if their home is noisy. ______
9. Neither heredity nor environment greatly affect students' progress in school. ______
10. Community expectations often motivate students to make better grades. ______

TIME ______

ERRORS ______

SKIMMING FOR OVERVIEW

How is skimming different from scanning (Lesson 6)? Both involve selective skipping at high speeds. *Skimming is reading for the general idea or the big picture. Scanning* is looking for exact answers to specific questions.

Some reading experts make a big point of skimming, and their estimates of 800 words per minute and up may frighten you. You may feel, "I can just barely read and comprehend at 200 wpm; how can I possibly read at 800 wpm?"

There are two good answers to that question. (1) You already have skimmed reading material at 800 wpm or even 1000 wpm or more. (2) Skimming is not the same as careful reading. In fact, some authors don't call it reading at all; they call it "semi-reading."

To go back to (1): when you look over and sort your mail, that's skimming. When you browse through the Sunday paper to see what's worth reading, that's skimming. When you flip through a paperback (*Beyond the Valley of the Dogs,* for example) while waiting in line at the check-stand, that's skimming. So you see you have done it naturally, without thinking. All a reading textbook can do is show you *when* to skim (and when to read slowly and carefully) and *why* to skim—and to provide practice.

The *when* and the *why* are all-important to the efficient reader and student. You should not start out on a reading task with a rate in mind—"I'm going to read at 200 wpm (or at 800 wpm)." You should start with a *purpose.* As you have learned in earlier lessons, if you want to find only the main idea and do not hold yourself responsible for memorizing details, you can read very rapidly. If you read for details, you must first locate the main idea and general outline, then fill in the details (see Lesson 4). However, you will find that you cannot read as fast.

If your purpose is any one of the following, you will not want to read carefully—at least, not at first. Instead, you will find yourself skimming:

1. to reread material you have already studied.
2. to sort out and discard, as with the junk mail in your home or office.
3. to "try before you buy"—or really read—a new book or magazine.
4. to keep informed in a general way about the news.
5. to review your lecture notes after class.
6. to see which reference materials might be useful to your term paper.
7. to be able to discuss the general content of a reading assignment in class, when you didn't have time to really read and study it.

You notice the use of the word *general.* Skimming should give you a general overview, not a detailed knowledge. You should look only for the

Answer Key: Ex. 8E
1, 10 (perhaps 5)

Answer Key: Ex. 8F
2, 5, 7

topic, the main idea, the major points. In expository (informative) prose, the writers and editors often help steer you with spaces or divisions, paragraphing, numbered lists, capital letters or italics, and headings and sub-headings. In a novel, you can skim quickly for setting, type of plot, the author's style, and so on. Good skimmers read selectively, completely skipping over some sentences, paragraphs, even whole pages. They know that they can always come back and read for details, if they wish.

Many students find it hard to relax and skim, even if they unconsciously do it outside of class. "I'm afraid to skip a word; I might miss something, or not follow the main idea." Being forced to skim the following reading selections should help you break out of that every-word pattern. You will not be skimming chemical formulas or mathematics; you will not be questioned about any details. Feel free to "once-over-lightly" at two or three times your usual reading speed. For example, if you read carefully at 250 wpm, you should be able to skim at 500 wpm and up. Beyond the rate of 1000 wpm, the eyes cannot physically "see" and "read" every word anyway, so expect to miss a lot of details. You can always come back to the selections later.

WORDS IN CONTEXT

Without using your dictionary, try to determine the meaning of each word in **boldface** print. Choose the definition that best fits the context—the way it is used in the sentence(s).

Short Reading 8H

1. There was just an immeasurable void that had its beginning and end, time, shape, and life in the mind of Taiowa the Creator. Then he, the infinite, conceived the **finite.**
   (a) sky **(b)** something having limits **(c)** the end **(d)** something that exists forever

2. You have created the universes and made them **manifest** in solids, waters, and winds, and put them in their proper places.
   (a) exceedingly beautiful **(b)** mysterious in nature **(c)** plainly apparent **(d)** in disorder

Long Reading 8I

3. You, Orunmila, who can **divine** the meanings of all things, instruct me further.
   (a) foretell **(b)** soothe **(c)** hasten **(d)** forget

4. So he put aside the making of humans and went to the palm trees to draw their inner fluid, out of which he made palm wine. When it was **fermented** he drank.
   (a) a sufficient quantity **(b)** cooled to an average temperature **(c)** having a vile taste **(d)** turned to alcohol

5. He instructed Agemo the **chameleon** to descend to the golden chain.
   (a) bodyguard **(b)** lizard that changes color **(c)** god of reptiles **(d)** chaperone at a dance

6. They were no longer clay, but people of blood, **sinews,** and flesh.
   (a) intelligence **(b)** weaknesses **(c)** tendons **(d)** corruption

7. But when the effects of the palm wine had worn off, Obatala saw that some of the humans he had made were misshapen, and **remorse** filled his heart.
   (a) delight **(b)** greed **(c)** terror **(d)** regret

Check your answers with the key on the bottom of page 212.

THEME FOR READING SELECTIONS: TALES OF IMAGINARY PEOPLE

Throughout time, every tribe or country has had a story to explain the origin of the world and the creation of people. These stories about the beginnings of our world are called creation myths. The reading selections in this Lesson are three myths, each drawn from a different area of the world. The first myth came from the ancient Greeks; it tells the story of Prometheus (pro meeth' yoose), the Titan or giant who created man. It also presents the beautiful Pandora, created by the gods, who was the first woman and the wife of Epimetheus (eppy meeth' yoose), brother of Prometheus. The second creation myth is an American Indian story told by the Hopis. It describes the creation of the first of the four worlds the Hopi Indians believe were formed, and it presents Spider Woman, who created life and people. The last myth is from the Yoruba people of Africa. In it you will meet the very human god Obatala as he prepares to start life on this earth. As you read, note the general similarities and differences among the three creation myths.

Imaginary Situation

You have an appointment with your English instructor in fifteen minutes to discuss the three myths that follow. Because you had to work overtime last night, you have not had a chance to read them yet and will have to bluff your way through. Now is the time to apply your skimming skills. As you read, grasp the basic story without concentrating a great deal on small details. Be sure to note sub-headings and try to follow the plot.

Exercise 8G—Short Reading

Try to *skim* the following selection in one minute. (Faster students should set a goal of one-half minute.) This exercise is nearly twice the length of earlier Short Readings; so skim as rapidly as you can for general ideas.

The Creation of Man and Woman

Miriam Cox

WPM

Two Brothers 2

After the war of the ages, Zeus had imprisoned or 12
otherwise punished all of the Titans except two. These were 22
Prometheus, whose name means "forethought," and his twin 30
brother Epimetheus, whose name means "afterthought." 36
Though they were Titans, they had fought with Zeus against 46
their own brothers because Prometheus, with his power to 55
foresee the future, had known that Zeus would win and 65
wanted to be on the victorious side. As a reward the two Titans 78
were allowed to roam the earth as they pleased. 87

Man, Made of Clay 91

To amuse himself, Prometheus often went down to the 100
seashore and molded figures of various shapes and sizes out of 111
the earth's clay. He became so pleased with his cleverness that 122
as each figure was completed he breathed life into it and took it 135
to his brother, saying, "Give this creature something by which 145
it may maintain and protect itself." So Epimetheus gave each 155
animal a special gift: swiftness to the deer, wings to the birds, 167
quills to the porcupine, a shell to the turtle. 176

Prometheus became increasingly skillful with practice. 182
One day he made the finest creature of all. He shaped it like 195
himself and the gods, causing it to stand upright with head 206
high. Proudly he said to Epimetheus, "This is Man, my master- 217
piece. Give him the best gift of all." 224

"But I have no more gifts," replied Epimetheus. "I have 234
given everything to the other animals." 240

Gift of Fire 243

Prometheus was deeply troubled. "Man cannot exist 250
without some way to protect himself. If I could give him fire, 262
he would be a match for any animal on earth." 272

So Prometheus journeyed to Mt. Olympus to get per- 280
mission from the king of the gods. "No!" thundered Zeus. "I 291
will never allow man to have fire, for with it he would become 304
too powerful. Fire shall be saved for the immortal gods alone!" 315

On the way back to earth Prometheus struggled with a 325
difficult decision. To defy Zeus meant terrible punishment for 334
himself; to obey meant that mankind would perish. But he did 345
not hesitate long. Straight to the sun he went, lighted a torch 357
from its flaming rays, and carried fire to earth. 366

Secretly he taught man how to use it for cooking his 377
food, making tools and weapons, and creating things of beau- 387
ty. A spark of the heavenly fire lit man's brain too, awakening 398
his emotions and enabling him to understand, to reason, and 408
to think. His superiority over all animals was complete. Man 418
was safe—but Prometheus was not. 424

Punishment for Prometheus 427

The angry Zeus sent his strongest servants, Force and 436
Violence, to capture Prometheus and carry him to the shaggy 446
crags of Mount Caucasus (kaw' kah suss), where they bound 454

Answer Key: Words in Context
1. (b) **2.** (c) **3.** (a) **4.** (d) **5.** (b) **6.** (c) **7.** (d)

him to the rocks with heavy chains. Then a fierce vulture was 466
sent to tear at his flesh and feed on his liver every day. That 480
his torment might go on forever, his body was renewed each 491
night. . . . 492

Woman, Made of Godly Gifts 497

The Olympian gods sat in council in the shining palace 507
of Zeus their king. "Man must be punished for daring to ac- 518
cept the gift of fire from Prometheus," he scowled. "We will 528
create woman!" 530
Thus it was that though man had been molded of 540
earth's muddy clay, woman was made by the gods themselves 550
of the exquisite materials in Olympus. Each god gave her a 561
special gift: intelligence, charm, beauty, grace, good humor, 569
gaiety, kindness, and many others. At the last moment, one 579
mischievous god contributed a generous portion of curiosity. 587
Delighted with their handiwork, the Olympians named 594
her Pandora (pan doe' rah), which means "all-gifted," since 601
each one of them had given her a present. 610
The gods did not want to part with the lovely maiden 621
they had created, but they instructed their messenger Hermes 630
(her' meez) to take her to earth and present her to Epime- 641
theus. Just as she left, Zeus gave her a golden box. "Never 652
open this!" he commanded. Pandora readily promised: with all 661
the lovely gifts the kind Olympians had given her, what did 672
this one little golden box matter? 678
Now Prometheus had warned his brother not to take 687
any presents from Zeus. But when Epimetheus saw Pandora, 696
he was completely captivated and accepted her joyfully as his 706
bride, the words of Prometheus forgotten. 712

Overcome with Curiosity 715

For a long time they were blissfully happy, and Pandora 725
learned to love the beautiful earth just as she had loved Mt. 737
Olympus. But more and more she wondered what was in the 748
mysterious golden box. . . . 751
One day when Epimetheus was away . . . she cautiously 759
opened the box just a crack, intending to close it at once. 771
But the lid fairly bounced out of her hands as, with a 782
flurry and rush of wings, thousands of tiny shrieking imps 793
swarmed into the air. . . . 797
Hearing her screams, Epimetheus rushed into the room 805
and the horde swept out through the open door, scattering in 816
all directions until it seemed as if the whole earth would be 828
covered with them. 831

Trouble Comes to Earth 835

"What have you done!" cried Epimetheus in horror. 843
"Because of you, never-ending misery has been loosed upon 852
the world. Those imps are Greed, Pain, Jealousy, Disease, 861
Hate, Bitterness, Cruelty, and Spite. Mankind will be plagued 870
by them forever!" 873
The terrified Pandora attempted to slam down the lid. 882
But in the very bottom she saw a shining gem whose soft radi- 895
ance began to fill the room. It was Hope, the one good thing 907
the gods had put in the box. . . . 914
It has remained with mankind ever since. 921

Mark the number of words read (or the number to the right of the last line read). Then immediately answer the questions below without referring to the selection.

1. According to this myth, the main reason woman was created was to
   - **(a)** reward Epimetheus for remaining loyal to Zeus.
   - **(b)** punish man for accepting the stolen fire.
   - **(c)** pay Prometheus for creating man.
   - **(d)** astonish and delight man with a bride.

2. In this story, the blame for the world's woes rests on Pandora's curiosity. **T F**

3. As punishment Prometheus was chained to a rock and vultures tore at his liver every day. **T F**

4. The one good thing in Pandora's box was Hope. **T F**

Check your answers with the key on the bottom of page 216, and record your scores below and on the progress chart in the Appendix.

WORDS PER MINUTE ______

% COMPREHENSION ______

Exercise 8H — Short Reading

Use the survey method (Lesson 7) before you begin to skim the following selection. Then try to *skim* the selection in one minute. (Faster students should set a goal of one-half minute.) This exercise is twice the length of earlier Short Readings; so skim as rapidly as you can for general idea.

The Creation of the First World

recorded and translated by Oswald White Bear Fredericks

WPM

Taiowa's Nephew Creates the Elements 5

But first, they say, there was only the Creator, Taiowa. 15
All else was endless space. There was no beginning and no 26
end, no time, no shape, no life. Just an immeasurable void that 38
had its beginning and end, time, shape, and life in the mind of 51
Taiowa the Creator. 54

Then he, the infinite, conceived the finite. First he cre- 64
ated Sótuknang to make it manifest, saying to him, "I have cre- 75
ated you, the first power and instrument as a person, to carry 86
out my plan for life in endless space. I am your Uncle. You are 100
my Nephew. Go now and lay out these universes in proper 111
order so they may work harmoniously with one another ac- 120
cording to my plan." 124

Sótuknang did as he was commanded. . . . 130

Taiowa was pleased. "You have done a great work ac- 139
cording to my plan, Nephew. You have created the universes 149
and made them manifest in solids, water, and winds, and put 160
them in their proper places. But your work is not yet finished. 172
Now you must create life and its movement to complete the 183
four parts of my universal plan." 189

Spider Woman Creates Life 193

Sótuknang went to the universe wherein was that to be 203
Tokpela, the First World, and out of it he created her who was 216
to remain on that earth and be his helper. Her name was Spi- 229
der Woman. 230

When she awoke to life and received her name, she 240
asked, "Why am I here?" 245

"Look about you," answered Sótuknang. "Here is this 253
earth we have created. It has shape and substance, direction 263
and time, a beginning and an end. But there is no life upon it. 277
We see no joyful movement. We hear no joyful sound. What is 289
life without sound and movement? So you have been given the 300
power to help us create this life. You have been given the 312
knowledge, wisdom, and love to bless all the beings you create. 323
That is why you are here." 329

She then created from the earth trees, bushes, plants, 338
flowers, all kinds of seed-bearers and nut-bearers to clothe the 348
earth, giving to each a life and name. In the same manner she 361
created all kinds of birds and animals—molding them out of 372
earth, covering them with her white-substance cape, and sing- 381
ing over them. . . . 383

Sótuknang was happy, seeing how beautiful it all was— 392
the land, the plants, the birds and animals, and the power 403
working through them all. Joyfully he said to Taiowa, "Come 413
see what our world looks like now!" 420

"It is very good," said Taiowa. "It is ready now for hu- 431
man life, the final touch to complete my plan." 440

Three Phases in the Creation of the First People 449

1. So Spider Woman gathered earth, this time of four 459
colors, yellow, red, white, and black; mixed with the liquid of 470
her mouth; molded them; and covered them with her white- 480
substance cape which was the creative wisdom itself. As before, 490
she sang over them the Creation Song, and when she un- 500
covered them these forms were human beings in the image of 511
Sótuknang. Then she created four other beings after her own 521
form. They were female partners, for the first four male 531
beings. 532

When Spider Woman uncovered them the forms came 540
to life. This was at the time of the dark purple light, the first 554
phase of the dawn of Creation, which first reveals the mystery 565
of man's creation. 568

2. They soon awakened and began to move, but there 577
was still a dampness on their foreheads and a soft spot on their 590
heads. This was at the time of the yellow light, the second 602
phase of the dawn of Creation, when the breath of life entered 614
man. 615

3. In a short time the sun appeared above the horizon, 625
drying the dampness on their foreheads and hardening the 634
soft spot on their heads. This was the time of the red light, the 648
third phase of the dawn of Creation, when man, fully formed 659
and firmed, proudly faced his Creator. 665

"That is the Sun," said Spider Woman. "You are meet- 675
ing your Father the Creator for the first time. You must always 686
remember and observe these three phases of your Creation. 695
The time of the three lights, the dark purple, the yellow, and 707
the red reveal in turn the mystery, the breath of life, and 719
warmth of love. These comprise the Creator's plan of life for 730
you as sung over you in the Song of Creation. . . . 740

Two Special Gifts 743

The First People of the First World did not answer her; 754
they could not speak. Something had to be done. Since Spider 765

Answer Key: Ex. 8G
1. (b) **2.** T **3.** T **4.** T

Woman received her power from Sótuknang, she had to call 775
him and ask him what to do. 782
All at once, with the sound as of a mighty wind, Sótu- 794
knang appeared in front of them. "I am here. Why do you 805
need me so urgently?" 809
Spider Woman explained. "As you commanded me, I 817
have created these First People. They are fully and firmly 827
formed; they are properly colored; they have life; they have 837
movement. But they cannot talk. That is the proper thing they 848
lack. So I want you to give them speech. Also the wisdom and 861
the power to reproduce, so that they may enjoy their life and 873
give thanks to the Creator." 878
So Sótuknang gave them speech, a different language to 887
each color, with respect for each other's difference. He gave 897
them the wisdom and the power to reproduce and multiply. 907
Then he said to them, "With all these I have given you 919
this world to live on and to be happy. There is only one thing I 934
ask of you. To respect the Creator at all times." . . . 944
So the First People went their directions, were happy, 953
and began to multiply. 957

Mark the number of words read (or the number to the right of the last line read). Then immediately answer the questions below without referring to the selection.

1. According to the tale, the first world was formed by
- **(a)** the Supreme God, Taiowa.
- **(b)** Taiowa's nephew.
- **(c)** Spider Woman.
- **(d)** the combined efforts of Spider Woman and Taiowa's nephew.

2. The Song of Creation was part of the process of creating life. **T** **F**

3. The First People were created in two stages. **T** **F**

4. One of the special gifts the First People received was the gift of speech. **T** **F**

Check your answers with the key on the bottom of the next page. Record your scores below and on the progress chart in the Appendix.

WORDS PER MINUTE ______

% COMPREHENSION ______

Exercise 8I — Long Reading

LENGTH: 1682

First *survey* the following selection by reading the subheadings and first and last paragraphs. Then *skim* the following selection as rapidly as you can for the general idea. Attempt to skim three times your usual reading speed. Wait for a signal from your instructor before you begin reading.

The Descent from the Sky

a story from the Yoruba People

The God Olurun and Other Deities

In ancient days, at the beginning of time, there was no solid land here where people now dwell. There was only outer space and the sky, and, far below, an endless stretch of water and wild marshes. Supreme in the domain of the sky was the orisha, or god, called Olorun. . . . Also living in that place were numerous other orishas, each having attributes of his own, but none of whom had knowledge or powers equal to those of Olorun.

Among them was Orunmila, also called Ifa, the eldest son of Olorun. To this orisha Olorun had given the power to read the future, to understand the secret of existence and to divine the processes of fate. There was the orisha Obatala, King of the White Cloth, whom Olorun trusted as though he also were a son. . . . These and the other orishas living in the domain of the sky acknowledged Olorun as the owner of everything and as the highest authority in all matters. Also living there was Agemo, the chameleon, who served Olorun as a trusted servant.

Obatala's Idea

Down below, it was the female deity Olokun who ruled over the vast expanses of water and wild marshes, a grey region with no living things in it, either creatures of the bush or vegetation. This is the way it was, Olorun's living sky above and Olokun's domain of water below. Neither kingdom troubled the other. They were separate and apart. The orishas of the sky lived on, hardly noticing what lay below them.

All except Obatala, King of the White Cloth. He alone looked down on the domain of Olokun and pondered on it,

Answer Key: Ex. 8H
1. (d) **2.** T **3.** F **4.** T

saying to himself: "Everything down there is a great wet monotony. It does not have the mark of any inspiration or living thing." And at last he went to Olorun and said: "The place ruled by Olokun is nothing but sea, marsh and mist. If there were solid land in that domain, fields and forests, hills and valleys, surely it could be populated by orishas and other living things."

Olorun answered: "Yes, it would be a good thing to cover the water with land. But it is an ambitious enterprise. Who is to do the work? And how should it be done?"

Obatala said: "I will undertake it. I will do whatever is required."

Four Recommendations for Obatala

He left Olorun and went to the house of Orunmila, who understood the secrets of existence, and said to him: "Your father has instructed me to go down below and make land where now there is nothing but marsh and sea, so that living beings will have a place to build their towns and grow their crops. You, Orunmila, who can divine the meanings of all things, instruct me further. How may this work be begun?"

Orunmila brought out his divining tray and cast sixteen palm nuts on it. He read their meanings by the way they fell. He gathered them up and cast again, again reading their meanings. And when he had cast many times he added meanings to meanings, and said: "These are the things you must do: Descend to the watery wastes on a chain of gold, taking with you a snail shell full of sand, a white hen to disperse the sand, a black cat to be your companion, and a palm nut. That is what the divining figures tell us."

The Golden Chain Is Made

Obatala went next to the goldsmith and asked for a chain of gold long enough to reach from the sky to the surface of the water.

The goldsmith asked, "Is there enough gold in the sky to make such a chain?"

Obatala answered: "Yes, begin your work. I will gather the gold." Departing from the forge of the goldsmith, Obatala went then to Orunmila, Eshu and the other orishas, asking each of them for gold. They gave him whatever they had. Some gave gold dust, some gave rings, bracelets or pendants. Obatala collected gold from everywhere and took it to the goldsmith.

The goldsmith said, "More gold is needed."

So Obatala continued seeking gold, and after that he again returned to the goldsmith, saying, "Here is more metal for your chain."

The goldsmith said, "Still more is needed."

Obatala said, "There is no more gold in the sky."

The goldsmith said, "The chain will not reach to the water."

Obatala answered: "Nevertheless, make the chain. We shall see."

The goldsmith went to work. When the chain was finished he took it to Obatala. Obatala said, "It must have a hook at the end."

"There is no gold remaining," the goldsmith said.

Obatala replied, "Take some of the links and melt them down."

The goldsmith removed some of the links, and out of them he fashioned a hook for the chain. It was finished. He took the chain to Obatala.

Obatala's Descent

Obatala said, "Now I am ready." He fastened the hook on the edge of the sky and lowered the chain. Orunmila gave him the things that were needed—a snail shell of sand, a white hen, a black cat, and a palm nut. Then Obatala gripped the chain with his hands and feet and began the descent. The chain was very long. When he had descended only half its length. Obatala saw that he was leaving the realm of light and entering the region of greyness. A time came when he heard the wash of waves and felt the damp mists rising from Olokun's domain. He reached the end of the golden chain, but he was not yet at the bottom, and he clung there, thinking, "If I let go I will fall into the sea."

While he remained at the chain's end thinking such things, he heard Orunmila's voice from above, saying, "The sand."

So Obatala took the snail shell from the knapsack at his side and poured out the sand.

Again he heard Orunmila call to him, saying this time, "The hen."

Obatala dropped the hen where he had poured the sand. The hen began at once to scratch at the sand and scatter it in all directions. Wherever the sand was scattered it became dry land. Because it was scattered unevenly the sand formed hills and valleys. When this was accomplished, Obatala let go of the chain and came down and walked on the solid earth that had been created. The land extended in all directions, but still it was barren of life.

Obatala named the place where he had come down Ife. He built a house there. He planted his palm nut and a palm tree sprang out of the earth. It matured and dropped its palm seeds. More palm trees came into being. Thus there was vegetation at Ife. Obatala lived on, with only his black cat as a companion.

The Sun Shines on Earth

After some time had passed, Olorun the Sky God wanted to know how Obatala's expedition was progressing. He instructed Agemo the chameleon to descend the golden chain. Agemo went down. He found Obatala living in his house at Ife. He said: "Olorun instructed me this way: He said, 'Go down, discover for me how things are with Obatala.' That is why I am here."

Obatala answered, "As you can see, the land has been created, and palm groves are plentiful. But there is too much greyness. The land should be illuminated."

Agemo returned to the sky and reported to Olorun what he had seen and heard. Olorun agreed that there should be light down below. So he made the sun and set it moving. After that there was warmth and light in what had once been Olokun's exclusive domain.

Creation of People

Obatala lived on, with only his black cat for a companion. He thought, "Surely it would be better if many people were living here." He decided to create people. He dug clay from the ground, and out of the clay he shaped human figures which he then laid out to dry in the sun. He worked without resting. He became tired and thirsty. He said to himself, "There should be palm wine in this place to help a person go on working." So he put aside the making of humans and went to the palm trees to draw their inner fluid, out of which he made palm wine. When it was fermented he drank. He drank for a long while. When he felt everything around him softening he put aside his gourd cup and went back to modeling human figures.

But because Obatala had drunk so much wine his fingers grew clumsy, and some of the figures were misshapen. Some had crooked backs or crooked legs, or arms that were too short. Some did not have enough fingers, some were bent instead of being straight. Because of the palm wine inside him, Obatala did not notice these things.

And when he had made enough figures to begin the

populating of Ife he called out to Olorun the Sky God, saying, "I have made human beings to live with me here in Ife, but only you can give them the breath of life." Olorun heard Obatala's request, and he put breath in the clay figures. They were no longer clay, but people of blood, sinews and flesh. They arose and began to do the things that humans do. They built houses for themselves near Obatala's house, and in this way the place Obatala named Ife became the city of Ife.

Obatala's Pledge

But when the effects of the palm wine had worn off Obatala saw that some of the humans he had made were misshapen, and remorse filled his heart. He said: "Never again will I drink palm wine. From this time on I will be the special protector of all humans who have deformed limbs or who have otherwise been created imperfectly." Because of Obatala's pledge, humans who later came to serve him also avoided palm wine, and the lame, the blind and those who had no pigment in their skin invoked his help when they were in need.

TOTAL SKIMMING TIME ______

Immediately answer the questions below without referring to the selection.

1. Choose the statement that best summarizes the events in the tale.
   (a) Olorun formed the world with the aid of the chameleon, his trusty servant.
   (b) Obatala descended to the wastes below on a chain of gold.
   (c) With the aid of some sand, a hen, a cat, and a palm nut, Obatala formed the earth.
   (d) Drinking too much palm wine can lead to unhappy consequences.

2. The supreme god was Olorun. **T F**

3. The area where the earth was formed was originally full of fire. **T F**

4. The idea to descend to the region below was Obatala's. **T F**

5. Obatala made the golden chain himself. **T F**

6. Because of its eggs, the hen was taken on the descent below. **T F**

7. The tale provides an explanation of how imperfection came to exist in the world. **T F**

8. People were made out of clay. **T F**

Check your answers with the key on the bottom of the next page. Then turn to the Rate Chart in the Appendix to get your words per minute for this selection. Finally, record your scores below and on the progress chart in the Appendix.

WORDS PER MINUTE ______

% COMPREHENSION ______

Bonus Questions (Scanning)

1. What was the name of the chameleon who served Olorun as a trusty servant?

____

2. What was *Ife?* ______________________________

Percentage Chart for Comprehension Check

Errors	0	1	2	3	4	5	6	7	8
% Right	100	88	75	63	50	38	25	13	0

Answer Key: Ex. 8I
1. (c) **2.** T **3.** F **4.** T **5.** F **6.** F **7.** T **8.** T **1.** Agemo **2.** The place where Obatala settled on earth, which later became a city of the same name.

Lesson 9

Exercise 9A—Phrase Perception (Variation)

Note: The key phrase may be repeated more than once.

key phrase

1. plush velvet lining	push velvet linings lush velvet lining	plush velvet lining plush velvet lining	very plush living
2. speaking to group	spoken to group speaking to group	speeding to place peaking to point	reaching group
3. pasting gold parts	pasting partial gold casting gold parts	hold pasted parts pasting gold parts	partial gold paste
4. holding hands high	holding hands high holding hands high	holding high hands holding hands high	holding high hand
5. say nothing to him	nothing said to him say not to him	say more to him say nothing to him	say nothing to him
6. long slender legs	long spending days long slender legs	along slender lines long slender leg	long slender legs
7. place for dinghy	place for dinghy place for dinghy	place for dimple pace for dinghy	a dingy place
8. eating good jerkin	eating food jerkily eating with jerks	wearing good jerseys eating bad jerkin	eating good jerkin
9. left-handed batter	left-handed batter left-handed batters	left-handed batter left-handed batter	right-handed batter
10. dealing with pathos	dealing with pathos dealing with pathos	dealing with bathos dealing with paths	dealing with patience
11. has the button	has the butter has the buttons	was the button has the button	has the button
12. spoken with candor	speak for candy spoken with candor	spoken candidly spoken with candor	poke the canine
13. that pungent odor	punctured motor punished child	that pungent odor	the pungent odor
14. an obscure person	an obsessed person an obscure son	an obscure person a secure person	an observed person
15. two in the dark	two in the dark two in the bank	two in the dark ten in the dark	two in the park
16. one forlorn girl	one forlorn curl one farm girl	one foreign girl one forlorn girl	one forlorn girl
17. sleeping dogs lying	sleeping dogs lying sleeping dogs lying	the dogs lying late sleeping dogs	creeping dogs lying

18. taking out garbage	taking garbage taking out garbage	taking out baggage raking up garden	taking in garbage
19. more narrow minds	more national binds more narrow minds	more narrow minds more narrow minds	more rational minds
20. carrying crates	carrying a crate carrying crates	parrying cracks carrying crackers	raising rates

TIME _______

ERRORS _______

Exercise 9B—Phrase Perception (Variation)

Note: The key phrase may be repeated more than once.

key phrase			
1. eating ice cream	making ice cream eating iced scones	eating ice cream eating ice cream	heating ice cream
2. picking up sticks	picking up sticks picking up sticks	picking up sticks picking dead sticks	packing up stacks
3. gnawing the bone	gnawing the bones knowing the bone	throwing the stone gnawing the bone	gnawing the bone
4. empty the basket	empty the waste basket empty the bucket	empty two baskets empty the baskets	empty the basket
5. filling the tooth	filling the tooth all the hole	filling the teeth filling the tooth	filing the tooth
6. shoes all shined	sun all shining shoes all shined	shores all shiny shoe all shined	shoes all shined
7. the Monkey Trial	the Monkey Trial the Monkeys' Trail	the Monkey Trail the Monkey tried	the Monkey's Trial
8. a chilling frost	a chilled frosting a chilly frog	a chilling frost a killer frost	a chilling frost
9. pen on the table	pen in the table pen on the tablet	pencil on the table pen on the table	pen on the table
10. news of the week	news of the weak news of the week	blues of the bleak news of the week	new on the beak
11. sat in the sun	sat in the sun sitting in the sun	seat with your son spit on the seat	not in the sun
12. drinking the coffee	drinking the coffee drank your coffee	drinking the coke drunk your coffee	blinking an eye
13. viewing a bad film	viewing a sad film reviewing a film	viewing a bad film viewing a bad film	viewing bad films

Answer Key: Ex. 9A
Repeated once: 2, 3, 8, 14, 18, 20
Repeated three times: 4, 9, 19
Others repeated twice

14. under milkwood	under milkwoods and the milkwood	under milkworm under millwood	under milkwood
15. spared a dime	speared a dime spared a dame	a spared dime spared a dime	a dim space
16. lightning flash	lightning flash lightning splash	light flash lighter flash	lightening flash
17. my older brother	my older brother my old mother	my old brother my older brothers	my older brother
18. peace with honor	peaceful honor peace with humor	peace with honesty piece of honor	peace with honor
19. evaded the draft	evaded the draft evaded the drift	avoided the draft evading the draft	invaded the draft
20. different drummer	diffident drummer indifferent drumming	different drummer different drummer	difficult drummer

TIME _______

ERRORS _______

Exercise 9C—Word Comprehension (Variation)

Note: Look for the *antonym* (opposite word) of the key word among the words on the right. Most of the words in these exercises have appeared before in other Word Comprehension exercises and in "Words in Context."

key word					
1. clad	form	clod	clothed	undressed	closet
2. aware	adorn	share	oblivious	wear	alert
3. acute	pretty	dull	sharp	roar	scissors
4. bliss	horn	blend	bent	sadness	joy
5. prominent	obscure	promenade	noticeable	permit	aroma
6. absurd	drudge	foolish	about	blank	serious
7. sufficient	recall	scant	enough	locate	sustenance
8. stylish	sock	wicked	dated	fashionable	clothes
9. accurate	acorn	account	right	incorrect	render
10. humane	cruel	kindly	weird	humble	slack
11. criticize	stare	observe	movie	paternal	praise
12. brittle	brusque	crisp	unbreakable	brittle	candy
13. moderate	wheeze	expensive	reasonable	price	money
14. melancholy	disease	gloomy	cheerful	flag	brain
15. loose	tight	slack	lose	limb	goose
16. fatigued	tired	fang	rested	dangle	guest
17. hoist	foist	pearl	lower	raise	haul
18. depart	deport	leave	devil	arrive	partition
19. victor	winner	loser	vicious	veal	vice
20. spry	inactive	dream	active	perfect	lead

TIME _______

ERRORS _______

Answer Key: Ex. 9B
Repeated once: 4, 7, 11, 12, 14, 15, 16, 18, 19
Others repeated twice

Exercise 9D—Word Comprehension (Variation)

Note: Look for the *antonym* (opposite word) of the key word among the words on the right.

key word					
1. adept	change	awaken	skilled	frighten	awkward
2. compassion	mercy	cruelty	cleverness	warmth	forgiveness
3. cryptic	cynical	secret	affectionate	open	isolated
4. conscious	knowing	smart	unaware	moral	sleepy
5. hilarious	funny	act	marvel	droll	sad
6. competent	comfort	competitor	wily	inefficient	contrast
7. boisterous	quiet	dynamic	silly	careful	girlish
8. monotonous	boring	exciting	moment	extra	bright
9. colossal	quick	big	bask	small	column
10. esteem	respect	dishonor	team	status	flatter
11. probable	probe	likely	impossible	rich	perhaps
12. unrepentant	sorry	recent	appealing	inept	forward
13. listless	innocent	active	lazy	happy	bored
14. hub	center	wife	car	periphery	knob
15. agony	gone	pleasure	pain	again	wound
16. frugal	economical	weekly	generous	stingy	dance
17. remote	close	distant	vote	move	resent
18. dismay	diligent	grief	relief	sanity	joy
19. articulate	fluent	talkative	insincere	mouth	inarticulate
20. legible	unreadable	reachable	letter	armor	illegal

TIME ______

ERRORS ______

Exercise 9E—Phrase Comprehension (Variation)

Note: Mark every *noun* in the phrases below. (A noun expresses person, place, thing, or idea.) Each phrase has at least one noun; some have more than one. (Do not mark nouns used to modify other nouns. Example: in "*car* coat," *car* is used as an adjective and *coat* is the noun.)

1. international airport
2. cars swarming like flies
3. palm-tree-lined streets
4. concrete parking structures
5. monotonous recorded voice
6. droning the same words
7. "no parking"
8. "for loading and unloading"
9. "of passengers only"
10. taxi driving up
11. passenger in mink coat
12. baggage unloaded
13. porter receiving tip
14. doors swinging wide
15. checked-in at ticket counter
16. going through security check
17. rushing down concourse
18. high heels clicking
19. running up escalator
20. arrival at gate
21. a scramble for ticket
22. seat assignment by window
23. flight delayed
24. tension in voices
25. police rushing by
26. rumors of bomb
27. the waiting in lobby
28. eyes staring at mink
29. cold plastic cushions
30. cigarette butts underfoot
31. smell of stale smoke
32. spilled soft drinks
33. paper-thin hamburgers
34. grease on chins
35. children running by
36. soldier kissing wife
37. the chatter in foreign languages
38. another flight announcement
39. passengers boarding plane
40. smiling stewardess
41. settled in first class
42. near a window
43. sipping on champagne
44. fastening seat belt
45. no smoking
46. demonstration by stewardess
47. captain's voice on speaker
48. apology for delay
49. smooth take-off
50. explosion in air

TIME ______

ERRORS ______

Exercise 9F—Phrase Comprehension (Variation)

Note: Mark every *noun* in the phrases below. Each phrase has at least one noun; some have more than one.

1. quiet rural scene
2. narrow dirt road
3. four-room sharecropper shack
4. outhouse in back
5. with no door
6. big shade trees
7. used tires in yard
8. patches of grass
9. chickens scratching around
10. tin roof shining
11. porch falling down
12. big cracks in walls
13. faint smell of urine
14. rain-stained wallpaper
15. straight-backed chairs
16. with cowhide bottoms
17. wood-burning stove
18. iron bedstead
19. chipped green paint
20. old feather mattress
21. with split seams
22. homemade kitchen table
23. wooden bench underneath
24. peas boiling on stove
25. cut green onions
26. pork frying in pan
27. biscuits in oven
28. sunset over pine trees
29. milking time near
30. the farmer's daughter
31. milkbucket swinging
32. carefully unwiring gate
33. walking through cowpen
34. rain-soaked ground
35. boots burying in mud
36. pigs grunting low
37. plow mules blinking
38. ramshackle barn
39. cow in stall chewing cud
40. and flicking flies
41. head against cow's belly
42. hands working like machines
43. hound dog watching
44. squirt on dog's head
45. hound dog leaping
46. milkbucket full
47. back in the kitchen
48. milk through strainer
49. biscuits done
50. supper on table

TIME ______

ERRORS ______

Answer Key: Ex. 9C
1. undressed **2.** oblivious **3.** dull **4.** sadness **5.** obscure **6.** serious **7.** scant **8.** dated **9.** incorrect **10.** cruel **11.** praise **12.** unbreakable **13.** expensive **14.** cheerful **15.** tight **16.** rested **17.** lower **18.** arrive **19.** loser **20.** inactive

Answer Key: Ex. 9D
1. awkward **2.** cruelty **3.** open **4.** unaware **5.** sad **6.** inefficient **7.** quiet **8.** exciting **9.** small **10.** dishonor **11.** impossible **12.** sorry **13.** active **14.** periphery **15.** pleasure **16.** generous **17.** close **18.** joy **19.** inarticulate **20.** unreadable

Answer Key: Ex. 9E
1. airport **2.** cars, flies **3.** streets **4.** structures **5.** voice **6.** words **7.** *parking **8.** *loading, unloading **9.** passengers **10.** taxi **11.** passenger, coat **12.** baggage **13.** porter, tip **14.** doors **15.** counter **16.** check **17.** concourse **18.** heels **19.** escalator **20.** arrival, gate **21.** scramble, ticket **22.** assignment, window **23.** flight **24.** tension, voices **25.** police **26.** rumors, bomb **27.** waiting, lobby **28.** eyes, mink **29.** cushions **30.** butts **31.** smell, smoke **32.** drinks **33.** hamburgers **34.** grease, chins **35.** children **36.** soldier, wife **37.** chatter, languages **38.** announcement **39.** passengers, plane **40.** stewardess **41.** class **42.** window **43.** champagne **44.** belt **45.** smoking **46.** demonstration, stewardess **47.** voice, speaker **48.** apology, delay **49.** take-off **50.** explosion, air
*Note: Parking, loading, and unloading are gerunds, which function as nouns.

Answer Key: Ex. 9F
1. scene **2.** road **3.** shack **4.** outhouse, back **5.** door **6.** trees **7.** tires, yard **8.** patches, grass **9.** chickens **10.** roof **11.** porch **12.** cracks, walls **13.** smell, urine **14.** wallpaper **15.** chairs **16.** bottoms **17.** stove **18.** bedstead **19.** paint **20.** mattress **21.** seams **22.** table **23.** bench **24.** peas, stove **25.** onions **26.** pork, pan **27.** biscuits, oven **28.** sunset, trees **29.** time **30.** daughter **31.** milkbucket **32.** gate **33.** cowpen **34.** ground **35.** boots, mud **36.** pigs **37.** mules **38.** barn **39.** cow, stall, cud **40.** flies **41.** head, belly **42.** hands, machines **43.** dog **44.** squirt, head **45.** dog **46.** milkbucket **47.** kitchen **48.** milk, strainer **49.** biscuits **50.** supper, table

WORDS IN CONTEXT

Without using your dictionary, try to determine the meaning of each word in **boldface** print. Choose the meaning below that best fits the context—the way it is used in the sentence.

Short Reading 9H

1. When Golda graduated as valedictorian of her class, her mother was **elated.**
   (a) relieved **(b)** calm **(c)** joyful **(d)** determined
2. Papa had, for once, sided with her—**albeit** rather faintly.
   (a) even though **(b)** in addition **(c)** since **(d)** therefore
3. And with the war came dire reports of increased **pogroms.**
   (a) injuries **(b)** draft calls **(c)** economical hardship **(d)** organized massacres
4. Her mission: to try to stir the **complacent** American Jewish youth, awaken them to the philosophies and the necessities of Labor Zionism.
   (a) selfish **(b)** self-satisfied **(c)** wealthy **(d)** excitable
5. His daughter, to stand on a soap box **exhorting** people on the street!
   (a) pleading with **(b)** singing to **(c)** giving warnings to **(d)** shouting at

Long Reading 9I

6. She had her own way of showing her displeasure—not to yell or even to scold, but to greet her son at all times with an **impassive** stare.
   (a) showing no emotions **(b)** hostile **(c)** angry **(d)** deceptively sweet
7. She inquired scrupulously into his plans for the future and, **eliciting** no assurance that he was even willing to entertain the notion of college, she closed him out completely.
   (a) forcing **(b)** drawing forth **(c)** begging for **(d)** winning
8. Johnson saw the trip, when he talked about it later, in cartoon **imagery.**
   (a) lies **(b)** drawings **(c)** mental pictures **(d)** funny stories

Check your answers with the key on the bottom of the next page.

THEME FOR READING SELECTIONS: TALES OF REAL PEOPLE

Before you read the selections in this Lesson, think about what kind of person becomes a public figure—whether politician or entertainer. What qualities led Elvis Presley, a poor shy Southern boy, to become a legendary singer for almost three decades? What caused Golda Meir to break with Jewish tradition for women and become one of the first women to be elected as head of state? What drove our late President Lyndon Johnson, who hated school, to continue his education and go into politics?

Imaginary Situation

Your boss has lent you a book of biographical sketches, hoping they will inspire you to work harder. He has asked you three times if you have read the sketches on Presley, Meir, and Johnson, but you have not looked at them. Your boss has asked you to dinner tonight to discuss your job performance, and you have accepted because you want to ask him for a raise. You know he will ask you again about the sketches. You have only fifteen minutes to read all three, but you must be able to discuss them intelligently with your boss.

Exercise 9G – Short Reading

Try to *skim* the following selection in one minute. (Faster students should set a goal of one-half minute.) This exercise is nearly twice the length of earlier Short Readings: so skim as rapidly as you can for the general idea.

Elvis Presley's First Concert

Red West, Sonny West, and Dave Hebler as told to Steve Dunleavy

WPM

In 1948, when Elvis was thirteen, his father, Vernon 9
Presley, decided it was time to leave the tiny shotgun home in 21
Tupelo. The big city across the border might afford a chance 32
for higher pay and a shot at the good life. He packed all the 46
household goods into a green Plymouth one night and the 56
family headed for Memphis. . . . 60

Like most transplanted kids in a new town, Elvis with- 70
drew into a shell of timidity and shyness. . . . When he was 80
fourteen he wanted a bike for Christmas. The Presleys couldn't 90
afford it. But they did manage to scrape up twelve dollars for a 103
guitar. With a few lessons from his uncle, Vester Presley, Elvis 114
was soon able to pluck away at the main chords. . . . 124

While Red West as a young teenager was practicing to 134
become a bone-crusher on the football field, Elvis stayed at 144
home, practiced his guitar and began developing a singing 153
voice at the First Assembly Church of God, a tiny, rickety struc- 165
ture on Adams Street in Tupelo. 170

Red recalls Presley's telling him on a dozen occasions 179
that his mother remembered three-year-old Elvis slipping off 187
her lap at a church service and running down to the choir. 199
There his little voice would try to follow the singing. It gave 211
him his first contact with music and that stayed with him. "Peo- 223

Answer Key: Words in Context
1. (c) **2.** (a) **3.** (d) **4.** (b) **5.** (c) **6.** (a) **7.** (b) **8.** (c)

ple are always talking about where he got his natural ability 233
from," says Red. "That little sonofabitch was singing his ass off 244
back in that church in Tupelo. And when he was about nine he 257
would sing trios with his mother and father. . . ." 265

Later, in Memphis, he would wander through the black 274
section of town, the famous Beale Street, and listen to the 285
blacks wail their blues. The influence was so strong that people 296
said Presley's first records sounded like a black voice inside a 307
white body. . . . 309

Elvis Presley, save for the long hair, rated as being high- 320
ly forgettable in a school that measured its respect quotient on 330
whether you could pound through a defensive line or whether 340
you could knock a guy on his butt. Elvis really couldn't handle 352
any of that, so there was no place for him to go down in Humes 367
High School history until midway through his final year. 376

"One of the big events of the year was the school variety 388
concert," Red recalls. "It consisted of about thirty acts. . . . 397
The person who ran the show was a history teacher who taught 409
Elvis. I think she always had a soft spot for Elvis because he was 423
so polite toward her. I put an act in the show. I played the 437
trumpet and I got together a guitar and a bass. It was a heck of 452
a big day and we were all very nervous. I didn't take much 465
notice of all the others because I was so intent on my own." 478

The rules of the concert were that whoever got the big- 489
gest applause would be given the honor of having an encore 499
and would be declared the winner. Red recalls he had finished 510
his act when he got the shock of his life, seeing Elvis come out 524
on the stage with his guitar. "To be honest, I never thought he 537
would have the guts to get out there in front of those people. 550
He just never impressed me as being that brave. I never even 562
knew he sang, but I was to get a surprise." 572

Elvis shuffled timidly onto the stage. His shyness, how- 581
ever, was offset by his elaborately combed crowning glory—his 590
Vaseline-walled hair—and a bright red shirt. Then it hap- 600
pened. Elvis put one foot up on a chair to act as a prop, and he 615
started to plunk away at the tune, "Old Shep." Then he 626
whipped into a fast song, then a ballad. Red West smiles, "Hell, 638
do you know while Elvis was singing the love songs, there was 650
one lady teacher crying?" 654

"And there were other teachers who had tears in their 664
eyes. When he finished his show, the kids went crazy; they ap- 674
plauded and applauded. They just went mad. He was an easy 685
winner. At first Elvis just stood there, surprised as hell. He 696
seemed to be amazed that for the first time in his life someone, 709
other than his family, really liked him. I'll never really know 720
when Elvis got bitten by the bug of loving the applause of the 733
audience, but my guess is that it happened right then in 744
Humes High School. At last, it seemed, he had found a way to 757
make outsiders love him. 761

"He still to this day craves that live audience yelling and 772
screaming for him. Of course, it's the same with most perform- 783
ers, but with Elvis I think it goes all the way back to the time at 798
school where the only time he made a mark was on stage. I saw 812
it that day. As shy as he was, he had a definite magic on stage. 827
After the show, he just seemed to go back to being ordinary old 840
Elvis. But on stage he had control." 847

Mark the number of words read (or the number to the right of the last line read). Then immediately answer the questions below without referring to the selection.

1. Red thinks Elvis Presley's first high school performance was important because Elvis
   - (a) humiliated himself by being too shy to sing loudly enough to be heard.
   - (b) sang well enough but made little impression on his audience.
   - (c) realized his impact on an audience.
   - (d) was cheered by the students and jeered by the teachers.

2. Elvis' strongest early influences were church singing and Negro blues. **T** **F**

3. Elvis was popular in high school because of his football achievements. **T** **F**

4. In spite of the loud applause, Elvis lost the contest. **T** **F**

Check your answers with the key on the bottom of page 240. Record your scores below and on the progress chart in the Appendix.

WORDS PER MINUTE ______

% COMPREHENSION ______

Exercise 9H—Short Reading

Try to *skim* the following selection in one minute. (Faster students should set a goal of one-half minute.) This exercise is nearly twice the length of earlier Short Readings; so read as rapidly as you can for general idea. Try to incorporate the Survey technique as you skim. Remember that what you survey (title, subtitles, topic sentences, etc.) gives you the general idea.

from *Golda: The Life of Israel's Prime Minister*

Peggy Mann

WPM

The Struggle with Her Parents Over Her Education 8

When Golda graduated as valedictorian of her class, her 17
mother was elated. Now the girl could work full time in the 29
grocery store. Even in America girls were not expected to go to 41
high school! 43

Golda, however, expected to go. And after some tearful 52
arguments, her parents agreed. Papa had, for once, sided with 62
her—albeit rather faintly. Perhaps he felt guilty that he, the 73
breadwinner, actually earned so little. He was a wise, gentle, 83
and scholarly man, but not cut out for business. . . . 92

She had decided to become a teacher because such a 102
profession was "intellectually and socially useful." Mama, 109
however, had found out that married women were not per- 119
mitted to teach in the local schools. "You want to be an old 131
maid?" she had screamed at Golda. "*That's* what you're study- 141
ing for?" 142

Papa now sided strongly with Mama. Either Golda must 151
quit school and go to work like other sensible girls her age, or 164
she must transfer to a business school to be trained in subjects 176
which would help her get a job and, who knows, a husband 188
too. . . . 189

[After running away from home and living with her 198
married sister in Denver for two years, Golda won this battle 209
too. She returned to Milwaukee to finish high school.] 218

Golda's Determination for a Jewish Homeland 224

Golda was still in high school when the First World War 235
broke out in Europe. And with the war came dire reports of 247
increased pogroms. The Jewish Pale of Settlement lay, unfor- 256
tunately, in the very territory where Russian and German- 264
Austrian armies clashed most often in violent battle. When the 274
White Russian Army fled in retreat they slaughtered Jews in 284
that section for being German sympathizers. When the Rus- 293
sians swept back and Germans fled from the same section, *they* 303
murdered Jews for being Russian spies. 309

The White Russian armies and their bitter opponents, 317
the Germans, seemed to agree on one tenet only: anti-Semi- 327
tism. And they had ample opportunity for carrying out their 336
battle cry: death to the Jews. For of the ten million Jews in 348
Europe, eight million lived in the Russian and Austro-Hun- 357
garian empires. 358

Millions of Jews were rendered homeless. Committees 365
were organized to raise funds for the ever-swelling ranks of 375
Jewish refugees who fled from one town to the next, trying to 387
keep out of the way of the armies. Golda worked with People's 399
Relief and with an organization called Aid in Need, formed by 410
Jewish workers in Milwaukee to help hungry and homeless 419
European Jews. . . . 421
She felt broken apart inside. For nights she could not 431
sleep. What *good* did it do, running around, making speeches, 441
collecting money for a new generation of suffering, displaced, 450
wandering Jews? There had to be a better answer than this. 461
There *had* to be one place in the world where Jews could at last 475
be free from persecution. There *had* to be a Jewish homeland. 486
And it must be created as soon as possible. All her beliefs sud- 498
denly solidified into one single purpose. As soon as she could 509
she would go to Palestine and devote her life to this goal. She 522
joined Poale Zion, the Labor Zionist Party. . . . 529

Golda's Talent as a Speaker 534

She set about making money for her passage to Pales- 543
tine. She worked part time at the Sixteenth Street and North 554
Avenue branch of the Milwaukee Public Library. In the spring 564
of 1916 she graduated. . . . She entered Milwaukee Normal 572
School for Teachers and took a part-time job at a Yiddish- 583
speaking folk school which advocated Labor Zionism. But even 591
this seemed too far removed from her goal. So she started 602
speaking for the Labor Zionists' Poale Zion. 609
The organization soon discovered that the eighteen- 616
year-old girl had a remarkable talent as a speaker. They sent 626
her on speaking engagements around the country. Her mis- 634
sion: to try to stir the complacent American Jewish youth, 644
awaken them to the philosophies and the necessities of Labor 654
Zionism. 655
One Friday night she was scheduled to speak in Milwau- 665
kee, not in a meeting room or an auditorium. She would speak 676
on a street corner. Standing on a soap box. 685
Her father heard about the plan and was horrified. 694
Women, he thundered at Golda, did not *do* such things! His 705
daughter, to stand on a soap box exhorting people on the 716
street! "If you dare to go ahead with that speech," he threat- 728
ened, "I'll come down there and pull you off home by your 739
braids!" 740
"I'm sorry, Papa," Golda said, firmly, "but the speech 749
has already been announced." 753

Answer Key: Ex. 9G
1. (c) **2.** T **3.** F **4.** F

She took the precaution of telling members of Poale 762
Zion that her father might create a scandal that evening, and 773
since she did not cherish the notion of being dragged off the 785
soap box, she asked that they form a protective circle around 796
her as she spoke. 800

This was done. But it was almost unnecessary, for the 810
crowd which gathered on the street corner that night was so 821
large that Moshe Mabovitch would have had a hard time shov- 832
ing his way through. Most of the bystanders had stopped out of 843
curiosity. It was not every day that one saw an attractive young 855
girl standing on a soap box and talking about a faraway land 867
called Palestine. They soon found themselves spellbound, 874
caught up by Golda's impassioned oratory. 880

As she spoke, Golda noticed her father at the edge of 891
the crowd; noticed thankfully that he did not, after all, seem 902
bent on making a scene. 907

Afterward, Poale Zion members gathered around her 914
with congratulations. It was a fine speech. One of the best she 926
had ever made. . . . 929

When she got home, her mother was sitting at the kitch- 940
en table sewing. 942

"Where's Papa?" 944

"In bed." 946

Bluma looked up. She was smiling a little. "He came in. 957
He sat down. He shrugged. He said, 'Where did she get this 969
talent for speaking?' Then he stood up. He said, 'God knows 980
what this girl may be able to do!' And he went to bed." 993

From that night onward the Mabovitches offered no 1001
more objections to anything Golda wanted to do. They seemed 1011
to realize that they had somehow bred a very special child. 1022
Their best contribution now would be not to interfere. . . . 1031

Many years later, when the new country called Israel 1040
was about to be born, its leader, David Ben-Gurion, would 1050
proclaim: "Some day when our history is written it will say 1061
that there was a Jewish woman who raised the money which 1072
made this nation possible." 1076

The Jewish woman he referred to was Golda. 1084

Mark the number of words read (or the number to the right of the last line read). Then immediately answer the questions below without looking back at the selection.

1. As a young girl, Golda had
- **(a)** a willingness to do anything to please her parents.
- **(b)** a saucy, pert charm that won over her parents.
- **(c)** a strong desire to get married.
- **(d)** an extraordinary speaking ability and a dedication to a homeland for Jews.

2. Golda's father always supported her—even against her mother's wishes. T F

3. Golda started working for a Jewish homeland during World War I. T F

4. Her father was never reconciled to her speaking in public. T F

Check your answers with the key on the bottom of page 244. Record your scores below and on the progress chart in the Appendix.

WORDS PER MINUTE _______

% COMPREHENSION _______

Exercise 9I—Long Reading

LENGTH: 1542

Survey the following selection by reading title, subtitles, first sentences in every subdivision, and first and last paragraphs. Then skim as rapidly as you can for the general idea. Attempt to skim three times your usual reading speed. Wait for a signal from your instructor before you begin reading.

from *Lyndon Johnson and the American Dream*

Doris Kearns

Lessons from His Father

"One of the first things I remember about my daddy," Johnson said, "was the time he cut my hair. When I was four or five, I had long curls. He hated them. 'He's a boy,' he'd say to my mother, 'and you're making a sissy of him. You've got to cut those curls.' My mother refused. Then, one Sunday morning when she went off to church, he took the big scissors and cut off all my hair. When my mother came home, she refused to speak to him for a week. . . ."

The . . . tension between father and son reveals itself in a story Johnson later told about his first experience killing an animal. "In the fall and the spring, I spent every moment when I wasn't in school out in the open. With the other boys, I went hunting squirrels and rabbits. I carried a gun and every now and then I pointed it at the animals but I never wanted to kill any of them. I wanted only to know that I could kill if I had to. Then one day my daddy asked me how did it happen that I was the only boy in the neighborhood who had never shot an animal. Was I a coward? The next day I went back into the hills and killed a rabbit. It jumped out at me from behind a bush and I shot it in between the eyes. Then I went to the bathroom and threw up. . . ."

Conflict with His Mother

Just the same, Johnson seemed to endure his father's testing far better than his mother's gloomy silence. . . . Indeed, she had refrained for months from commenting about his mediocre performance in school or his frequent evenings on the town with his friends. She had her own way of showing her displeasure—not to yell or even to scold, but to greet her son at all times with an impassive stare. She made no secret of the fact that his drinking, fast driving, and generally aggressive behavior displeased her. Nor did she conceal the repugnance she felt at the reputation he had established in school as a sluggish student who treated everything as a joke. Johnson knew by his mother's withdrawal that he had not lived up to the splendid vision she had held of him as a boy.

When Johnson graduated from high school in May, 1924, Rebekah allowed her quarrel with her son to surface at last. When she spoke, daily taking him to task for his slovenly manner, she had, as Johnson later described it, "a terrible knifelike voice."

She inquired scrupulously into his plans for the future and, eliciting no assurance that he was even willing to entertain the notion of college, she closed him out completely. During supper she would direct her remarks to her husband and her younger children, never so much as confirming Lyndon's existence. Directly after supper, she went to bed.

"We'd been such close companions, and, boom, she'd abandoned me. I wanted to please her, but something told me I'd go to pieces if I went to college. I'd just finished ten years of sitting inside a school; the prospect of another four years was awful. It would make me a sissy again and I would lose my daddy's respect. . . ."

Trip to California

Yet our concern here is not simply with the conflicts from which Lyndon Johnson suffered, but with how he surmounted or utilized these conflicts, adapting them to the realities of his life. And here the interesting biographical fact is that Johnson knew enough at the age of fifteen to know that he simply had to get away.

That summer—the summer of 1924—the opportunity arrived. A group of Johnson's friends had decided to leave home and go to California. For each of the boys the trip no doubt meant something different—adventure, the hope of work. There was a report, one of the boys later recollected, that money out there grew on trees and that a person had but to reach up and get it. Lyndon, youngest of the group, listened in as they made their plans; he watched as they fixed up the old Model T that would carry them West. He wanted desperately to go along, but he knew that his parents would never allow him to leave. "Going was one hell of a problem," he said. "I decided I'd just say to my mother and father that I was going West with the boys. I knew it would be an emotional scene, but one night I decided to look them straight in the eye and reveal my plans. But when I reached the front door of my house, I began to shiver uncontrollably. At last, I went in. They sat opposite one another at the kitchen table. My sisters and brother were there. I tried to speak, but I couldn't say a goddamn word. I lost my nerve."

One week later, before the sun came up on a Monday morning, the boys took off in their Model T. At the last minute, Johnson decided, without asking or telling anyone, to go with them. He jumped into the car. "Here I am," he said. "Let's hurry along and be on our way."

During the entire trip Johnson walked around carrying his suitcase as though it were incredibly heavy and had within it enough clothes to last a family of twenty for fifteen years. His companions could not imagine why Johnson took so much along and yet wore the same clothes day after day. Then one afternoon the baling wire that Johnson had used to tie up the suitcase came loose and it opened on the street. Out rolled the sum of Johnson's worldly possessions—a straw hat!

The Vagabond

Johnson saw the trip, when he talked about it later, in cartoon imagery. He recounted brushes with gruff poker players, scenes of burying money in underground holes, and fancies of reliving his grandfather's life on the frontier.

But the old frontier had promised economic and spiritual independence, and in California, in 1924, that independence was not easy to secure. Indeed, Johnson was barely able to survive on the grapes he picked, the dishes he washed, and the cars he fixed. Just the same, he remembered living happily for a time in different places. Free of both his mother and his father, he found he had an immense curiosity about the differ-

Answer Key: Ex. 9H
1. (d) **2.** F **3.** T **4.** F

ent kinds of people with whom he worked—the field hands in the Imperial Valley, the cooks in the all-night cafés, the garage mechanics in the big cities. He found himself constantly entertaining his fellow workers with stories and jokes. People seemed to like him; they admired his quickness.

Johnson lived the vagabond life for nearly a year; then, when his money dried up completely, he took a job in Los Angeles as a clerk to a criminal lawyer. The job was no accident. The lawyer was a cousin of Rebekah's. There Lyndon stayed for another year, until one August day in 1926 when, suddenly, faced with an offer of a ride to Texas, he decided that after two years' absence he was ready to return.

The Decision

Johnson would long remember this trip back home; he later theatrically designated it *the* moment when he found his vocation of politics. On the trip, as Johnson recounted it, he thought a great deal about his parents. "I still believed my mother the most beautiful, sexy, intelligent woman I'd ever met and I was determined to recapture her wonderful love, but not at the price of my daddy's respect. Finally, I saw it all before me. I would become a political figure. Daddy would like that. He would consider it a manly thing to be. But that would be just the beginning. I was going to reach beyond my father. I would finish college; I would build great power and gain high office. Mother would like that. I would succeed where her own father had failed; I would go to the Capitol and talk about big ideas. She would never be disappointed in me again."

Johnson reached his boyhood home on a Sunday afternoon. When he walked inside the door, he carried with him an air of pride and self-respect. At supper that night, there was, as he remembered it, much conversation. Later, left in his room, he knew that somehow things were different. He was ready to embark on his future career.

Perhaps the trip was, as Johnson believed, a turning point, marking the transition from childhood to adulthood. The separation from home obviously helped to distance Lyndon in a positive way from his mother's ceaseless pressure. And the resolve he felt that night he returned certainly showed up in the rapid successes he achieved once he entered college. But turning points are rarely as dramatic as we remember them to be. Despite his resolution, Lyndon stayed away from the study of books for another six months, taking, instead, a job with a road gang. Finally, one hot afternoon in February, 1927, he went to his mother and said: "All right, I'm sick of working just with my hands and I'm ready to try and make it with my brain."

Immediately answer the questions below without referring to the selection.

1. Choose the statement that best expresses the main idea.
   - **(a)** Johnson's parents' conflicting expectations of him helped shape his personality and career goals.
   - **(b)** Johnson's decision to become a politician was primarily to please his mother.
   - **(c)** His decision to become a politician was primarily to please his father.
   - **(d)** After much difficulty, Johnson finds his true vocation.
2. One might infer that Johnson's drinking, running around, and neglecting school was partly to keep his father from thinking he was a sissy. **T F**
3. Johnson liked to go hunting and bring in game for the family. **T F**
4. Johnson's mother habitually nagged her son about his behavior. **T F**
5. Johnson initially did not want to go to college. **T F**
6. He took a suitcase full of clothes and books with him to California. **T F**
7. In California, he worked at various jobs for a year, then as a clerk for a lawyer for another year. **T F**
8. He claimed that it was on his trip back from California that he decided to become a politician. **T F**

Check your answers with the key on the bottom of this page. Then turn to the Rate Chart in the Appendix to get your words per minute for this selection. Finally, record your scores below and on the progress chart in the Appendix.

WORDS PER MINUTE ______

% COMPREHENSION ______

Bonus Questions (Scanning)

1. When did Johnson graduate from high school? ______________________
2. Where in California did he work as a field hand? ______________________

Percentage Chart for Comprehension Check

Errors	0	1	2	3	4	5	6	7	8
% Right	100	88	75	63	50	38	25	13	0

Answer Key: Ex. 91
1. (a) **2.** T **3.** F **4.** F **5.** T **6.** T **7.** T **8.** T **1.** May, 1924 **2.** Imperial Valley

Lesson 10

Exercise 10A—Phrase Perception (Variation)

Note: Each column of twenty items has only one key phrase. Mark each repeated phrase. Work through both columns vertically before checking your time.

key phrase

livid with fear

lived with fear
livid with fear

loved with fear
loved with tears

living with fear
living with fears

livery of fear
lively with wear

livid with fear
alive with fear

livid ears
lively ears

in living color
livid with fear

living on fear
lived without fear

lives with fear
livid with fear

alive with fleas
liquid with fear

key phrase

singed his finger

singed his finger
singed his fins

signal his finish
signing his finish

signal the swingers
singed his finger

singed his fingers
signed the singers

singed two fingers
singe her finger

singer's fingers
singe my fingers

singing of fingers
unhinged with anger

singing of anger
singed his finger

sign this finger
signed with fingers

singed his finger
Band-aid, please!

TIME ________

ERRORS ________

Exercise 10B — Phrase Perception (Variation)

Note: Each column of twenty items has only one key phrase. Mark each repeated phrase. Work through both columns vertically before checking your time.

key phrase

tract of land

track of land
track landing

attract land
tractor on land

traction on land
tract of land

trace of land
trace island

tract of land
trace inland

trace the island
tract or land

race for land
track the landing

tract of land
tracing the hand

trance of mind
race to land

tract of land
contract for land

key phrase

curry favor

curry favors
carry favors

famous curry
carry flavor

the cur you favor
cherry flavor

carrying favors
cure favorite

cursory favor
curry flavoring

curry favor
savor the curry

hurry the favor
curious favor

curry for four
crawl for favors

can I favor
care for few

curry favor
furry favors

TIME ________

ERRORS ________

Exercise 10C—Word Comprehension (Variation)

Note: Look for the *antonym* (opposite word) of the key word among the words on the right.

key word					
1. sanitary	sanity	clever	clean	serious	dirty
2. miserly	surly	stingy	generous	miserable	missed
3. plausible	false	unbelievable	credible	praise	ironic
4. antipathy	disinterest	fondness	pathway	hatred	antics
5. indigestible	rotten	gourmet	digestible	swallow	indignant
6. turbulent	churning	hurried	engine	agitated	calm
7. dissect	sew up	look over	under	cut up	decent
8. hoist	trailer	foist	raise	lower	slack
9. indisposed	placed	rejected	healthy	decided	ill
10. disengage	ring	separate	bind	gadget	lose
11. comply	constant	fly	common	consent	defy
12. eloquent	pronounce	tongue-tied	bilingual	well-said	written
13. pomposity	porous	situation	male	humility	sadness
14. ferocity	tenderness	wildness	treaty	seniority	gladness
15. eradicate	revolt	erase	permanent	establish	avoid
16. customary	second	first	practice	rare	usual
17. balk	cooperate	gyrate	stop	pause	finish
18. grotesque	bizarre	huge	ordinary	clumsy	artistic
19. legible	writing	unreadable	book	readable	reading
20. sinister	evil	ladylike	wholesome	unrelated	moral

TIME ______

ERRORS ______

Answer Key: Ex. 10A
"livid with fear" repeated 4 times
"singed his finger" repeated 4 times

Answer Key: Ex. 10B
"tract of land" repeated 4 times
"curry favor" repeated 2 times

Exercise 10D—Word Comprehension (Variation)

Note: Look for the *antonym* (opposite word) of the key word among the words on the right.

key word					
1. lament	celebrate	glue	fail	pass	mourn
2. disqualified	referee	loser	qualified	unqualified	entrance
3. nimble	athletic	slow-moving	frantic	agile	sorrowful
4. delete	replace	add	omit	dilute	change
5. abate	adore	push	subside	magical	increase
6. anti-war	battle	flag	anecdote	warrior	pro-war
7. idolize	godly	church	converse	degrade	worship
8. compel	force	ask	argue	shave	pay
9. superfluous	necessary	quantity	extra	powerful	great
10. spurn	wound	reject	accept	spoon	aid
11. ornate	jewelry	beautiful	elaborate	plain	ugly
12. non-entity	nonsense	unknown	entire	tire	famous
13. surly	tender	pleasant	bad-tempered	fearful	certain
14. indelible	erasable	invisible	permanent	understood	distant
15. dismantle	destroy	disrupt	put together	take back	take apart
16. replica	original	graphic	copy	repent	regain
17. illegible	readable	unwritten	ignorant	unreadable	uneducated
18. renown	foreign	famous	recent	restful	unknown
19. agreement	common	defiance	argue	compliance	care
20. tedious	tender	calm	interesting	work	boring

TIME ______

ERRORS ______

Exercise 10E—Sentence Comprehension

key sentence: Who can protest and does not is an accomplice in the act. (The Talmud)

1. If you do not protest about some wrongful act, you are as guilty as the actor. ______
2. Ignorance of the law is no excuse. ______
3. Silence is golden. ______
4. Protest and dissent are seldom useful to society. ______
5. Silent disagreement is one good way to combat evil. ______
6. Free speech and dissent can act as curbs on unlawful acts. ______
7. Indifference or silence about a crime is the same as helping the criminal. ______
8. A responsible person does not keep quiet about injustice. ______
9. Group protest is more effective than individual protest. ______
10. Good always wins out over evil. ______

TIME ______

ERRORS ______

Answer Key: Ex. 10C
1. dirty **2.** generous **3.** unbelievable **4.** fondness **5.** digestible **6.** calm **7.** sew up **8.** lower **9.** healthy **10.** bind **11.** defy **12.** tongue-tied **13.** humility **14.** tenderness **15.** establish **16.** rare **17.** cooperate **18.** ordinary **19.** unreadable **20.** wholesome

Answer Key: Ex. 10D
1. celebrate **2.** qualified **3.** slow-moving **4.** add **5.** increase **6.** pro-war **7.** degrade **8.** ask **9.** necessary **10.** accept **11.** plain **12.** famous **13.** pleasant **14.** erasable **15.** put together **16.** original **17.** readable **18.** unknown **19.** defiance **20.** interesting

Exercise 10F—Sentence Comprehension

key sentence: There is a strong correlation in reading between concentration and comprehension.

1. Ability to concentrate in reading is closely related to understanding what is read. ______
2. Paying careful attention when reading increases comprehension. ______
3. Concentrating on punctuation makes oral reading more effective. ______
4. The ability to comprehend long difficult passages correlates directly to intelligence. ______
5. Reading rapidly improves both comprehension and concentration. ______
6. Reading comprehension is improved by good concentration. ______
7. Many corporations have encouraged executives to learn speed reading. ______
8. The challenge of reading every other line improves concentration. ______
9. Good readers choose a reading environment without distracting noises and sights. ______
10. Retention of factual detail is dependent upon reading the material twice. ______

TIME ______

ERRORS ______

DETERMINING INFERENCE

So far in this book you have tried to find the main idea of each reading. You have also read to understand and recall exact details. Now you will learn another skill: reading for inferences. It's a slightly higher level skill than the other two, or perhaps we should say "lower," since you must read *beneath* the surface.

An inference is an idea that the speakers or writers do not state openly, but intend you to understand anyway. Through their words, they *imply* (or suggest) something. From their words, you *infer* something (or draw a conclusion). Sometimes the inference is obvious. In fact, the act of speaking or writing seldom avoids inference completely. Very seldom are we presented with surface facts only; almost automatically, we look behind, under, or ahead of the simple facts. We practice inference constantly in our daily lives. The healthy human mind cannot exist without making inferences from facts and evidence.

For example, the factual statement, "There's the bus" usually implies something. Perhaps you must hurry to gather up your belongings and take out the exact change. Perhaps, if you have waited on the bus bench for over an hour, the words "At last!" are implied. Or the chance that you may make your dental appointment after all may be implied.

Actually, the first reading skill—finding the main idea—may have already involved you in some inferring. If the writers have not clearly stated their main idea in so many words, so that you have had to find a single overall topic for a cluster of details, you have practiced inference.

Seeing implications or inferences might be called "reading between the lines." But be careful not to read too much into the words. If Sandra says to Steve, "There's the bus," and he answers, "Do you think I'm blind?" or "Why don't you want to talk with me?" he may be guilty of inferring too much from the evidence of her simple statement. (Of course, if he has met Sandra before, his inference may be based on a lot of good solid evidence!)

Inferences can be extremely simple, drawn from simple facts. For instance, common sense tells us that "Dogs barking all night" implies "Many sleepless neighbors," which leads to "Many irate neighbors," which can logically lead to phone calls, letters to the editor, and perhaps police action.

At other times inference can require close careful reading and examination of all the evidence. Examples of subtle inference might be found in a political speech, a housing contract, the text of a new law, or the entire style, setting, and character development of a novel.

Whether a simple or complex task, the ability to draw inferences is based first on a correct literal comprehension of the words, and second on the careful interpretation of the literal meaning. The trained reader does

Answer Key: Ex. 10E
1, 7, 8 (perhaps 6)

Answer Key: Ex. 10F
1, 2, 6 (perhaps 9)

not immediately leap to "Well, *my* opinion has always been that. . . .," or "My imagination is really taking off from here," without *first* determining: "This is what the author *intended me to infer*."

Follow these steps cautiously in the following descriptive narrative.

In the living room, the grandmother sat in her usual chair. She looked down at her lap while one hand absently stroked the other. The mother pressed the drip-dry men's shirts, one after the other and hung them on hangers with more than the usual thump of her iron and clanking of the hangers. Every few minutes she glanced at the wall clock, with a worried twitch of her eyebrows. Davey, the 10-year-old, ran into the room and turned on the television. But the mother pushed past him, snapped it off, and gritted between her teeth, "You can't have that boob tube on tonight!" He opened his mouth in surprise, then turned, and ran out slamming the door. Once again, the iron thumped, the shirt hangers clanked. To the two women, the hands of the clock seemed to be paralyzed.

1. What is the main idea or topic of this paragraph?

___

2. What are some of the stated details, and how are they organized?

___

___

3. What are some of the simple unstated facts?
Example: The wearer of the shirts—the father?—is not home.

___

4. What deeper inferences can you make about this situation?

___

Answers

1. The *main idea* seems to be the setting of a mood in a scene. Here, the mood is one of nervous waiting by two women.

2. *Stated details:* Three people are mentioned: a mother who is ironing silently, a grandmother who is sitting silently, and a ten-year-old who is not allowed to watch his usual TV program. The mother watches the clock anxiously. And so on. (The details are arranged in a chronological time sequence.)

3. *Unstated details:* The two women share the same feeling of anxiety. The mother seems irritated by the 10-year-old's behavior. He must usually watch TV, since he seems surprised at being scolded.

4. *Deeper inferences:* Someone—the father?—is late coming home. Something is about to happen, which the women know about and expect but the 10-year-old doesn't. It is not a pleasant something—the details all express tension in the air.

PRACTICE PARAGRAPHS—INFERENCE AND LOGIC

Choose the answer that best completes each paragraph. Consider clues such as transition words and logic patterns (example, contrast, comparison, cause-effect, etc.) in making your choice.

A. When a person uses her peripheral vision, she uses her ability to see to the left and right and above and below the point where her eyes fix. A driver uses her peripheral vision when she drives. She sees not only directly ahead of her car, but she is aware of cars behind her and on both sides. She sees "out of the corners of her eyes." Similarly, a reader who uses her peripheral vision can read faster by seeing

(a) cars on each side.
(b) more than one word at a glance.
(c) one whole word at a time.
(d) spots in front of her eyes.

B. When a geologist suggested that the Washington "scablands" had been made by a gigantic flood, many other scientists disagreed. Now, however, a satellite photo seems to confirm his idea. Today, the geologist's suggestion

(a) is widely accepted.
(b) is as hotly disputed as ever.
(c) has been forgotten.
(d) is known to be false.

C. It takes energy to produce energy for our use. For example, building the Alaskan pipeline and transporting the oil to users takes considerable energy. Extracting oil from difficult locations, or coal from low-grade ore, or electricity from a poorly-placed dam, can cost almost as much energy as is realized from the final product. This is why experts searching for new energy sources must

(a) balance the energy used for production against the net energy gained.
(b) concentrate on coal, oil, and electricity.
(c) concentrate on sources other than coal, oil, and electricity.
(d) concentrate on persuading people to use less energy.

D. One reads more efficiently by getting a "mental set"—preparing to read the material or zeroing in on the subject. One effective method is to *Survey* the article: read the title, author's name, subtitles, and first and last paragraphs. Having done this, the reader will then

(a) have no need actually to read the material.
(b) have set his mind to reading everything in the article except the first and last paragraphs.
(c) be able to take a rest.

(d) be able to understand more when he reads the material because he has a general idea of the content.

E. Most scientists believe that the continents of North America and Europe were joined around 200 million years ago. Since that time, these continents have been drifting apart at a rate of two inches per year. As they drifted apart the Atlantic Ocean formed between them. Based on this theory,

(a) the Atlantic Ocean is getting smaller.
(b) the Pacific Ocean is getting larger.
(c) the Atlantic Ocean is getting larger and the Pacific smaller.
(d) The Atlantic Ocean is getting deeper and colder.

Check your answers with the key on the next page.

WORDS IN CONTEXT

Without using your dictionary, try to determine the meaning of each word in **boldface** print. Choose the meaning below that best fits the context—the way it is used in the sentence.

Short Reading 10G

1. Over the years, out of an **innate** sense of respect, I imagine, I have refused to smother women with outdated courtesies.
   (a) learned **(b)** inborn **(c)** artistic **(d)** reluctant

Short Reading 10H

2. He may be responded to in a **solicitous** tone in which the rejection is hidden behind "supportive" words.
   (a) expressing concern **(b)** hypocritical **(c)** sarcastic **(d)** harshly critical
3. Or, he'll be put down with **derogatory** comments about his intelligence or adequacy.
   (a) truthful **(b)** insulting **(c)** angry **(d)** complimentary
4. He is now in the process of building a permanent, **latent** reservoir of self-hate and abuse that threatens to pour through.
   (a) late **(b)** last **(c)** potential **(d)** deep

Long Reading 10I

5. She had planned a funny little story about the deeply humorous **pomposity** of executives.
   (a) sophistication **(b)** jokes **(c)** mannerisms **(d)** self-importance

Check your answers with the key on the bottom of page 260.

Answer Key: Practice Paragraphs—Inference

A. *(b).* [This is the only possible answer in this paragraph. The person who reads "more than one word at a glance" can read two or three times as fast as the person who reads (c) "one whole word at a time." Note the transition word *similarly,* which points out the similarity between the driver who sees more than one car and the reader who sees more than one word. Answers (a) and (d) are irrelevant.]

B. *(a).* [This is the only answer that provides the contrast set up by *however* in the second sentence.]

C. *(a).* [This answer provides the result of preceding statements about energy costing so much to produce.]

D. *(d).* [This is the only answer that expresses the concept of reading "more efficiently." Note the transitions "having done this" and "then" set up a cause-effect relationship.]

E. *(c).* [If the Atlantic is between two continents continually drifting apart, then the Atlantic is obviously getting larger—and the Pacific on the other side of the earth would therefore be getting smaller.]

THEME FOR READING SELECTIONS: BEYOND SEX ROLES

These selections deal with a hot social issue: women's liberation (and the related men's liberation). All three readings make a point about how difficult it is for people to play roles expected of them because of their sex. The first, by Jack Smith, popular *Los Angeles Times* columnist, expresses the confusion over changes in etiquette because of women's liberation. Another, from Herb Goldberg's *The Hazards of Being Male,* delves into the pressures on men to succeed. The last, from *Ms.* magazine, has become a classic in the feminist movement. It describes the awakening of women to an awareness of the roles they have been forced into.

Imaginary Situation

You are going to a party tonight where you will be in a crowd of liberal sophisticated people. One of the guests will be feminist, Gloria Steinem. You know the feminist movement will be a major topic of discussion and you want to sound well-informed and fairminded.

Exercise 10G — Short Reading

Try to read the following selection in one minute. Remember to look for the topic, the main idea, and the supporting details. Also try to read deeper for inference. (What do the details imply?)

Men's Liberation from Etiquette

Jack Smith

WPM

One of the blessings for men in women's liberation, ac- 9
cording to the feminist magazine *Ms.*, is that men are no longer 21
obliged to pay women the stylized courtesies of the etiquette 31
book. 32

"Goodby Emily, Goodby Amy," says Jane Trahey in an 41
article on the new manners. Ms. Trahey declares that a per- 51
fectly able woman no longer has to act helpless in public. She 63
no longer need allow a man to steer her about by the elbow, 76
pull out chairs, open doors and otherwise act as if he were 88
dealing with a dummy. 92

Ms. Trahey points out that women do not need help 102
getting in and out of cars. "Women get in and out of cars twen- 116
ty times a day with babies and dogs. Surely they can get out by 129
themselves at night just as easily." 135

She also says there is no reason why a man should walk 147
on the outside of a woman on the sidewalk. "Historically, the 158
man walked on the inside so he caught the garbage thrown out 170

of a window. Today a man is supposed to walk on the out- 182
side. A man should walk where he wants to. So should a wom- 195
an. If, out of love and respect, he actually wants to take the 207
blows, he should walk on the inside—because that's where 217
muggers are all hiding these days." 223

As far as manners are concerned, I suppose I've always 233
been a feminist. Over the years, out of an innate sense of re- 245
spect, I imagine, I have refused to smother women with out- 256
dated courtesies. 257

It is usually easier to follow rules of social conduct than 268
to depend on one's own taste. But rules may be safely broken, 280
of course, by those of us with the gift of natural grace. For 293
example, when a man and woman are led to their table in a 306
restaurant and the waiter pulls out a chair, the woman is 317
expected to sit in the chair. That is according to Ms. Amy 329
Vanderbilt. I have always done it the other way, according to 340
my wife. 342

It came up only the other night. I followed the hostess 353
to the table and when she pulled the chair out I sat on it, quite 368
naturally, since it happened to be the chair I wanted to sit in. I 382
had the best view of the boats. 389

"Well," my wife said, when the hostess had gone, "you 399
did it again." 402

"Did what?" I asked, utterly baffled. 408

"Took the chair." 411

Actually, since I'd walked through the restaurant ahead 419
of my wife, it would have been awkward, I should think, not to 432
have taken the chair. I had got there first, after all. 443

Also, it has always been my custom to get in a car first, 456
and let the woman get in by herself. This is a courtesy I insist 470
on as the stronger sex, out of love and respect. In times like 483
these, there are muggers lurking about. It would be foolhardy 493
indeed to put a woman in a car and then shut the door on her, 508
leaving her at the mercy of some lout who might well be 520
crouching in the back seat. 525

Mark the number of words read (or the number to the right of the last line read). Then immediately answer the questions below without referring to the selection.

Answer Key: Words in Context
1. (b) **2.** (a) **3.** (b) **4.** (c) **5.** (d)

1. In most matters of etiquette, the author
   (a) allows his wife to decide.
   (b) follows the rules in etiquette books.
   (c) puts his wife's interests first.
   (d) relies on his own judgment.

2. The author is mildly poking fun at the whole question of etiquette and women's liberation. **T F**

3. Ms. Trahey points out that women with babies and dogs do need to be helped in and out of cars. **T F**

4. The author says he always gets in a car first to protect his wife. **T F**

Check your answers with the key on the bottom of the next page, and record your scores below and on the progress chart in the Appendix.

WORDS PER MINUTE _______

% COMPREHENSION _______

Exercise 10H—Short Reading

Try to read the following selection in one minute. Read carefully for inference.

from *The Hazards of Being Male*

Herb Goldberg, Ph.D.

WPM

A young boy learns to value himself in terms of achiev- 11
ments, successes, and victories. The message is brought home 19
to him constantly, both in direct and indirect ways: When he 30
runs faster, speaks better, wins a game, reads earlier, gets a 41
higher grade, shows more strength, or does anything that 50
demonstrates his superiority over other young boys, his father 59
proudly calls him "my son" and together with his mother they 70
brag about his accomplishments to others. 76
Periodically, however, he'll be reminded that even 83
though he does certain things well he must never rest on his 95
laurels, because he lives in a world that only has room for the 108
best, a world with little space or sympathy for a loser. A loser is 122
defined by the saying, "A miss is as good as a mile." In effect, 136
anyone who isn't a winner is a loser. 144
Indirectly, he will get the same kinds of messages when 154
he hears his mother talking about how good someone else's 164
boy is at doing something. He'll come to understand the un- 175
derlying message there which is, "Wouldn't it be great if you 185
were that good too!" 189

Throughout those early years when he does win or suc- 199
ceed he will be praised and otherwise rewarded. He will be 209
treated in a special way that makes him feel proud of himself 221
and good inside. 224

However, when he loses, fails, acts in a clumsy or inef- 235
fectual, weak, or incompetent way, he'll feel particularly his 243
father's, and often also his mother's, disapproval and rejection. 252
Perhaps this won't be expressed directly. He may be respond- 262
ed to in a solicitous tone in which the rejection is hidden be- 274
hind "supportive" words such as, "It's O.K. You'll do better 284
next time," "Nobody can win them all," "It's not whether you 295
win or lose, it's how you play the game." The rejection however 307
is clearly implied in subtle tones by the fact that when he does 320
win or succeed he is responded to with enthusiasm. When he 331
doesn't, even though the words are "kind," the emotional tone 341
behind them is muted, lukewarm, or negative. 348

If his parents are not psychologically sophisticated, the 356
feedback he will receive when he doesn't perform well will be 367
more direct. Perhaps he will be rejected in favor of a better 379
performing sibling. Or, he'll be put down with derogatory 388
comments about his intelligence or adequacy. 394

As a growing boy he will increasingly internalize paren- 403
tal and other attitudes that he hears until he becomes his own 414
parent. That is, he will develop his own inner voice that will say 427
nice things to him to make him feel good when he performs 439
well or wins, and will insult, gnaw at him, and put him down 452
when he doesn't do as well or better than his peers. 463

He is now in the process of building a permanent, latent 474
reservoir of self-hate and abuse that threatens to pour through 485
whenever he fails to achieve. This reservoir will dampen even 495
his greatest triumphs, as even in "victory" he will always be 506
focusing on those who are "better" than himself. He now has a 518
built-in motor that will forever be driving him toward success 529
goals. 530

Mark the number of words read (or the number to the right of the last line read). Then immediately answer the questions below without referring to the selection.

1. The message a young boy gets from his parents about success and failure is that
   - **(a)** he gets approval as long as he does his best.
   - **(b)** he gets approval for success and disapproval, however subtle, for failure.

Answer Key: Ex. 10G
1. (d) **2.** T **3.** F **4.** T

(c) he gets approval from his father only for winning but gets approval from his mother whether or not he wins.
(d) he must be critical of himself in order to achieve.

2. The implication is that men are uncomfortable in the role their parents impose on them as achievers and winners. **T** **F**

3. A boy will not feel rejected if his parents reassure him kindly that "Nobody can win them all" when he loses. **T** **F**

4. In defense, a boy will develop an inner voice to reassure himself when he performs badly. **T** **F**

Check your answers with the key on the bottom of the next page, and record your scores below and on the progress chart in the Appendix.

WORDS PER MINUTE ______

% COMPREHENSION ______

Exercise 10I — Long Reading

LENGTH: 1008

Read the following selection as rapidly as you can but read deeper for inference. Wait for a signal from your instructor before you begin reading.

Click!

Jane O'Reilly

Women are beginning to experience that click! of recognition—that moment of truth that brings a gleam to our eyes and means the revolution has begun. Those clicks are coming faster, and women are getting angry. Not redneck-angry from screaming because we are so frustrated and unfulfilled, but clicking-things-into-place-angry. We have suddenly and shockingly seen the basic lack of order in what has been believed to be the natural order of things.

One little click turns on a thousand others.

In Houston, Texas, a friend of mine stood and watched her husband step over a pile of toys on the stairs, put there to be carried up. "Why can't you get this stuff put away?" he mumbled. Click! "You have two hands," she said, turning away.

Last summer I got a letter from a man who wrote: "I do not agree with your last article, and I am cancelling my wife's subscription." The next day I got a letter from his wife saying, "*I* am not cancelling *my* subscription." Click!

On Fire Island my weekend hostess and I had just finished cooking breakfast, lunch, and washing dishes for both. A male guest came wandering into the kitchen just as the last dish was being put away and said, "How about something to eat?" He sat down, expectantly, and started to read the paper. Click! "You work all week," said the hostess, "and *I* work all week, and if you want something to eat, you can get it, and wash up after it yourself."

In New York last fall, my neighbors—named Jones—had a couple named Smith over for dinner. Mr. Smith kept telling his wife to get up and help Mrs. Jones. Click! Click! Two women radicalized at once.

A woman I know in St. Louis, who had begun to enjoy a little success writing a grain company's newsletter, came home to tell her husband about lunch in the executive dining room. She had planned a funny little story about the deeply humorous pomposity of executives, when she noticed her husband rocking with laughter. "Ho ho, my little wife in an executive dining room." Click!

Last August, I was on a boat leaving an island in Maine. Two families were with me, and the mothers were discussing the troubles of cleaning up after a rental summer. "Bob cleaned up the bathroom for me, didn't you, honey?" she confided, gratefully patting her husband's knee. "Well, what the hell, it's vacation," he said fondly. The two women looked at each other, and the queerest change came over their faces. "I got up at six this morning to make sandwiches for the trip home from this 'vacation,' " this first one said. "So I wonder why I've thanked him at least six times for cleaning the bathroom?" Click! Click!

In suburban Chicago, the party consisted of three couples. The women were a writer, a doctor, and a teacher. The men were all lawyers. As the last couple arrived, the host said, heartily, "With a roomful of lawyers, we ought to have a good evening." Silence. Click! "What are we?" asked the teacher. "Invisible?"

In an office, a political columnist, male, was waiting to see the editor-in-chief. Leaning against a doorway, the columnist turned to the first woman he saw and said, "Listen, call Barry Brown and tell him I'll be late." Click! It wasn't because she happened to be an editor herself that she refused to make the call.

In the end, we are all housewives, the natural people to turn to when there is something unpleasant, inconvenient or inconclusive to be done. It will not do for women who have jobs to pretend that society's ills will be cured if all women are

Answer Key: Ex. 10H
1. (b) **2.** T **3.** F **4.** F

gainfully employed. In Russia 70 percent of the doctors and 20 percent of the construction workers are women, but women still do *all* the housework. Some revolution. As the Russian women's saying goes, it simply freed us to do twice the work.

They tell us we are being petty. The future improvement of civilization could not depend on who washes the dishes. Could it? Yes. The liberated society—with men, women and children living as whole human beings, not halves divided by sex roles—depends on the steadfast search for new solutions to just such apparently unimportant problems, on new answers to tired old questions. Such questions as:

Denise works as a waitress from 6 A.M. to 3 P.M. Her husband is a cabdriver, who moonlights on weekends as a doorman. They have four children. When her husband comes home at night, he asks: *"What's for dinner?"*

Jonathan and Joanne are both doctors. They have identical office hours. They come home in the evening to a dinner cooked by the housekeeper. When they go to bed, he drops his clothes on the floor and she picks them up. In the morning he asks: *"Where is my pink and orange striped shirt?"*

In moments of suburban strife, Fred often asks his wife, Alice, "Why haven't you mended my shirt and lubricated the car? *What else have you got to do but sit around the house all day?"*

According to insurance companies, it would cost Fred $8,000 to $9,000 a year to replace Alice's services if she died. Alice, being an average ideal suburban housewife, works 99.6 hours a week—always feeling there is too much to be done and always guilty because it is never quite finished. Besides, her work doesn't seem important. After all, Fred is paid for doing whatever it is he does. Abstract statistics make no impact on Alice. "My situation is different," she says. Of course it is. All situations are different. But sooner or later she will experience—in a blinding click—a moment of truth. She will remember that she once had other interests, vague hopes, great plans. She will decide that the work in the house is less important than reordering that work so she can consider her own life.

The problem is, what does she do then?

TOTAL READING TIME ______

Immediately answer the questions below without referring to the selection.

1. Choose the statement that best expresses the main idea.
   - **(a)** Men must arm themselves against a female revolution.
   - **(b)** Women are beginning to realize the unfairness of their being totally responsible for housework.
   - **(c)** Women are beginning to prefer careers to housework.
   - **(d)** A woman's place is in the kitchen.
2. According to the author, one can expect women in the future to demand a live-in maid. **T F**
3. Click! means the shock of recognition when a woman sees a chore to be done. **T F**
4. The men in the examples take a woman's role as homemaker for granted. **T F**
5. The problem of sex discrimination in Russia has been solved. **T F**
6. Insurance companies estimate that it would cost approximately $9,000 annually to replace a housewife's services. **T F**
7. The author seems to be saying that despite the fact that women are often frustrated and unfulfilled, they still believe the natural order of things to be for their best. **T F**
8. As in Russia, working women in America are still almost totally responsible for the care of home and family. **T F**

Check your answers with the key on the bottom of page 268. Then turn to the Rate Chart in the Appendix to get your words per minute for this selection. Finally, record your scores below and on the progress chart in the Appendix.

WORDS PER MINUTE ______

% COMPREHENSION ______

Bonus Questions (Scanning)

1. How many times did Bob's wife thank him for cleaning the bathroom? ______
2. What percent of construction workers in Russia are women? ______

Percentage Chart for Comprehension Check

Errors	0	1	2	3	4	5	6	7	8
% Right	100	88	75	63	50	38	25	13	0

Answer Key: Ex. 10I
1. (b) **2.** F **3.** F **4.** T **5.** F **6.** T **7.** F **8.** T **1.** 6 **2.** 20

Lesson 11

Exercise 11A—Phrase Perception (Variation)

Note: Each column of twenty items has only one key phrase. Mark each repeated phrase. Work through both columns vertically before checking your time.

key phrase

bear in mind

bear in window
bears in mind

bears in the wind
bear in winter

bare in mind
beer in mind

bear in mind
bearing minds

mindless bear
barring minds

bear in mind
bear in mid-winter

bear in mind
bear on your mind

hear in mind
hear in the wind

read your mind
bear in mind

read and mind
bearing in mind

key phrase

the right station

the eighth station
the bright station

the richest station
the right stanchion

the right state
the right station

the mighty station
a right station

the rigged station
the right states

the station's right
the right stallion

tight little station
the right station

the straight station
the fight station

the right station
the fighting station

the night station
the right station

TIME ______

ERRORS ______

Exercise 11B — Phrase Perception (Variation)

Note: Each column of twenty items has only one key phrase. Mark each repeated phrase. Work through both columns vertically before checking your time.

key phrase

cope with life

copout from life
cope with strife

cope with life
copper has life

coping with life
cape with knife

cop wins life
cope with light

cops with lifer
cope with life

come with life
run from life

cope within
coping with line

cope with line
coping wins life

cold without life
cope with life

cope with knife
poke with knife

key phrase

a slow drawl

a low trawler
a low shawl

a low drawling
as low a drawl

a lower drawl
a slight frawl

a slow down
a slow drawl

a slow crawl
as slowly crawl

a southern drawl
a slow draw

as slow a draw
a slow drowning

a slow howl
a low drawl

a slow drawl
a loud drawl

our slow drawl
a slow drawl

TIME ______

ERRORS ______

Exercise 11C—Word Comprehension (Variation)

Note: Look for the *antonym* (opposite word) of the key word among the words on the right.

key word					
1. obscure	cautious	vague	obstacle	clear	open
2. reprimand	reply	scold	joke	frown	compliment
3. deplore	differ	approve	depend	dig	disapprove
4. mute	talkative	moon	hard	loud	silent
5. wane	hag	increase	stubborn	waste	decline
6. destitute	poor	future	rich	hollow	humble
7. imply	suggest	regulate	hinder	refer	infer
8. deceased	alive	body	dead	coffin	decent
9. valiant	brave	pretentious	cowardly	villain	soldier
10. sham	wrap	master	pretend	real	shake
11. secrete	hasty	uncover	send	hide	treat
12. wary	cautious	tired	postponed	wasteful	careless
13. abhor	like	horde	detest	attitude	horrible
14. arid	acid	filled	wet	dusty	dry
15. trivial	previous	treatment	masterful	important	petty
16. apprentice	veteran	appreciate	learner	carpenter	scholar
17. amputate	hold out	sew on	cut off	risk	break
18. smite	strike	small	caress	fight	shoot
19. expire	expand	die	breathe in	spirit	live
20. forego	send	give in	win	give up	force

TIME _______

ERRORS _______

Answer Key: Ex. 11A
"bear in mind" repeated four times
"the right station" repeated four times

Answer Key: Ex. 11B
"cope with life" repeated three times
"a slow drawl" repeated three times

Exercise 11D—Word Comprehension (Variation)

Note: Look for the *antonym* (opposite word) of the key word among the words on the right.

key word					
1. rove	wander	drive	fall	stay	raise
2. deficient	lacking	sufficient	failing	define	subtraction
3. dormant	wake	active	sleeping	forgetful	weak
4. compile	erect	gather	divide	finish	scatter
5. eccentric	common	metric	radical	electric	odd
6. segregate	multiply	race	integrate	melt	separate
7. tolerable	acceptable	lasting	complete	unbearable	welcome
8. oblivious	obvious	conscious	carefree	unaware	memorable
9. diverse	alike	poetry	drive	different	rare
10. annihilate	elate	destroy	anniversary	construct	analyze
11. discretion	judgment	talk	abandon	gossip	belief
12. droll	dramatic	trick	amusing	rude	serious
13. demure	mature	extroverted	immoral	shy	decent
14. despondent	depressed	writer	disciple	happy	bland
15. immature	mature	unripe	imitate	empty	developing
16. diligent	different	difficult	lazy	toil	hard-working
17. accessible	convenient	sensible	available	excessive	closed
18. naive	dumb	native	sophisticated	young	innocent
19. crucial	crude	special	little	trivial	weak
20. furtive	active	false	candid	sneaky	quick

TIME _______

ERRORS _______

Exercise 11E—Phrase Comprehension (Variation)

Note: Mark every *verb* in the phrases below. (A verb expresses action or state of being.) Some phrases have none.

1. 32° temperature
2. good butchering weather
3. neighbors come early
4. catch razorback hog
5. shoot in head
6. right between eyes
7. stab in heart
8. 6-inch knife blade
9. bleed until drained
10. drop in huge vat
11. of scalding water
12. hair comes off
13. scrape off remaining hair
14. wash hog well
15. hog now white
16. tie up back legs
17. swing hog off ground
18. take the knife
19. rip downwards
20. through the breastbone
21. stop at neck
22. saw off head
23. remove liver and heart
24. remove intestines
25. wash out intestines
26. soak for 2 or 3 days
27. fry intestine walls
28. southern delicacy—chitlings
29. saw down backbone
30. lay 2 halves on table
31. cut hind quarter off
32. for the ham
33. take out ribs
34. cut between
35. front and back quarter
36. for bacon
37. front quarter
38. is for roasts
39. pork chops are
40. from backbone
41. take the trimmings
42. of lean meat
43. grind up together
44. 1/4 fat and 3/4 lean
45. add seasoning
46. makes sausage
47. give to neighbors
48. their fair share
49. everybody has
50. meat for winter

TIME ______

ERRORS ______

Exercise 11F—Phrase Comprehension (Variation)

Note: Mark every *verb* in the phrases below. Some phrases have none.

1. the long drive home
2. is a rainy night
3. the thunder thunders
4. the lightning lights
5. family in car
6. the children fight
7. hillbilly singer whines
8. on the radio
9. cigar smoke in air
10. air too warm
11. wife studies map
12. small explosion is heard
13. a blown-out tire
14. low curses inside
15. drives over to side
16. coveralls over dress
17. husband with umbrella
18. puts block under wheel
19. prevents rolling
20. flashlight on
21. flares around car
22. opens trunk
23. gets out tools
24. jack and tire irons
25. jacks up car
26. only a little
27. removes hub cap
28. loosens lug nuts
29. jacks it up higher
30. removes lug nuts
31. flat tire off
32. replaces with new tire
33. lug nuts on
34. lowers the jack
35. tightens lug nuts
36. hub cap back on
37. tools into trunk
38. flat tire into trunk
39. wife washes hands
40. husband lowers umbrella
41. back in the car
42. children asleep on seat
43. engine starts quickly
44. headlights on
45. windshield wipers on
46. cigar lights up
47. nasal voice sings
48. on the radio
49. the open road
50. the long drive home

TIME ______

ERRORS ______

Answer Key: Ex. 11C
1. clear **2.** compliment **3.** approve **4.** talkative **5.** increase **6.** rich **7.** infer **8.** alive **9.** cowardly **10.** real **11.** uncover **12.** careless **13.** like **14.** wet **15.** important **16.** veteran **17.** sew on **18.** caress **19.** live **20.** win

Answer Key: Ex. 11D
1. stay **2.** sufficient **3.** active **4.** scatter **5.** common **6.** integrate **7.** unbearable **8.** conscious **9.** alike **10.** construct **11.** abandon **12.** serious **13.** extroverted **14.** happy **15.** mature **16.** lazy **17.** closed **18.** sophisticated **19.** trivial **20.** candid

Answer Key: Ex. 11E
3. come **4.** catch 5. shoot 7. stab 9. bleed **10.** drop 12. comes 13. scrape **14.** wash **16.** tie **17.** swing **18.** take **19.** rip **21.** stop **22.** saw **23.** remove **24.** remove **25.** wash **26.** soak **27.** fry **29.** saw **30.** lay **31.** cut **33.** take **34.** cut **38.** is **39.** are **41.** take **43.** grind **45.** add **46.** makes **47.** give **49.** has

MORE PRACTICE PARAGRAPHS—INFERENCE

The following paragraphs are characterizations drawn from the writings of well-known authors. By paying careful attention to the details in each character sketch, you will be able to *infer* the dominant impression the author wants to create.

A. Miss Abbott had a pink nose and came from a small town in South Mississippi. She pronounced words like "night," "bright," and "sight" with the *i*'s prolonged and nasal, a sure sign of hill-country origins. The only book she read through and through, she told us, was the Bible, and you lived to believe her, and to rue the day she got hold of that book. . . . Miss Abbott's religion was Christianity by fear and by rote—so tenacious it got you by the extremities and never let go; . . . she wanted you to believe she herself was in radio contact with the Deity, and had hung the moon for Him on day number six. When she talked about the time she had been saved, a moist glint began creeping into her eyes, which invariably meant the sermon was on its way. She learned to play a little plastic flute, the kind you could get in Woolworth's for a quarter, and she would play us rousing hymns and Christian marches, heedless of the saliva trickling down that instrument onto the floor. After the music she would preach to us on sin and redemption, there being more of the former than the latter, or what the Old Testament said about niggers or Japs, or why we would all end up in hell if God caught us in a backfire. She would not drink Coca-colas, she said, because of their alcoholic content. Sometimes she would lapse into a sweet, unexpected silence, and gaze out the nearest window for endless minutes. Her features would be bathed in gentle peace. Then I knew Miss Abbott was praying to herself.

from *North Toward Home* by Willie Morris

1. The author's attitude toward Miss Abbott is one of
(a) respect. **(b)** ridicule. **(c)** affection. **(d)** hatred.

2. List the details that suggest Miss Abbott was a hypocrite.

____

____

____

____

B. (1) He was a rich man: banker, merchant, manufacturer, and what not. (2) A big, loud man, with a stare, and a metallic laugh. (3) A man made out of a coarse material, which seemed to have been stretched to make so much of him. (4) A man with a great puffed head and forehead, swelled veins in his temples, and such a strained skin to his face that it seemed to hold his eyes open, and lift his eyebrows up. (5) A man with a pervading appearance on him of being inflated like a balloon, and ready to start. (6)

A man who could never sufficiently vaunt himself a self-made man. (7) A man who was always proclaiming, through that brassy speaking-trumpet of a voice of his, his old ignorance and his old poverty. (8) A man who was the Bully of humility.

from *Hard Times* by Charles Dickens

1. Most of the sentences (or fragments) in this paragraph describe the man's physical appearance. Which three sentences make implications about his *internal* make-up? ______________

2. The words "Bully" and "humility" in the last sentence seem contradictory. Explain how they fit in this characterization.

____

____

____

C. Miss Baez sat very still in the front row. She was wearing a longsleeved navy-blue dress with an Irish lace collar and cuffs, and she kept her hands folded in her lap. She is extraordinary looking, far more so than her photographs suggest, since the camera seems to emphasize an Indian cast to her features and fails to record either the startling fineness and clarity of her bones and eyes or, her most striking characteristic, her absolute directness, her absence of guile. She has a great natural style, and she is what used to be called a lady. . . . Joan Baez was a personality before she was entirely a person, and like anyone to whom that happens, she is in a sense the hapless victim of what others have seen in her, written about her, wanted her to be and not to be. The roles assigned to her are various, but variations on a single theme. She is the Madonna of the disaffected. She is the pawn of the protest movement. She is the unhappy analysand. She is the singer who would not train her voice, the rebel who drives the Jaguar too fast, the Rima who hides with the birds and the deer. Above all, she is the girl who "feels" things, who has hung on to the freshness and pain of adolescence, the girl ever wounded, ever young.

from "Joan Baez" by Joan Didion

1. The author's description of Joan Baez is full of
(a) sarcasm. **(b)** respect and sympathy. **(c)** complete admiration. **(d)** criticism.

Answer Key: Ex. 11F
2. is **3.** thunders **4.** lights **6.** fight **7.** whines **11.** studies **12.** is heard **15.** drives **18.** puts **19.** prevents **22.** opens **23.** gets **25.** jacks **27.** removes **28.** loosens **29.** jacks **30.** removes **32.** replaces **34.** lowers **35.** tightens **39.** washes **40.** lowers **43.** starts **46.** lights **47.** sings

2. What is meant by the statement that Miss Baez is "the hapless victim of what others have seen in her"?

____

____

____

Check your answers with the key on the next page.

WORDS IN CONTEXT

Without using your dictionary, try to determine the meaning of each word in **boldface** print. Choose the meaning below that best fits the context—the way it is used in the sentence.

Short Reading 11G

1. She was a dear little creature, so **guileless** and good-natured.
   (a) smiling **(b)** simple **(c)** foolish **(d)** passionate
2. Even Miss Pinkerton, that **austere** and god-like woman, ceased scolding her after the first time.
   (a) stern **(b)** violent **(c)** religious **(d)** pompous

Short Reading 11H

3. She looked like a child, but she had the dismal **precocity** of poverty.
   (a) misery **(b)** symptoms **(c)** horrors **(d)** maturity
4. Her father, **reprobate** as he was, was a man of talent.
   (a) artist **(b)** loving father **(c)** morally unprincipled person **(d)** gambler

Long Reading 11I

5. You must go away from here and from the **impertinences** of these men.
   (a) impudences **(b)** hostile behavior **(c)** conversation **(d)** importance

Check your answers with the key on the bottom of page 282.

THEME FOR READING SELECTIONS: CONFLICTS IN LITERATURE

The following selections are from a nineteenth century British novel, *Vanity Fair,* by William Makepeace Thackeray. The Short Readings each in-

Answer Key: Practice Paragraphs—Inference

A. 1. *(b).* [All the descriptive details are negative, but not to the point of (d) hatred.]
2. Christianity by fear and rote; belief that she had a special connection to God; emphasis on sin; refusal to drink Coca-colas; racist attitudes.

B. 1. *6, 7, 8* [These sentences are the only ones giving personality traits.] **2.** His loud, aggressive boasting of his modest beginnings explain the contradiction in terms.

C. 1. *(b).* [The only other possible answer is (c), but the description is too realistic to be one of complete admiration.] **2.** Her public has assigned her the roles of "Madonna of the disaffected," "pawn of the protest movement," and "the unhappy analysand." Didion suggests that it is difficult to live up to all these images.

troduce the two major characters—Amelia and Rebecca, a study in contrasts—during their school days. The Long Reading reunites them almost two decades later for a final conflict.

Imaginary Situation

You are reading a story about a legendary family feud that you have always been curious about. Even though the setting is a century ago, you may find that you can identify with the two characters.

Exercise 11G—Short Reading

Try to read the following selection in one minute. Read carefully for inference.

Amelia
from *Vanity Fair*

William Makepeace Thackeray

WPM

Now Miss Amelia Sedley was a young lady who de- 10
served all that Miss Pinkerton [the schoolmistress at Chiswick 18
Hall] said in her praise. Amelia could sing like a lark, dance 30
gracefully, embroider beautifully, and spell as well as the dic- 40
tionary itself. She also had such a kindly, smiling, tender, gen- 50
tle, generous heart of her own. She won the love of everybody 61
who came near her, from Miss Pinkerton herself down to the 72
poor girl in the scullery, and the one-eyed tartwoman's daugh- 83
ter. She had twelve intimate and bosom friends out of the 93
twenty-four young ladies. 97

Even envious Miss Briggs never spoke ill of her. High 107
and mighty Miss Saltire (Lord Dexter's grand-daughter) al- 116
lowed that Amelia's figure was genteel. And as for Miss Swartz, 126
the rich girl from St. Kitt's, on the day Amelia went away, she 139
was in a passion of tears. They were obliged to send for Dr. 152
Floss and make her tipsy. 157

Amelia was a dear little creature, so guileless and good- 168
natured. I am afraid, however, that her nose was rather short 178
than otherwise, and her cheeks a great deal too round and red 190
for a heroine. But her face blushed with rosy health, and her 202
lips with the freshest of smiles. She had a pair of eyes, which 215
sparkled with the brightest and honestest good humor, except 224
indeed when they filled with tears, and that was a great deal 236
too often. For that silly thing would cry over a dead canary 248
bird; or over a mouse, that the cat had seized upon; or over the 262
end of a novel, were it ever so stupid. 271

And as for saying an unkind word to her, were any per- 283
sons hardhearted enough to do so—why, so much the worse for 294
them. Even Miss Pinkerton, that austere and god-like woman, 304
ceased scolding her after the first time. Although she no more 315
comprehended sensibility than she did algebra, she gave all 324
masters and teachers particular orders to treat Miss Sedley 333
with the utmost gentleness, as harsh treatment was injurious 342
to her. 344

Mark the number of words read (or the number to the right of the last line read). Then immediately answer the questions below without referring to the selection.

1. Amelia's most admired qualities were
   (a) her singing and dancing.
   (b) her sparkling eyes and fresh smile.
   (c) her embroidery and spelling.
   (d) her sensitivity and kindness.
2. The author is making fun of Amelia in the line, "for that silly thing would cry over a dead canary bird." T F
3. The author is making fun of Miss Swartz, who went into a passion of tears at Amelia's departure. T F
4. Miss Pinkerton was kind to Amelia because she was a sensitive, though strict, schoolmistress. T F

Check your answers with the key on the bottom of page 284, and record your scores below and on the progress chart in the Appendix.

WORDS PER MINUTE ______

% COMPREHENSION ______

Answer Key: Words in Context
1. (b) **2.** (a) **3.** (d) **4.** (c) **5.** (a)

Exercise 11H — Short Reading

Try to read the following selection in one minute. Read carefully for inference.

Rebecca
from *Vanity Fair*

William Makepeace Thackeray

WPM

Rebecca was seventeen when she came to Chiswick, and 9
was bound over as an articled pupil. Her duties were to talk 21
French. Her privileges were to live cost free, with a few guineas 33
a year and gather scraps of knowledge from the professors who 44
attended the school. She was small and slight in person, pale, 55
sandy-haired, and with eyes habitually cast down. When they 65
looked up they were very large, odd, and attractive. 74

By the side of many tall and bouncing young ladies in 85
the establishment, Rebecca Sharp looked like a child, but she 95
had the dismal precocity of poverty. Many a dun had she 106
talked to and turned away from her father's door. Many a 117
tradesman had she coaxed and wheedled into good-humor, 126
and into the granting of one meal more. She sat commonly 137
with her father, who was very proud of her wit, and heard the 150
talk of many of his wild companions — often but ill-suited for a 163
girl to hear. But she had never been a girl, she said; she had 177
been a woman since she was eight years old. 186

The rigid formality of Chiswick Hall suffocated her. 194
The prayers and the meals, the lessons and the walks, which 205
were arranged with a monotonous regularity, oppressed her 213
almost beyond endurance. She looked back to the freedom and 223
the beggary of her old home with so much regret that every- 235
body, herself included, fancied she was consumed with grief for 245
her father. She had a little room in the garret, where the maids 258
heard her walking and sobbing at night. But it was with rage, 270
not grief. She had not been much of a dissembler, until now 282
her loneliness taught her to pretend. She had never mingled in 293
the society of women. Her father, reprobate as he was, was a 305
man of talent. His conversation was a thousand times more 315
agreeable to her than the talk of such of her own sex as she 329
now encountered. 331

The pompous vanity of the old schoolmistress, the fool- 340
ish good humor of her sister, the silly chat and scandal of the 352
elder girls, and the frigid correctness of the governesses equal- 362
ly annoyed her. She had no soft maternal heart, this unlucky 372
girl; otherwise the prattle and talk of the younger children, 382
with whose care she was chiefly entrusted, might have soothed 392
and interested her. She lived among them for two years, and 403

not one was sorry that she went away. The gentle, tenderheart- 414
ed Amelia Sedley was the only person to whom she could at- 424
tach herself in the least. And who could help attaching herself 435
to Amelia? 437
The happiness, the superior advantages of the young 445
women round about her, gave Rebecca inexpressible pangs of 454
envy. She determined at any rate to get free from the prison in 467
which she found herself, and now began to act for herself. For 479
the first time she began to make connected plans for the fu- 491
ture.

Mark the number of words read (or the number to the right of the last line read). Then immediately answer the questions below without referring to the selection.

1. Rebecca might be most admired for
(a) her wit and her large eyes.
(b) her sympathy and tolerance.
(c) her robust looks.
(d) her popularity with the other girls.

2. Her being at Chiswick Hall caused her to change. **T** **F**

3. She didn't make friends with any of the other girls—not even Amelia. **T** **F**

4. The author presents Rebecca as a totally unsympathetic character. **T** **F**

Check your answers with the key on the bottom of page 286, and record your scores below and on the progress chart in the Appendix.

WORDS PER MINUTE ______

% COMPREHENSION ______

Answer Key: Ex. 11G
1. (d) **2.** F **3.** T **4.** F

Exercise 11I—Long Reading

LENGTH: 916

Read the following selection as rapidly as you can but read deeper for inference. Wait for a signal from your instructor before you begin reading.

The Sacrifice from *Vanity Fair*

William Makepeace Thackeray

[Many years pass; both Amelia and Rebecca marry and have a son each. Amelia becomes a widow and is courted for years to no avail by a Major Dobbin, a gentle, dependable man. She refuses to marry him in memory of her late husband, the more exciting George Osborne.

Rebecca, in the meantime, has been deserted by her husband because she had been taking presents from another man and probably had been unfaithful. Her son is also taken away from her, an act which does not upset her unduly. She has been living a life of not-too-genteel poverty when she is rescued by Amelia and taken into her home—against Dobbin's wishes. He knows her reputation and character.

Rebecca takes advantage of her improved situation and lives a little more discreetly. She soon becomes aware that Amelia is pining for Major Dobbin, who has gone away. He finally gave up on his courtship of Amelia because of her stubborn clinging to her husband's memory. The two women go to Bath where Amelia is being courted by two unsuitable men—old friends of Rebecca's.]

"She mustn't stay here," Rebecca reasoned with herself. "She must go away, the silly little fool. She is still whimpering after that gaby of a husband—dead (and served right!) these fifteen years. She shan't marry either of these men. No, she shall marry the bamboo-cane [Major Dobbin]. I'll settle it this very night."

So Rebecca took a cup of tea to Amelia in her private apartment. She found that lady in the company of her miniatures, and in a most melancholy and nervous condition. She laid down the cup of tea.

"Thank you," said Amelia.

"Listen to me, Amelia," said Rebecca, marching up and down the room before the other, and surveying her with a sort of contemptuous kindness. "I want to talk to you. You must go away from here and from the impertinences of these men. I won't have you harassed by them; and they will insult you if you stay. I tell you they are rascals. Never mind how I know them. I know everybody. You are no more fit to live in the world than a baby in arms. You must marry, or you and your precious boy will go to ruin. You must have a husband, you fool. One of the best gentlemen I ever saw has offered you a hundred times, and you have rejected him, you silly, heartless, ungrateful little creature!"

"I tried—I tried my best, indeed I did, Rebecca," said Amelia, "but I couldn't forget—." She finished the sentence by looking up at her husband's portrait.

"Couldn't forget *him!*" cried out Rebecca, "that selfish humbug, that low-bred cockney-dandy, that padded booby, who had neither wit, nor manners, nor heart. He was no more to be compared to your friend with the bamboo-cane than you are to Queen Elizabeth! Why, the man was weary of you, and would have jilted you, but that Dobbin forced him to keep his word. He owned it to me. He never cared for you. He used to sneer about you to me, time after time. He made love to me the week after he married you."

"It's false! It's false, Rebecca!" cried out Amelia, starting up.

"Look there, you fool," Rebecca said, still with provoking good humor. She took a little paper out of her belt, opened it, and flung it into Amelia's lap. "You know his handwriting. He wrote that to me—wanted me to run away with him. He gave it to me under your nose, the day before he was shot—and served him right!" Rebecca repeated.

Amelia did not hear her; she was looking at the letter. It was that which George had put into the bouquet and given to Rebecca on the night of the Duke of Richmond's ball. It was as she said: the foolish young man had asked her to go away with him.

Amelia's head sank down, and she commenced to weep. Her head fell to her bosom, and her hands went up to her eyes. And there for awhile, she gave way to her emotions, as Rebecca stood on and regarded her. Who shall analyze those tears, and say whether they were sweet or bitter? Was she most grieved because the idol of her life was tumbled down at her feet? Or was she indignant that her love had been so despised? Or was she glad because the barrier was removed which modesty had placed between her and a new, a real affection? "There is nothing to forbid me now," she thought. "I may love him with all my heart now. Oh, I will, I will, if he will but let me, and forgive me." I believe it was this feeling which rushed over all the others which agitated that gentle little bosom.

Indeed, she did not cry so much as Rebecca expected—the other soothed and kissed her—a rare mark of sympathy with Rebecca. She treated Amelia like a child, and patted her head. "And now let us get pen and ink, and write to him to

Answer Key: Ex. 11H
1. (a) **2.** T **3.** F **4.** F

come this minute," she said.

"I—I wrote to him this morning," Amelia said, blushing exceedingly.

Rebecca screamed with laughter, and the whole house echoed with her shrill laughter.

Immediately answer the questions below without referring to the selection.

1. Choose the statement that best expresses the main idea.
   (a) Amelia was a good woman and Rebecca a bad one.
   (b) Both Rebecca and Amelia had human frailties and virtues.
   (c) Amelia was foolish for sacrificing her life for a worthless man.
   (d) Rebecca's sacrifice, telling Amelia the truth about her husband, was for nothing.

2. For all her faults, Rebecca was a loving mother. **T F**

3. Rebecca seemed to have selfish motives for telling Amelia about her husband. **T F**

4. Amelia wouldn't marry Major Dobbin because of loyalty to her late husband. **T F**

5. According to Rebecca, Amelia's husband respected his wife even though he was unfaithful to her. **T F**

6. Amelia had no way of knowing whether Rebecca was telling her the truth about her husband. **T F**

7. The author believed Amelia's tears were because
   (a) her husband had been unfaithful.
   (b) because he hadn't loved her.
   (c) she was finally free to love Major Dobbin.
   (d) her idol had fallen.

8. Rebecca's shrill laughter at the end indicates that she recognizes the irony of her confession. **T F**

Check your answers with the key on the bottom of the next page. Then turn to the Rate Chart in the Appendix to get your words per minute for this selection. Finally, record your scores below and on the progress chart in the Appendix.

WORDS PER MINUTE ______

% COMPREHENSION ______

Bonus Questions (Scanning)

1. Who gave the ball the night before Amelia's husband was shot? ______________

2. How long had Amelia's husband been dead? ______________

Percentage Chart for Comprehension Check

Errors	0	1	2	3	4	5	6	7	8
% Right	100	88	75	63	50	38	25	13	0

Answer Key: Ex. 11I
1. (b) **2.** F **3.** F **4.** T **5.** F **6.** F **7.** (c) **8.** T **1.** Duke of Richmond **2.** 15 years

Lesson 12

Exercise 12A—Phrase Perception (Variation)

Note: Each column of twenty items has only one key phrase. Mark each repeated phrase. Work through both columns vertically before checking your time.

key phrase

immune to colds

immune to chills
immersed in colds

immune to colds
immune to cold

immune to cold
imagine colds

among these clods
inured to colds

immunity to colds
immune to colds

impugn my colds
immune to the cold

immense cold
immune to colds

an immense cold
immunize against colds

immunity to cold
immune to clods

immune to colds
immense coffin

key phrase

internal stress

eternal stress
international stress

internal stress
interminable stress

interior stress
internal stress

eternal rest
entirely stress

intrinsic stress
internal stress

enter the stress
eternal trees

internal stars
eternal stares

internal satire
internal stress

internal stress
interminable stars

interesting stress
interred dress

TIME ________

ERRORS ________

Exercise 12B — Phrase Perception (Variation)

Note: Each column of twenty items has only one key phrase. Mark each repeated phrase. Work through both columns vertically before checking your time.

key phrase

varsity baseball

university baseball
version of baseball

varsity basketball
various baseballs

varnished baseballs
varsity baseball

various basketballs
university base walls

university baseball
inner city baseball

varsity baseball
varsity baseball

verse about baseball
varsity team

varsity racketball
variation baseball

varsity baseball
vanished baseball

varsity baseball
next year, the pros!

key phrase

uncanny look

uncanny book
uncanny brook

unkind look
uncanny look

granny look
uncanny hook

uncanned cook
a nanny look

uncanny look
unplanned book

unplanned look
unmanned boat

banned book
unfanned food

uncared-for look
unkind cook

uncalled-for look
uncanny look

uncanny look
must be a witch

TIME ______

ERRORS ______

Answer Key: Ex. 12A
"immune to colds" repeated four times
"internal stress" repeated five times

Answer Key: Ex. 12B
"varsity baseball" repeated five times
"uncanny look" repeated four times

Exercise 12C—Word Comprehension (Variation)

Note: Look for whole-part relationships and mark the part(s). To illustrate this relationship: a *toe* is a part of the whole *foot;* a *fender* is a part of the whole *car.* (Words expressing this relationship are common transitions between ideas in writing.) There may be more than one answer.

Example:

orange	basket	~~peel~~	lamp	~~seed~~	glue

key word					
1. bottle	bat	mother	neck	cells	steak
2. lamp	base	chair	arm	shade	ankle
3. kangaroo	scales	ear	sorrow	lipstick	pouch
4. skirt	trousers	shoes	zipper	dress	rascal
5. stocking	heel	nails	collar	hammer	toe
6. wagon	horse	wheel	road	cloud	thunder
7. desert	traffic	whistle	sand	oak	red
8. ocean	water	dream	briefcase	salt	paper
9. book	rug	binding	branch	words	page
10. bank	golf	basketball	money	vault	nightclub
11. apple	core	cider	seed	foot	peel
12. saw	grass	blade	check	handle	magazine
13. bathroom	tub	stove	soap	refrigerator	towel
14. egg	skillet	shell	yolk	boil	white
15. classroom	desk	logs	mink	blackboard	cat
16. pen	file	ink	sweater	ring	tissue
17. fish	hair	wings	scales	legs	pencil
18. street	plane	notes	box	fire	pavement
19. telephone	elephant	cord	lips	receiver	teeth
20. watch	belt	cushion	stem	chain	crystal

TIME ________

ERRORS ________

Exercise 12D—Word Comprehension (Variation)

Note: Look for whole-part relationships and mark the part(s). There may be more than one answer.

key word					
1. body	stocking	arm	hat	pill	leg
2. house	home	family	roof	steps	rake
3. shoe	track	sole	sock	shadow	heel
4. car	engine	trip	selfish	wheel	accident
5. lawn	lost	grass	virtue	knife	bird
6. cigarette	cigar	teeth	tobacco	board	picture
7. flower	vase	petal	cut	stem	plant
8. face	veil	neck	nose	nail	lips
9. kitchen	stove	bed	sink	car	bathroom
10. tree	forest	leaf	meadow	trunk	branch
11. hand	finger	toenail	shoe	wrist	palm
12. forest	wagon	trees	street	dream	firm
13. office	clouds	rabbit	desk	tennis	typewriter
14. cow	horse	hoof	plow	farm	pouch
15. eye	brow	kneecap	iris	honor	pupil
16. pencil	park	lead	paper	eraser	powerful
17. bird	wing	sky	snake	scales	bathroom
18. coat	hat	stockings	sleeve	hanger	collar
19. window	scene	pane	door	frame	factor
20. hammer	tongs	blade	handle	tongue	hatchet

TIME _______

ERRORS _______

Answer Key: Ex. 12C
1. neck **2.** base, shade **3.** ear, pouch **4.** zipper **5.** heel, toe **6.** wheel **7.** sand **8.** water, salt **9.** binding, words, page **10.** money, vault **11.** core, seed, peel **12.** blade, handle **13.** tub, soap, towel **14.** shell, yolk, white **15.** desk, blackboard **16.** ink **17.** scales **18.** pavement **19.** cord, receiver **20.** stem, chain, crystal

Exercise 12E—Phrase Comprehension (Variation)

Note: Mark each noun that represents an animate object (containing human or animal life). Example: the fat finger. Some phrases have none; some have more than one.

1. the overcast sky
2. high on a hill
3. towering stone mansion
4. howl of a coyote
5. a door creaking
6. the monkey's paw
7. the whistling wind
8. the chain clanking
9. sudden glimpse of mummy
10. candles snuffed out
11. a starving black rat
12. the mad doctor
13. in a dank, dark basement
14. blood on the coat
15. a twisted arm hanging
16. glaring bloodshot eyes
17. one foot sliding behind
18. sharpening of a blade
19. eyes on last victim
20. hoarse croaking laugh
21. footsteps up the stairs
22. whining cries of a child
23. lightning outside a window
24. vultures hovering above
25. bat wings rustling in attic
26. bedroom on West Wing
27. pale sleeping girl
28. under a red velvet spread
29. the slim trembling hand
30. an eyelid flutters
31. stirred by unknown fears
32. bird caught in a trap
33. steps coming closer
34. claw-like hand reaches out
35. doorknob slowly turning
36. heavy door creaking open
37. frightened eyes piercing the dark
38. blade illuminated by lightning
39. shrill scream shatters quiet
40. desperate struggle begins
41. knife near throat
42. lips loom near
43. yellowed teeth bared
44. fangs pierce throat
45. not a drop wasted
46. body falls to floor
47. mad doctor dead
48. the pink flush returns
49. to girl's pale cheeks
50. Vampira strikes again

TIME ______

ERRORS ______

Answer Key: Ex. 12D
1. arm, leg **2.** roof, steps **3.** sole, heel **4.** engine, wheel **5.** grass **6.** tobacco **7.** petal, stem **8.** nose, lips **9.** stove, sink **10.** leaf, trunk, branch **11.** finger, palm **12.** trees **13.** desk, typewriter **14.** hoof **15.** iris, pupil **16.** lead, eraser **17.** wing **18.** sleeve, collar **19.** pane, frame **20.** handle

Answer Key: Ex. 12E
4. coyote **6.** paw **11.** rat **12.** doctor **15.** arm **16.** eyes **17.** foot **19.** eyes, victim **22.** child **24.** vultures **25.** wings **27.** girl **29.** hand **30.** eyelid **32.** bird **34.** hand **37.** eyes **41.** throat **42.** lips **43.** teeth **44.** fangs, throat **46.** body **47.** doctor **49.** cheeks **50.** Vampira

Exercise 12F—Phrase Comprehension (Variation)

Note: Mark each noun that represents an animate object (has human or animal life). Some phrases have none; some have more than one.

1. small southern town
2. five hundred people
3. the courthouse square
4. magnolia trees on lawn
5. old men on benches
6. whittling and spitting
7. old pick-up trucks
8. bird splattered windshield
9. farmer walking into courthouse
10. to pay his taxes
11. farmer's wife shopping
12. six dry-goods stores
13. horse and wagon
14. causing traffic jam
15. coon dog scratching fleas
16. noon-day sun shining
17. long, hot summer
18. spilled ice cream cone
19. on the pavement
20. flies buzzing around
21. teenagers lined up
22. outside the movie house
23. *Son of Swamp Monster*
24. store clerk rushing
25. back to work
26. shirtsleeves rolled up
27. perspiration on arms
28. college kids hanging around
29. the local dairy treat
30. waitress chewing gum
31. boy on motorcycle
32. roars up
33. waitress giggles
34. manager comes out
35. shakes his fist
36. only bank in town
37. customers lined up
38. cashiers handling money
39. children in cowboy boots
40. scuffling on floor
41. mothers grabbing hands
42. holding on tight
43. sound of music
44. and marching feet
45. trumpets off-key
46. the high school band
47. around the courthouse square
48. hands waving
49. hearts beating
50. too much excitement

TIME ______

ERRORS ______

WORDS IN CONTEXT

Without using your dictionary, try to determine the meaning of each word in **boldface** print. Choose the meaning below that best fits the context—the way it is used in the sentence.

Long Reading 12G

1. Evie thought of the washing erupting **convulsively** onto the line as the woman next door hung up each garment with controlled violence.
   (a) cleanly **(b)** blowing gently in the wind **(c)** shaking violently **(d)** suddenly

2. She got into bed, took a **nembutal,** and fell asleep.
   (a) pep-pill **(b)** tranquilizer **(c)** aspirin **(d)** vitamin

3. Evie grew to know the woman . . . by her **soliloquy** as she talked to herself, the words inaudible but the tone clear. . . .
   (a) dramatic monologue **(b)** crisp dialogue **(c)** whistling sounds **(d)** heavy breathing

4. . . . the fatigued tread of the woman, her face drained of everything but **lassitude.**
   (a) anger **(b)** fear **(c)** grief **(d)** listlessness

5. Filled with **torpor,** the dogs were quiet now, lazy, growing fat as they ambled reluctantly at the end of their rope leashes, to crawl back and lie **somnolent.**

5A. torpor
(a) too much food **(b)** inactivity; apathy **(c)** dreams of rabbits **(d)** sickness

5B. somnolent
(a) playing dead **(b)** without moving **(c)** sleepy **(d)** hungry

Check your answers with the key on the bottom of page 300.

THEME FOR READING SELECTIONS: INTERPRETING LITERATURE

As you progressed through this workbook, you have had the opportunity to read a variety of short articles, mostly non-fiction. The selections from mythology and from "Conflicts in Literature" have offered a taste of fiction, or literature. The reading selection in this Lesson allows you the

Answer Key: Ex. 12F
2. people **5.** men **8.** bird **9.** farmer **11.** wife **13.** horse **15.** dog, fleas **20.** flies **21.** teenagers **23.** Son, Monster **24.** clerk **27.** arms **28.** kids **30.** waitress **31.** boy **33.** waitress **34.** manager **35.** fist **37.** customers **38.** cashiers **39.** children **41.** mothers, hands **44.** feet **46.** band **48.** hands **49.** hearts

opportunity to read a longer work of fiction, an ironic short story from *Alfred Hitchcock Presents Stories for Late at Night.*

Imaginary Situation

A teacher you respect has asked you to read this short story and write a short critique to read to your English class. He points out that it has more than one possible interpretation. You realize that you must read and evaluate it carefully to avoid making a superficial analysis.

Exercise 12G — Long Reading

LENGTH: 1825

Read the following selection as rapidly as you can but read carefully to evaluate as you read. Wait for a signal from your instructor before you begin reading.

The People Next Door

Pauline C. Smith

"Well, how are you getting along with your new neighbor?" Ed asked.

Evelyn looked down at the knitting in her lap. "All right," she said.

"I talked with her a few minutes before dinner, while I was out in the yard. They used to live in California, she said. Seemed like a nice, ordinary woman."

Evelyn held up the wool, inspected it. "She did?"

"You like her all right, don't you?"

"I guess so."

"It gives you someone for company during the day. Keeps you from thinking about yourself too much," he persisted.

"I don't see her much. Sometimes I talk to her when she's hanging the wash on the line."

"Well, it's good for you," he said briskly, the clinical look taking over his face.

Evelyn picked up the wool again and clicked the needles. The knitting was a form of prescription.

"She hangs out her washing as if she was angry at it," she said. "She puts the clothespins on the shirts as if she were stabbing them."

"Evie!" His tone was sharp.

"Well, she does," Evelyn persisted. "Maybe it's because there's so many shirts. Fourteen of them. Two clean shirts every day. Perhaps her husband has a phobia about clean shirts."

Ed rattled his newspaper as he lowered it.

"Evie," he said, "you mustn't imagine things! You mustn't try to find phobias and neuroses in everything anybody does. It isn't healthy. I should think you'd have had enough of analyzing and being analyzed all this last year since your breakdown."

Evie thought of the washing erupting convulsively onto the line as the woman next door hung up each garment with controlled violence.

"Maybe she's tired of washing and ironing so many shirts every week," she said. "Maybe she's sick to death of it. Maybe that's why she seems to be stabbing the shirts with the clothespins."

"Evie, you're almost well now!" Ed was speaking with forced calm. "You can't afford to let your imagination run away about every simple little thing. It isn't healthy. You'll have a relapse."

"I'm sorry, Ed." She picked up the wool again. "I won't imagine things."

"That's a good girl." He relaxed. "She tell you what her husband does?"

"He's a salesman," Evelyn said, needles clicking. "He sells cutlery to restaurants—knives and cleavers and things."

"You see?" Ed remarked. "Salesmen have to be neat. That's why he wears so many shirts."

"Is it?" Evelyn studied the sweater. The gray wool was very unexciting. She decided she would work a little pattern into it—red, maybe. "Have you ever seen him?"

"No." Ed removed his glasses and polished them. "Have you?"

"Every morning. He leaves for work a little while after you do. His car is parked in their driveway, right by our kitchen window. I see him while I'm doing the breakfast dishes."

Ed turned the pages of his newspaper to the sport section.

"What's he like?"

"He's very tall and thin. His mouth is thin, like a knife. He wears gray all the time. He makes me think of a gray snake."

"Evie!" Ed's voice was angry now. "Stop that!"

"All right." She stood up. "I guess I'll go to bed now."

In her bedroom, she stood for a moment at the window. There was a light on next door—one window was an orange oblong. She got into bed, took a nembutal, and fell asleep.

Answer Key: Words in Context
1. (c) **2.** (b) **3.** (a) **4.** (d) **5A.** (b) **5B.** (c)

Over the clean suds of dishwater each morning she saw the man next door appear, stride quickly to his car and get in with his sample case—tall, his features as sharp as the knives he sold, his eyes hooded. Then the car would start, rattle off and he would be gone.

Through her brief appearances in the back yard, Evelyn grew to know the woman; by her long strides to the refuse can where she would clatter the lid off, throw in her paper-wrapped bundle with an over-arm motion, clang the lid back; by her short, fierce tussle with a garment on the clothesline; by her soliloquy as she talked to herself, the words inaudible but the tone clear—sometimes a grumbling complaint and sometimes a violently fierce monolog. Evelyn grew to know her, she felt, quite well. And sometimes at night she would hear sounds from next door. Not very loud sounds; not conversation. Muffled sounds. You would have to use imagination to say they were sounds of anger, or perhaps of pain. And she had promised Ed not to let herself imagine things . . .

When the car had been sitting in the driveway for two days, she mentioned it to Ed. He lowered his paper.

"Oh?" he said politely. "Is he sick?"

"Maybe he is. I haven't seen her, either."

"You'd better go over, hadn't you? Maybe they're both sick."

"No. I don't want to go over there."

He glanced at his paper, then at his wife. "Why not? You've talked to her. It would be the kind thing to do."

Evelyn bent over her occupational therapy, the knitting on her lap. "She might think I was snooping."

Aggravation and indulgence struggled in Ed's face. At last, he said mildly, "I don't think she'd think that."

"She might."

Through one more day without backyard clangor, Evelyn listened and watched while the house next door slept.

On the next day the woman next door emerged to hang out her washing. She no longer moved with a controlled fury. She handled the pieces of wash, even the shirts, as if they were fabric, inanimate and impersonal—no longer as if she wrestled a hated opponent.

Stepping to the dividing fence, Evelyn rested her hands on the palings. She leaned over. "I see your husband's car in the driveway . . ." she began.

The words seemed to filter slowly through the other woman's mind, to arrange themselves in her brain to make a sense which startled her. She looked at the car, then back at Evelyn.

"He took a trip." Her expression was suddenly veiled and withdrawn. She wet her lips with the tip of her tongue.

"He's gone off to a convention. It was too far to drive. He took the train and left the car for me."

"Oh, that's it," Evie said politely. "We were afraid he was sick."

"No, he's not sick. He's not sick at all."

Abruptly the woman backed away, spare-lipped mouth moving as if to utter further words of explanation that would reduce the unusual to the commonplace. Then she turned, stepped through her back door and locked it behind her.

"The man next door is out of town," Evelyn told Ed that evening.

He smiled. "So you went over, after all."

"No."

"Oh? You talked to her, though?"

"Yes. I talked to her." Evelyn bent over the knitting. "She took the car and went away this afternoon."

Rustling the paper, Ed settled to read.

"She wasn't gone long. When she came back, she had two big dogs in the car with her."

He lowered the paper. "She did?"

"Two big thin dogs," described Evelyn. "She tied them in the back yard using the clothesline to tie them to the clothes pole. She had a big wash this morning and after it dried, she went and got the dogs and tied them with the clothesline."

"Maybe she's scared while her husband's gone. And she got them for watchdogs."

"Maybe."

Now Evelyn felt ready to give up the nembutal she had used to get her to sleep all these months. Pushing the little bottle of sleeping tablets far back on the bedside table, she lay down. She thought of the woman next door, the dogs and the car in the driveway . . . the woman, the dogs and the car . . .

At last, she rose to pace through the darkened house.

Standing at the kitchen window, she looked out at the night to see a button of light cross the yard next door. Her eyes followed it. She heard a plop, a snarl and a growl—then the gulping, snuffling sound of hunger being satisfied. The light made an arc and moved back to the house and was lost.

For a long time she stood at the window, then she went to her bedroom, took a nembutal and fell asleep . . .

"She doesn't like the dogs," Evelyn told Ed several days later.

"She doesn't have to. They're watchdogs, not pets."

"She walks them every day. She unties their ropes from the clothes pole and goes off with them. When she comes back, she's tired and the dogs are tired. Then after dark she gives them a big dinner."

Evie thought of them, the slip-slap drag of the animals,

their lolling tongues—the fatigued tread of the woman, her face drained of everything but lassitude. Of the way she re-tied them to the clothes pole, knotting, knotting and re-knotting the ropes while they lay, eyes closed, panting, satiated.

"What does she say about her husband? Seems to me that convention is lasting awfully long."

"She doesn't say anything. She just walks the dogs. Walks them and feeds them."

Ed laid down his paper. "Evie," he said, "Don't you talk with her any more?"

Holding the needles tightly, Evelyn looked at him. "I don't see her to talk with her. She just walks the dogs. She doesn't hang anything on her line any more because she doesn't have any line. She doesn't seem to do anything in the yard except untie the dogs and tie them up again."

"Well, that's too bad. I wanted you to have some company. Maybe you could walk . . ."

"No! I don't want to walk with her or the dogs." Evelyn dropped the knitting on the chair as she left for bed . . .

Filled with torpor, the dogs were quiet now, lazy, growing fat as they ambled reluctantly at the end of their rope leashes, to crawl back and lie somnolent.

Evelyn was knitting quietly. The sweater was almost finished; the drab, uninteresting sweater with the bright little pattern of scarlet she had added. "She took the dogs away in the car today," she told Ed on Friday.

Ed looked at her over his glasses. "She did?"

"And she came back alone. Then she went in the house, got two suitcases, came out, put them in the car and drove off."

"Maybe that's why she took the dogs away—she's going on a trip."

"She's going on a trip all right."

"Or perhaps the upkeep was too high." Ed yawned, and polished his glasses, fitted them carefully on his nose. "She shouldn't have exercised them so much. It made them too hungry." He opened his paper and placed it across his knees. "Must have cost her plenty to feed the brutes."

Evie pulled the needles from the yarn and folded the sweater. She stood. The thing was a pattern, its design all finished.

"I don't think it did," she said. "I don't think it cost her hardly anything at all."

Immediately answer the questions below without referring to the selection.

1. Evie's interpretation of the events next door is that
   (a) the woman doesn't like her husband and sends him away.
   (b) the woman hates her husband so much she kills him.
   (c) the couple have a loud argument, and he leaves her.
   (d) the man has gone on a business trip.
2. What does this statement, "She put clothespins on the shirts as if she were stabbing them," imply about the later disappearance of the man next door? ______________________________
3. Evie weaves a pattern of red into the gray sweater she is knitting. What might this bit of red symbolize (or represent)? ______________________________
4. When the car next door remains in the driveway a couple of days, the woman tells Evie her husband is sick. **T F**
5. Why does Ed encourage Evie to be friendly to the people next door? ______________________________
6. What does Evie think the murder weapon is? ______________________________
7. Evie tells her husband in the last sentence that feeding the dogs didn't cost the lady next door anything. What does this statement imply? ______________________________
8. Why didn't Evie tell Ed her interpretation of the events next door? ______________________________

Check your answers with the key on the bottom of the next page. Then turn to the Rate Chart in the Appendix to get your words per minute for this selection. Finally, record your scores below and on the progress chart in the Appendix.

WORDS PER MINUTE ______

% COMPREHENSION ______

Bonus Questions

1. Scan the story for the lines containing knife imagery (example: see quotation in question 2), and briefly list the images below.

______________________________ ______________________________

______________________________ ______________________________

2. There are two possible interpretations of the story. (1) *The woman next door killed her husband as Evie suggests.* (2) *Evie is slipping back into insanity and only imagines the woman killed her husband.* Choose one of these interpretations and write a brief paragraph justifying your choice. Choose your supporting details directly from the story.

____

____

____

____

____

Percentage Chart for Comprehension Check

Errors	0	1	2	3	4	5	6	7	8
% Right	100	88	75	63	50	38	25	13	0

Answer Key: Ex. 12G

1. (b) **2.** that she wishes she were stabbing the owner of the shirts and later does stab him *or* that Evie reads too much into the woman's actions because of her own hostility toward Ed **3.** The obvious answer is "blood." [The red makes the pattern in the sweater complete, just as murder is the final piece in the puzzle next door.] Another possibility is that the red in the dull gray symbolizes excitement (the couple next door) in her dull life. **4.** F **5.** Because of her former illness, he seems to consider an interest in her neighbors to be good therapy. **6.** the man's knives. **7.** She thinks the woman disposed of her husband's body by feeding it to the dogs. **8.** She evidently thinks he wouldn't believe her. She might even be afraid he will think she is having another nervous breakdown—especially in view of his reactions to some of her earlier statements about the couple.

Bonus: **1.** "as if she were stabbing them"
"stabbing the shirts with clothespins"
"His mouth is thin, like a knife."
"his features as sharp as the knives he sold"
2. (Check with your instructor.)

Homework

How to Use the Dictionary

You are probably thinking now that you already know how to use the dictionary. You know the alphabet so you know how to look up a word; you can find the correct spelling if you have an idea of how the word starts; and you know how to find the meaning of a word.

You have only just *begun* to learn how to use the dictionary, however. When you look up the definition of a word, do you know why that word might have up to fourteen different definitions listed? Which one do you pick?

There are around twenty other kinds of information (besides spelling and definition) that can be given about a word. How many can you think of? Do you know how to use the aids in the front or back of your dictionary? Perhaps you have never looked at these aids before or after the alphabetized list of words. Also, how do you learn to pronounce words you do not know? Can you pronounce an unfamiliar word after you look it up in your dictionary?

You will find the answers to these questions and to many, many more while working through the following exercise.

Exercise 1

For this exercise you need a large unabridged (uncut) dictionary, an abridged hardcover dictionary, and a paperback dictionary. The exercise might be done as a class project, small group work, or individual work. When you finish, you will know the differences between the three types of dictionary and which dictionary to choose for a particular problem. (Remember, you can find all three types of dictionary in your library if they are not available at home or in the classroom.)

1. How many entries (the alphabetized words plus information such as spelling, definition, etc.) are in each dictionary?
   Tip: You do not have to count the words or the pages.

   In the unabridged dictionary ____________________

   In the abridged hardcover dictionary ____________________

   In the paperback dictionary ____________________

2. What special sections or charts do you find in the abridged hardcover dictionary that are not in the paperback?

   ____

   What special sections or charts do you find in the unabridged dictionary that are not in the abridged hardcover?

   ____

3. Most paperback dictionaries do not have a special biography section. Therefore where can you find Albert Einstein's birthdate in your paperback dictionary? ______________________________

____

4. Look in all three dictionaries and find the page numbers for the chart of abbreviations and symbols used in the entries of each dictionary.

   In the unabridged dictionary ______________________________

   In the abridged hardcover dictionary ______________________________

   In the paperback dictionary ______________________________

5. On what page do you find information about usage labels?

   In the unabridged dictionary ______________________________

   In the abridged hardcover dictionary ______________________________

   In the paperback dictionary ______________________________

6. Find the guide words (two words above the line of each page of entries) in any of the dictionaries. Explain how these guide words help you find a word more quickly. ______________________________

____

7. Find the main pronunciation key in all three dictionaries. Then find the pronunciation key at the bottom of every other page throughout any of the dictionaries. Explain how the sample words in the pronunciation key help you pronounce words. ______________________________

____

8. How is the pronunciation of a word set apart from the rest of the entry? ________

____

How is the etymology (origin) of a word set apart from the rest of the entry?

____

9. Draw the symbol for "derived from" in the etymology for an entry. __________

10. Look up a couple of words that have long entries and list at least ten different kinds of information given about the words. (Remember, give the *type* of information, not the information itself. Two answers are given.)

spelling	______________
definitions	______________
______________	______________
______________	______________
______________	______________

Check the answers with your instructor.

Exercise 2

Do this exercise individually using a paperback dictionary recommended by your instructor.

1. Give the complete title of your dictionary. ______________________

____

2. When was Richard M. Nixon born? ______________________
3. What is the capital of Rhode Island? ______________________
4. **(a)** What verb forms are given for the regular verb *reward?*

   ____

   (b) What verb forms are given for the irregular, intransitive verb *lie?*

   ____

5. List all the parts of speech for *cool.* (Give the whole word, not the abbreviation for the part of speech.) ______________________

   ____

6. Rewrite the following words, showing their syllable division the same way your dictionary does.

   (a) examination ______________________

   (b) commodious ______________________

   (c) valedictorian ______________________

   (d) euthanasia ______________________

7. Give the plural spelling of the following words.

   (a) belief ______________________

   (b) elf ______________________

   (c) sister-in-law ______________________

   (d) phenomenon ______________________

   (e) tomato ______________________

   (f) sash ______________________

   (g) thesis ______________________

   (h) fox ______________________

8. How many definitions are listed for *order?* ______________________

9. Give the complete etymology for the following words. (Do not use abbreviations.)

   (a) bane ______

   (b) lollipop ______

   (c) obloquy ______

   (d) quarry ______

10. What is a slang definition for *squeal?* ______

11. (a) What is the preferred or central definition for *regular?* ______

    (b) What is the definition for *sharp* used in music? ______

    ______

12. What is the definition for *relief* used in baseball? ______

    ______

13. What do the following abbreviations stand for?

    (a) M.A. ______

    (b) R.I. ______

    (c) ck. ______

    (d) Bart. ______

14. (a) Give the definition of the suffix *-ic.* ______

    (b) Give two words ending in *-ic.* ______

15. (a) Give the definition of the prefix *intra-.* ______

    (b) Give two words beginning with the prefix *intra-.* ______

16. When you add suffixes to many words, you must double a final consonant, drop an *e*, or add an *i*. Your dictionary gives these inflectional changes. Look up the correct spelling for the following words, and write the complete word (root plus suffix) in the blank.

    (a) courage + ous ______

    (b) convey + ing ______

    (c) patrol + ed ______

    (d) acknowledge + ment ______

17. Look up the definitions for these commonly confused pairs of words. Then write a sentence using each word. Make sure your sentences clearly show the difference between the words in each pair.

(a) continuous ______

continual ______

(b) principle ______

principal ______

(c) allusion ______

illusion ______

(d) implication ______

inference ______

18. How do you find the number *4* or *8* in your dictionary? ______

______

19. **(a)** Does your dictionary have word combinations like *radio frequency?* ______

(b) Would *radio frequency* come before or after *radiology?* ______

(c) Would the entry *William McKinley* come before the entry *Machiavellian* in your dictionary? ______

(d) Would the word *Ma* come before or after McKinley and Machiavellian?

______

20. Write all the pronunciation symbols and marks for the following words. Using the pronunciation key at the bottom of every other page, prepare to pronounce the words in class.

(a) ungulate ______

(b) desuetude ______

(c) satyriasis ______

(d) farinaceous ______

(e) demesne ______

(f) dementia ______

(g) Zeitgeist ______

(h) deleterious ______

Check the answers with your instructor.

TWENTY WAYS TO COMPLIMENT YOUR FRIENDS

Read the following carefully to determine how the descriptive adjectives in **boldface print** are used.

It was the ten-year reunion for class of 1968, Puddle Creek High School. As Mark drove down the winding old Puddle Creek Road, he thought of some of his old classmates that he hoped to see. He was especially curious to see the [1]**agile** Sally Faye. He loved to watch her [2]**lithe** young body moving on the basketball court. She could weave and bob and dribble her way across the court and sink a basket in a flash of the eye. Sally Faye was well-coordinated off the court too. He remembered her [3]**nimble** fingers flying across the typewriter and piano keys with equal skill.

Another person he hoped to see was Randall, the senior class president. How Mark envied his speaking ability! Randall was [4]**articulate** on every subject, always able to talk convincingly about anything. He was so [5]**fluent** that he made even the speech teachers seem like stammering, stuttering idiots in comparison. Mark would never forget how [6]**eloquent** Randall was in defending senior class privileges—every reason [7]**plausible.**

The person Mark was sure would attend was the [8]**affable** Artie Joe. This good-natured class clown would probably be the first to arrive and the last to leave. He would keep the alumni amused with his [9]**droll** remarks. Though he poked fun at everyone, his jokes were [10]**benign;** they had no bite.

Mark knew the most outstandingly dressed couple there would be the favorite class sweethearts, Ginger Lee and Freddy. She would be looking [11]**exotic** in some rich-colored, gypsy-style, swirling dress to match her striking dark features and flashing eyes. He would look [12]**immaculate** as usual, dressed in [13]**impeccable** taste. He would probably be wearing an expensively tailored three-piece suit, perhaps beige and brown, with a handmade tie. This inseparable couple would know all the latest dance steps.

And surely Phyllis would be there—[14]**vivacious** as ever. Her [15]**effervescent** personality would sparkle and shine, brightening up the party. She would dazzle them all with her [16]**scintillating** wit.

Mark was curious if Alphonse, the class brain, would honor them with his presence. He used to be jealous that Alphonse seemed [17]**proficient** in all subjects, seeming to have no weak areas. He was equally [18]**diligent** in every course, spending as much time in English as in Math or P.E. His study habits were [19]**exemplary.** He studied four hours a day, every day, at the same time and same place. He always studied at a desk, sitting in a straight-back chair, with good lighting over his left shoulder. His answers in class were [20]**astute,** right on the mark.

As Mark drove through the night, he worried that he might still be in awe of these shining lights of the Puddle Creek class of 1968.

Exercise

Pick the best definition for the words to the left as they were used in the preceding passage.

1. *agile* **(a)** aggravating **(b)** active **(c)** clumsy
2. *lithe* **(a)** limber **(b)** brittle **(c)** muscular
3. *nimble* **(a)** slow **(b)** strong **(c)** quick
4. *articulate* **(a)** speaking well **(b)** artistic **(c)** talking a lot
5. *fluent* **(a)** boastful **(b)** smooth talking **(c)** intelligent
6. *eloquent* **(a)** emotional **(b)** persuasive **(c)** loud
7. *plausible* **(a)** believable **(b)** possible **(c)** doubtful
8. *affable* **(a)** rich **(b)** funny **(c)** agreeable
9. *droll* **(a)** slapstick **(b)** complimentary **(c)** dryly comical
10. *benign* **(a)** poisonous **(b)** mild **(c)** healthy
11. *exotic* **(a)** unusual and striking **(b)** classy **(c)** beautiful but dumb
12. *immaculate* **(a)** slovenly **(b)** neat **(c)** spotless
13. *impeccable* **(a)** expensive **(b)** faultless **(c)** gaudy
14. *vivacious* **(a)** amusing **(b)** weird **(c)** lively
15. *effervescent* **(a)** bubbling **(b)** devious **(c)** kind
16. *scintillating* **(a)** sarcastic **(b)** sparkling **(c)** sweet
17. *proficient* **(a)** average **(b)** competent **(c)** recognized
18. *diligent* **(a)** hard working **(b)** smart **(c)** busy
19. *exemplary* **(a)** well organized **(b)** to be criticized **(c)** praiseworthy
20. *astute* **(a)** correct **(b)** shrewd **(c)** pompous

Check the answers with your instructor and record your score below.

% CORRECT ______

TWENTY WAYS TO INSULT YOUR ENEMIES

Read the following carefully to determine how the descriptive adjectives in **boldface print** are used.

Mark drove up to the old gymnasium, where the Puddle Creek High School reunion, class of 1968, was being held. He entered the brightly lit room, decorated with balloons and streamers. The first person he saw was former star athlete Sally Faye. What a shock! Her lithe young body had become fat. No longer agile, she had become [1]**slothful**—her movements slow and [2]**listless;** her once nimble fingers were now swollen and arthritic.

Mark ducked into another direction and bumped into Randall, Big Man on Campus, who immediately began boasting about his important executive position with an international banking firm. How could he ever have thought Randall fluent, Mark wondered to himself. The former class president was merely [3]**loquacious.** Randall's fluency with words now seemed [4]**glib.** His tone was [5]**condescending,** his whole manner [6]**supercilious.**

Fortunately they were interrupted by Artie Joe, formerly beloved class clown, loudly trying to get everyone's attention. People were shying away from his [7]**boisterous** behavior. His antics were too [8]**juvenile** and his jokes too [9]**asinine** for people pushing thirty to laugh at. As the evening progressed and Artie Joe dipped into the spiked punch more and more, he became [10]**surly** and threatening. His remarks were especially [11]**snide** to those who had laughed most at his jokes in high school.

At one point Mark saw Ginger Lee swirl by—but not with her class sweetheart Freddy. He was dancing with someone else on the other side of the gym, carefully avoiding contact with Ginger Lee. Ginger Lee no longer looked exotic to Mark. She now appeared too [12]**flamboyant.** Her dress was [13]**gaudy** with its loud clashing colors, beads, bows, ribbons, and ruffles. Her once distinctive dance style now seemed to Mark only [14]**eccentric.**

The years had been equally unkind to Freddy. Mark realized that Freddy's cool poise hid a [15]**humdrum** personality. His careful attire seemed conservative and unimaginative. Mark quickly became bored with his [16]**bland** conversation and drifted away to find the class genius, Alphonse. Alphonse told Mark that he was still in graduate school, working on his fourth degree. He seemed so pale and [17]**cadaverous** that he looked as if he had been in prison for ten years. He had dark circles under his eyes, and his frame appeared [18]**gaunt** from improper diet and lack of exercise. His conversation was [19]**tedious;** it was like talking with an encyclopedia. Alphonse's mind was so full of trivia that he wandered from one subject to another and back again in an [20]**incoherent** fashion.

Mark silently slipped out of the gym thinking that perhaps he had not turned out so badly after all.

Exercise

Pick the best definition for the words to the left as they were used in the preceding passage.

1. *slothful* **(a)** lazy **(b)** mean **(c)** sick
2. *listless* **(a)** without warmth **(b)** without ambition **(c)** without energy
3. *loquacious* **(a)** phony **(b)** very talkative **(c)** too friendly
4. *glib* **(a)** surface; too easy **(b)** using big words **(c)** bilingual
5. *condescending* **(a)** lowering oneself **(b)** insulting **(c)** hypocritical
6. *supercilious* **(a)** superficial **(b)** arrogant **(c)** easy to anger
7. *boisterous* **(a)** smelly **(b)** obnoxious **(c)** noisy
8. *juvenile* **(a)** immature **(b)** criminal **(c)** ignorant
9. *asinine* **(a)** retarded **(b)** silly **(c)** too serious
10. *surly* **(a)** rude **(b)** strong **(c)** cursing
11. *snide* **(a)** funny **(b)** stupid **(c)** sarcastic
12. *flamboyant* **(a)** showy **(b)** vulgar **(c)** greasy
13. *gaudy* **(a)** dull colored **(b)** cheaply colorful **(c)** too thin
14. *eccentric* **(a)** odd **(b)** clumsy **(c)** sexy
15. *humdrum* **(a)** singsong **(b)** boring **(c)** snappy
16. *bland* **(a)** low-voiced **(b)** colorless **(c)** loud
17. *cadaverous* **(a)** sickly **(b)** corpselike **(c)** evil
18. *gaunt* **(a)** ill **(b)** out of shape **(c)** thin and bony
19. *tedious* **(a)** tiresome **(b)** tender **(c)** depressing
20. *incoherent* **(a)** coarse **(b)** disordered **(c)** uninformed

Check the answers with your instructor and record your score below.

% CORRECT ______

WORD ANALYSIS

What is "word analysis"? It is one more way that a reader can unlock the meanings of words. You may learn a word through its use, in context; or you may use a dictionary; or you may consciously analyze the word. If English is your native language, you already practice word analysis unconsciously. For example, you know that the last word, *unconsciously,* in the previous sentence is the "way you practice." Why do you know this? Because of the little two-letter ending *-ly.* You probably also know that the two-letter beginning *-un,* means *not.* The whole word then means "without being conscious of doing it."

In this way, one English word can stand for several words, or for a whole phrase. If you can consciously learn how these word parts work, and memorize some uncommon parts as well as common ones, you can unlock even more words, especially in more difficult and technical reading. (What word beginnings and endings do you see in this sentence and the previous sentence?)

The three major parts of an English word are called the *root, prefix,* and *suffix.* In the remaining Homework sections you will learn how important these word parts are in unlocking the meaning to unfamiliar words. The root is discussed first, because it is the only essential part of the word. A word consists of *at least* a root. *We will* italicize *the* words *in this sentence which are root* words only. Do you see any beginnings or endings on those italicized words which can be removed and still leave a basic word? (Your answer should be no.)

But if you can remove a part, one that you have seen attached to many other words, and still have a basic word remaining, then that letter or part is probably a *prefix* or *suffix.* Can you do this to the words *removed, attached,* and *words?* If you took off a part from the beginning of the word, the part is called a *prefix.* If you took off a part from the end, it is called a *suffix.*

To remember the order of these three possible word parts in a word, read the word from left to right as usual → and think Prefix-Root-Suffix, or PRS. If you still forget your word parts think of this Word Animal, made of the letters P, R, and S (the eye is not a word part, only an eye!).

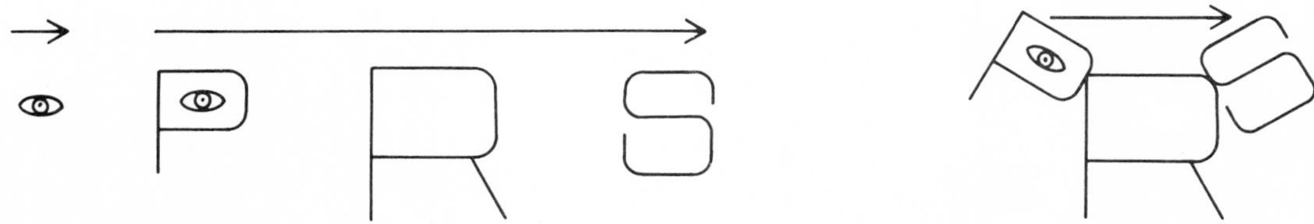

Now look at these words: *removed, incapable, rewording.* We have written the basic word below within the R or root. Add the detachable parts to the root, in the right place on the Animal. (The first one has been done for you.)

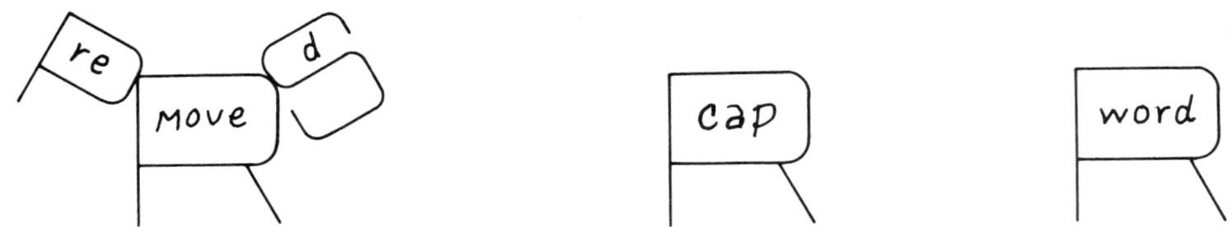

If you did this correctly, you are already a good Word Analyst!

Look at the table of contents again and notice how many Homework sections are devoted to roots, prefixes, and suffixes.

While eighty roots, forty prefixes, and forty-seven suffixes may sound like a lot of word parts to memorize, you probably know many of them already. If you do not, your vocabulary is gravely hampered, because these 167 parts are basic to the English language, and therefore extremely important. As you advance through your studies, you will learn dozens more, formally through learning lists like these, and informally through your reading and general vocabulary growth.

TWENTY COMMON GREEK AND LATIN ROOTS

We begin our word analysis with a list of twenty common root words that English has borrowed from two ancient languages, Latin and Greek. You will see these roots in many English words, often combined with prefixes and suffixes. Note that a borrowed root does not always make a familiar English word by itself. "Cent" and "cult," below, are whole words, but "cogni" and "cor" are not. (Also note that the root is usually a stressed syllable in a word.)

Directions: First memorize the root with its original meaning. Then study the example of the root at work in the English language. If you cannot determine the meaning of any example, look up the word in your dictionary. Then jot down any other examples you can think of.

Root	*Original Meaning*	*English Example*	*Your Examples*
1. aequus	equal, even	equivalent	________
		equinox	________
2. anima	breath, spirit,	animate	________
	mind	magnanimous	________
3. *ann, enn	year	annuity	________
		biennial	________
4. anthropo	man	anthropology	________
		philanthropy	________
5. *astro	star	astronomy	________
		astral	________
6. *aud, audit	to hear	auditory	________
		audio-frequency	________

7. *auto	self	automation	______
		autobiography	______
8. bellum	war	rebel	______
		belligerent	______
9. *bene	good, well	benefactor	______
		benign	______
10. *bio	life	autobiography	______
		biopsy	______
11. cap, cept	to take	capture	______
		accept	______
12. *capit	head	capitol	______
		caption	______
13. cede, ceed	to yield, to go	recede	______
		accessory	______
14. cent	hundred	centennial	______
		centimeter	______
15. *chron	time	chronological	______
		chronic	______
16. *civ	citizen	civility	______
		civilization	______
17. cogni	to know	connoisseur	______
		incognito	______
18. cor	heart	core	______
		courage	______
19. *crat, cracy	rule	plutocrat	______
		democracy	______
20. cult	to care for	cult	______
		agriculture	______

*Also presented in *Reading Faster and Understanding More, Book I* and included here for review.

Exercise

Directions: Use your knowledge of the original meaning of the root to choose the answer most closely related to the italicized word. Write the letter of the answer in the blanks. Do not look back at the list until finished.

______ **1.** In his weakened condition, he was barely *audible.*
(a) able to stand **(b)** visible **(c)** able to be heard

______ **2.** He crossed the Alps safely because he was *cognizant* of the dangers.
(a) concerned about **(b)** aware **(c)** unaware

______ **3.** As the word itself suggests, *biology* is the study of
(a) living things **(b)** chemical compounds **(c)** physical systems

_____ **4.** After taking a long draw from her cigarette, she slowly rose to her feet and toasted her new status of *centenarian.*
(a) winner of a marathon **(b)** someone who is one hundred years old **(c)** a type of veterinarian

_____ **5.** An *asterisk* gets its name from its _____ shape.
(a) starlike **(b)** circular **(c)** flower-like

_____ **6.** Attila and his Huns were noted for their *bellicose* tendencies.
(a) artistic **(b)** warlike **(c)** agricultural

_____ **7.** The beautiful streets, public buildings, and parks of the city of Santa Barbara are the source of much *civic* pride.
(a) architectural **(b)** of the citizens **(c)** financial

_____ **8.** No matter how hectic the workload in our office, my boss always responds with *equanimity.*
(a) enthusiasm **(b)** an even temperament **(c)** lots of laughs

_____ **9.** According to this *chronology,* you entered high school in 1968.
(a) high school yearbook **(b)** newspaper clipping **(c)** a list given in order of time

_____ **10.** Neal spends much of his time *cultivating* the friendship of his co-workers.
(a) tending to **(b)** ignoring **(c)** wishing for

_____ **11.** World power in the future may be controlled by the *technocrats.*
(a) space-age computers **(b)** those who rule technology **(c)** technical details

_____ **12.** The man gave his best friend's wife a *cordial* welcome.
(a) indifferent **(b)** frosty **(c)** friendly

_____ **13.** *Perennial* flowers are not only beautiful but practical since you need plant them only once.
(a) appearing in the spring **(b)** prize winning **(c)** reappearing yearly

_____ **14.** Rocks, though they may make nice pets, are still *inanimate.*
(a) not lasting in popularity **(b)** not alive **(c)** not warm and clever

_____ **15.** If I were a dictator, I know I would be a *beneficent* one.
(a) kind **(b)** scared **(c)** powerful

_____ **16.** "We have no evidence *anthropoids* inhabited this earth until relatively recently in the earth's history," intoned the professor.
(a) large horses **(b)** creatures resembling man **(c)** dinosaurs

_____ **17.** Through *autohypnosis* many people successfully change their lives.
(a) the power of positive thinking **(b)** deep hypnosis **(c)** self-hypnosis

_____ **18.** The task of the Tactical Air Command is to *intercept* enemy planes.
(a) assist **(b)** prevent progress of **(c)** send back

______ **19.** After hotly debating his point for several hours, he suddenly *conceded.*
(a) won **(b)** grew tired **(c)** gave in

______ **20.** *Per capita,* New Yorkers pay more in property taxes than residents of most other states.
(a) for each household **(b)** for each individual **(c)** for each family of four

Check the answers with your instructor and record your score below.

% CORRECT ______

TWENTY MORE GREEK AND LATIN ROOTS

Directions: As in the previous assignment, first memorize the root with its original meaning. Study the example of the root at work in the English language. If you cannot determine the meaning of any example, look up the word in your dictionary. Then jot down any other examples you can think of.

Root	*Original Meaning*	*English Example*	*Your Examples*
1. *cred, credit	to believe	credible	________
		creditor	________
2. cycle	wheel, circle	cycle	________
		cyclone	________
3. dem	people	democracy	________
		demographic	________
4. dent	tooth	denture	________
		indent	________
5. derma	skin	hypodermic	________
		pachyderm	________
6. *dic, dict	to say, to speak	indicative	________
		valedictorian	________
7. duc, duct	to lead	educate	________
		conductor	________
8. *fac, fact	to make	facile	________
		factory	________
9. *fin	end, to complete	finale	________
		infinite	________
10. *gen, gene	birth, origin	genealogy	________
		eugenics	________
11. geo	earth	geology	________
		geophysics	________
12. *gram	to write	diagram	________
		gramophone	________
13. *graph	to write	graffiti	________
		graphology	________
14. hetero	other	heterosexual	________
		heterodox	________
15. *homo	same	homeopathy	________
		homogeneous	________
16. hydra	water	hydraulic	________
		hydrogen	________
17. *jac, ject	to throw	eject	________
		interject	________

18. *log, logo	word, study	apology	______
		mineralogy	______
19. loqui, locut	talk	loquacious	______
		elocution	______
20. luc, lus	light	translucent	______
		illustrate	______

*Also presented in *Reading Faster and Understanding More, Book I* and included here for review.

Exercise

Directions: Using your knowledge of the original meaning of the root, choose the answer most closely related to the italicized word. Write the letter of the answer in the blank. Do not look back at the list until you have finished.

______ **1.** He is always *engendering* new designs.
(a) overlooking **(b)** creating **(c)** distrusting

______ **2.** She was able to *induce* her friends to follow her.
(a) flatter **(b)** threaten **(c)** lead

______ **3.** My childhood sweetheart has rushed me a *cryptogram.* [*Crypt* means "secret."]
(a) message written in secret code. **(b)** secret box of chocolates
(c) secret music box

______ **4.** *Dermabrasion* is a rubbing technique often used by beauty parlors.
(a) fingernail shaping **(b)** hair removal **(c)** skin scraping

______ **5.** According to the popular *dictum,* he is a man-on-the-go.
(a) philosophy **(b)** saying **(c)** advertisement

______ **6.** The fiery words of the *demagogue* swayed the crowd.
(a) one who agitates people with words **(b)** one who likes to hear himself talk **(c)** one who has a cause he is willing to die for

______ **7.** Even though she was dripping with sweat, it was hard for me to give any *credence* to her story about winning the cross-country race.
(a) sympathy **(b)** attention **(c)** belief

______ **8.** A daily use of *dentifrice* can save you hours of pain and agony later.
(a) common sense **(b)** household safety **(c)** floss for the teeth

______ **9.** The *calligraphy* on the invitation was very delicate and full of detail.
(a) handwriting **(b)** painting **(c)** scroll

______ **10.** "Apparently, my dear, her interest in her marriage was merely *cyclical,*" purred the lady from behind her fan.
(a) superficial **(b)** based on money **(c)** came and went

_____ **11.** The police pointed out that, oddly enough, the check for $1,000,000 bore a *facsimile* of my signature.
(a) sample **(b)** old version **(c)** reproduction

_____ **12.** He has a reputation for writing in a *colloquial* style.
(a) sincere **(b)** elegant and carefully structured **(c)** informal, like talking

_____ **13.** There was a tone of *finality* in his voice as he sang to the judge.
(a) completeness **(b)** sorrow **(c)** freshness

_____ **14.** His explanation helped to *elucidate* the difficult lesson in trigonometry.
(a) prepare **(b)** cast light on **(c)** tear apart

_____ **15.** *Homonyms* are words that have _____.
(a) similar sounds **(b)** opposite meanings **(c)** abbreviated forms

_____ **16.** A future source of world energy may lie in *geothermal* resources. [*Thermal* means "heat."]
(a) heat from the sun **(b)** heat from the sea **(c)** heat from the earth

_____ **17.** The *projectile* was found on my lawn.
(a) lizard-like creature **(b)** object that is thrown **(c)** carton of film

_____ **18.** The *hydroplane* made good time between Spain and Morocco.
(a) jet airplane **(b)** high-speed water craft **(c)** commuter plane

_____ **19.** A *eulogy* involves
(a) words **(b)** music **(c)** hormones

_____ **20.** I like a large college because the students are more likely to be *heterogeneous*.
(a) of the same sex **(b)** doing upper-division study **(c)** from varied backgrounds

Check the answers with your instructor and record your score below.

% CORRECT _____

EVEN MORE GREEK AND LATIN ROOTS

Directions: Again, memorize the common root with its original meaning. Notice how the original meaning helps explain the English word. Look up any word you do not know in your dictionary. Then jot down any other examples you can think of.

	Root	*Original Meaning*	*English Example*	*Your Examples*
1.	mania	madness, derangement	maniacal	________________
			nymphomania	________________
2.	manus	hand	manuscript	________________
			manacle	________________
3.	*metr	measure	seismometer	________________
			metrology	________________
4.	micro	small	microbe	________________
			microelectronics	________________
5.	*mit, miss	to send	intermittent	________________
			missive	________________
6.	mono	one	monogamy	________________
			monochrome	________________
7.	mor	dead	mortal	________________
			morgue	________________
8.	ocul	eye	binocular	________________
			monocle	________________
9.	*path	feeling, suffering	pathos	________________
			pathologist	________________
10.	ped	foot	pedestal	________________
			impediment	________________
11.	pel, puls	drive	propel	________________
			impulse	________________
12.	*phil, philo	to love	philander	________________
			philharmonic	________________
13.	*phobia	fear	hydrophobia	________________
			acrophobia	________________
14.	*phon	sound	phoneme	________________
			phonology	________________
15.	*photo	light	photosynthesis	________________
			photophobia	________________
16.	pod	foot	podium	________________
			tripod	________________
17.	*poly	many	polysyllable	________________
			polytechnic	________________
18.	pon, pos	to place	component	________________
			transpose	________________

19. *popul	people	populace	________
		populous	________
20. *port	to carry	portfolio	________
		rapport	________

*Also presented in *Reading Faster and Understanding More, Book I* and included here for review.

Exercise

Directions: Using your knowledge of the original meaning of the root, choose the answer most closely related to the italicized word. Write the letter of the answer in the blank. Do not look at the list until you have finished.

_____ **1.** My blind date was a bore; she carried on a constant *monologue* throughout the evening.
(a) conversation with strangers **(b)** pleasing chat **(c)** long, uninterrupted speech

_____ **2.** *Vox populi* is a term that means voice of the
(a) people **(b)** government **(c)** pope

_____ **3.** Her strong sense of ambition *compels* me to rest a lot.
(a) forbids **(b)** pays **(c)** drives

_____ **4.** Certain skin diseases respond well to *phototherapy.*
(a) chemicals **(b)** light **(c)** sound

_____ **5.** The king was recently *deposed* from his throne.
(a) removed **(b)** suffering from an illness **(c)** praised

_____ **6.** A *bibliophile* is a person who _____ books.
(a) mends **(b)** writes **(c)** loves

_____ **7.** The ideas in that book are dull and *pedestrian.*
(a) plodding **(b)** quoted often **(c)** sharply defined

_____ **8.** The *emissary* of the king is here and will not stop talking.
(a) messenger sent by another **(b)** foreign affairs officer **(c)** official historian

_____ **9.** She *manipulated* the cards so well everyone thought she was a gambler.
(a) bet **(b)** read **(c)** handled

_____ **10.** His thoughts have become *morbid* ever since he got that "D" on his assignment.
(a) about revenge **(b)** about death **(c)** about vacation

_____ **11.** The word *geometry* literally means _____ of the earth.
(a) division **(b)** measurement **(c)** worship

_____ **12.** She would have had a better time on their date if he weren't such an *egomaniac*. [*Ego* means "I."]
(a) independent and self-sufficient **(b)** suffering from poor eyesight **(c)** overly concerned with himself

_____ **13.** The psychiatrist helped him to overcome his many *phobias*.
(a) experiences **(b)** fears **(c)** problems

_____ **14.** He thought an *oculist* might discover the cause of his headaches.
(a) ear-nose-and-throat doctor **(b)** eye doctor **(c)** specialist in brain disorders

_____ **15.** My mother has a lot of *empathy* for other people.
(a) helpful advice **(b)** identification with feelings **(c)** secret anger

_____ **16.** Even though he often puts his foot in his mouth, he has never had to visit a *podiatrist*.
(a) nutritionist **(b)** speech therapist **(c)** foot doctor

_____ **17.** A *polygon* is a figure with _____ sides.
(a) seven **(b)** many **(c)** three

_____ **18.** Instead of keeping stacks of old newspapers, libraries usually put the information on *microfilm*.
(a) on tiny filmstrips **(b)** on recording tape **(c)** on large-screen television

_____ **19.** If our language had a *phonetic* spelling system, few people would make spelling errors.
(a) based on sound **(b)** based on historical developments **(c)** based on visual aspects

_____ **20.** Although her *deportment* is conventional, her ideas are sensational.
(a) way of carrying or conducting oneself **(b)** section or subdivision of an office **(c)** educational background

Check the answers with your instructor and record your score below.

% CORRECT _____

STILL MORE GREEK AND LATIN ROOTS

Directions: By this time you have begun to understand just how much our English language owes to the influence of Greek and Latin. Here are twenty more roots to add to your growing foundation. Again, memorize the root with its original meaning. Look up any word you do not know in your dictionary. Then jot down any other examples you can think of.

Root	*Original Meaning*	*English Example*	*Your Examples*
1. *psych	mind	psychoanalysis	__________
		psychopath	__________
2. rupt	to break	bankrupt	__________
		disrupt	__________
3. *scrib, script	to write	scribe	__________
		nondescript	__________
4. sect	to cut	insect	__________
		vivisect	__________
5. *sens, sent	to feel	sensation	__________
		sentient	__________
6. *spec, spect	to look at	spectrum	__________
		perspective	__________
7. spir	to breathe	inspire	__________
		conspire	__________
8. tain, ten	to hold	container	__________
		tenet	__________
9. *tele	distant	telecast	__________
		telekinesis	__________
10. *tempor	time	extemporaneous	__________
		temporal	__________
11. tend, tens	to stretch	extend	__________
		attention	__________
12. terra	earth	terrestrial	__________
		inter	__________
13. the	god	theology	__________
		atheist	__________
14. *therm	heat	thermal	__________
		thermodynamics	__________
15. vene, vent	to come	revenue	__________
		adventure	__________
16. vers, vert	to turn	anniversary	__________
		convert	__________
17. *vid, vis	to see	providence	__________
		visionary	__________

18. *viv, vit	to live, life	vivacious	________
		vital	________
19. *voc, vocat	to call	evoke	________
		avocation	________
20. volens	wishing, willing	volunteer	________
		benevolence	________

*Also presented in *Reading Faster and Understanding More, Book I* and included here for review.

Exercise

Directions: Using your knowledge of the original meaning of the root, choose the answer most closely related to the italicized word. Write the letter of the answer in the blank. Do not look back at the list until you have finished.

______ **1.** The general sent out an *invocation* for assistance.
(a) call **(b)** battalion **(c)** strategist

______ **2.** He longs to be on *terra firma* once again.
(a) the lake **(b)** the earth **(c)** the farm

______ **3.** To climb Mt. Whitney requires enormous *vitality.*
(a) liveliness and energy **(b)** muscular development **(c)** experience and courage

______ **4.** Be careful or you'll *rupture* that line!
(a) twist **(b)** drop **(c)** break

______ **5.** The *vista* before us had the beauty of a painting by Joseph Turner.
(a) lakeshore **(b)** view **(c)** attractive woman

______ **6.** Despite the difficulty of getting into medical school, she is *tenacious* in her desire to be a doctor.
(a) confident **(b)** uncertain **(c)** holding strong to

______ **7.** *Thermopane* glass is not a good conductor of ______.
(a) light **(b)** moisture **(c)** heat

______ **8.** Members of the delegation will *convene* at 3:00 P.M. in the bar.
(a) vote **(b)** meet **(c)** depart

______ **9.** Much to his pleasure he was named president *pro tem* of the service club.
(a) honorary **(b)** elect **(c)** for the time being

______ **10.** Whenever he winked at her, she would *avert* her eyes and groan.
(a) blink **(b)** turn away **(c)** widen

______ **11.** A *teletypewriter* is for material ______.
(a) to be used on television **(b)** that is transmitted from or sent afar **(c)** typed at extremely high speeds

______ **12.** With great zest he began to *dissect* the frog.
(a) cut up **(b)** eat **(c)** catch

______ **13.** Because of the hero's constant *introspection,* the play did not have much action in the first act. [*Intro* means "within."]
(a) love duets with the heroine **(b)** serious illness **(c)** soul searching

______ **14.** Most paper is unsuitable for making clothing because it lacks *tensile* strength.
(a) waterproof **(b)** fire-resistant **(c)** stretching

______ **15.** He was *insensible* to the fact he was standing on my hand.
(a) aware **(b)** unaware **(c)** unconcerned about

______ **16.** Except for a few *respiratory* problems, he is in excellent health.
(a) stomach **(b)** breathing **(c)** back

______ **17.** He asked for the *typescript* of the trial.
(a) tape-recording **(b)** news photos **(c)** typed copy

______ **18.** "Should you marry me," said the aging duke to the young woman, "I insist it be of your own *volition*."
(a) love **(b)** free will **(c)** need

______ **19.** *Psychosis* is a serious illness of the ______.
(a) liver **(b)** heart **(c)** mind

______ **20.** Maria is a *polytheist.*
(a) member of the union **(b)** believer in many gods **(c)** many talented student

Check your answers with your instructor and record your score below.

% CORRECT ______

HOMEWORK—LESSON 8

PREFIXES

In Lessons 4, 5, 6, and 7 you discovered the idea of word parts. You also learned some common root words that English has borrowed from Greek and Latin. Our Word Animal so far has only a body ⊏⊐. Now we will add a head! The word "prefix" is itself an example of a word made up of a root plus a prefix, or a P-R combination:

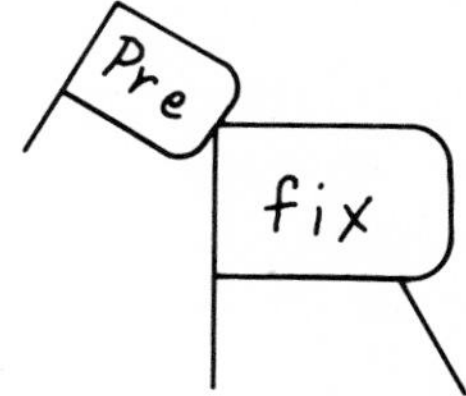

The head of an animal precedes, or goes before, the body. So what does "pre-" mean? ______ A prefix adds to, modifies, or reverses the meaning of the root.

TWENTY COMMON PREFIXES

Directions: Memorize this list of common prefixes, with their original meanings. Just as in root words, the original meaning of each prefix helps you understand the English word. Jot down any other examples you can think of. (Note: Prefixes seldom are usable English words by themselves. That is why they are listed here with hyphens.)

	Prefix	*Original Meaning*	*English Example*	*Your Examples*
1.	ab-	away from, down	abnormal, abate	______ ______
2.	ad-	to, toward	addict, adhere	______ ______
3.	ambi-, amphi-	on both sides, around	ambiguous amphitheater	______ ______
4.	arch-	chief, principal	archangel, archbishop	______ ______
5.	bi-	two	biannual, bifocals	______ ______
6.	circum-	around	circumnavigate, circumspect	______ ______
7.	con-, com-	with, together	congregate commence	______ ______

8. extra-	outside, beyond	extraneous, extradite	______ ______
9. inter-	among, between	interject, intermingle	______ ______
10. mal	bad, wrong	malice, maladjusted	______ ______
11. *in- (im-, il-, ir-) [in- may also mean inside]	not, opposite of	ineligible impeccable illegitimate irreligious	______ ______ ______ ______
12. *a-	not, without	amoral, atypical	______
13. *dis- [dis- may also mean apart]	not	dissimilar, disinterested	______ ______ ______
14. *un-	not	unreal, unlikely	______
15. *non-	not	nonproductive, nonaddictive	______
16. *in- [in- may also mean not]	inside, within	ingest, indebted	______ ______ ______
17. *intra-	inside, within	intramuscular, intramural	______
18. *e-, ex-	out, away from	egress exhale	______ ______
19. *de-	away, down	depart, depress	______
20. *dis-	apart	dismember, disperse	

*Also presented in *Reading Faster and Understanding More, Book I* and included here for review.

Exercise

Directions: Using your knowledge of the original meaning of the prefix, choose the answer most closely related to the italicized word. Write the letter of the answer in the blank. Do not look back at the list until you have finished.

______ **1.** The teacher said there were many *extraneous* ideas in my paper.
(a) deeply pondered **(b)** unusual **(c)** off the subject

______ **2.** For a speech teacher, he is almost *inarticulate.*
(a) not well spoken **(b)** overly talkative **(c)** having an accent

______ **3.** If you ask for her help, you will hear a great deal of sweet *circumlocution.*
(a) swearing **(b)** beating about the point **(c)** well-expressed eagerness

______ **4.** Formerly governments would *decapitate* lawbreakers.
(a) burn at the stake **(b)** cut off the head **(c)** put in the stocks

_____ **5.** If I say that I can *commiserate* with your misfortune, I mean that I _____.
(a) can comment on it objectively **(b)** sympathize with you **(c)** am glad it did not happen to me

_____ **6.** He would like to have that blemish *excised.*
(a) cut away **(b)** hidden **(c)** beautified

_____ **7.** A *binary* star is composed of _____ parts.
(a) two **(b)** ten **(c)** one hundred

_____ **8.** An *intracardiac* problem would be located _____ the heart.
(a) next to **(b)** under **(c)** inside

_____ **9.** My *archenemy* gives me reason to live.
(a) friend **(b)** former enemy **(c)** chief enemy

_____ **10.** After her *incarceration* was over, she began to live a successful life.
(a) being jailed in **(b)** graduation **(c)** medical operation

_____ **11.** My feelings about snakes are *ambivalent.*
(a) firmly decided **(b)** both for and against **(c)** negative

_____ **12.** Because of an allergy, she must wear things that are *nonmetallic.*
(a) man-made **(b)** not metal **(c)** plastic or metal

_____ **13.** "If you wish to be successful," said the famous musician, "you must not blindly *adhere* to the rules."
(a) stick to **(b)** ignore **(c)** revise in your favor

_____ **14.** He persists in believing that he is *unaccountable* for his bad luck.
(a) not responsible **(b)** deserving **(c)** about to change

_____ **15.** His brother always *interceded* for him when he got in trouble.
(a) was glad **(b)** pleaded his case **(c)** was sorry

_____ **16.** She is *disinclined* to change her opinion.
(a) not ready to **(b)** about to **(c)** known

_____ **17.** If I wish a *malady* upon you, I am hoping you have
(a) wealth **(b)** an illness **(c)** a good journey

_____ **18.** That movie was totally *asexual.*
(a) sexually suggestive **(b)** nonsexual **(c)** against sex

_____ **19.** The king *abdicated* his throne.
(a) secured the safety of **(b)** stepped up to **(c)** stepped down from

_____ **20.** He floats around as if he were *disembodied.*
(a) in a trance **(b)** removed from his body **(c)** on a natural high

Check the answers with your instructor and record your score below.

% CORRECT _____

NINETEEN ADJECTIVE SUFFIXES AND ONE ADVERB SUFFIX

In Lesson 10, you learned some (but not all!) of the suffixes that show a word is being used as a noun—electric*ian,* fix*er,* fix*ation,* national*ism,* and so on. In Lesson 11, you learned most of the verb suffixes that show a word is being used as an action word or a verb—electr*ify,* fix*ate,* national*ize,* and so on. This last group of suffixes is used to show that a word is being used as either an adjective or adverb.

Again, we should review what is meant by an adjective and an adverb. They are words that modify (describe) other words. An adjective describes a noun or pronoun; an adverb describes a verb, adjective, or another adverb. An adverb indicates how, when, where, why, or to what degree.

As in the last lesson, we can take a skeleton sentence and add an adjective and an adverb like this:

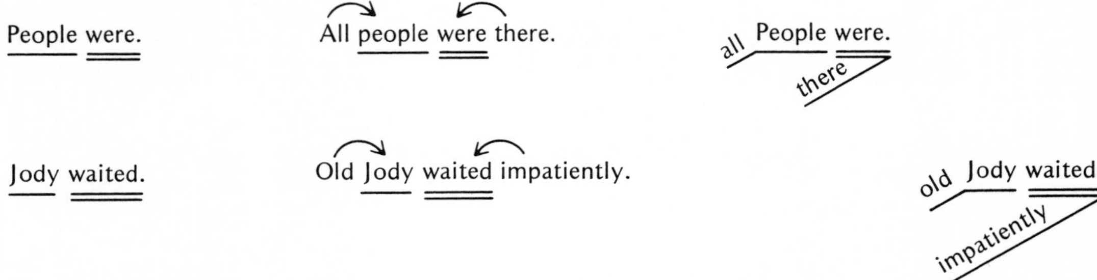

Is the adjective "old" in that sentence a root word, or does it also have a prefix and suffix? What about the adverb "impatiently"? If you say that "im" is a prefix and "ly" is a suffix, you have kept on top of the vocabulary building exercises so far.

Do you remember, from Lesson 10, the problem some students face when they want to describe a person as "wordy," "wordish," "wordal," "wordic," or "wordive"? These are all possible adjective endings, describing a noun, and English has so many that it is easy to be confused. Sometimes the only way to make the choice is to read and listen until "the *ear* knows." As in the noun suffixes in Lesson 10, as many as possible are grouped together by similar meaning.

Luckily, the adverb ending in English is usually "-ly," so you can learn that one easily and quickly. (Stop and underline carefully the adverb endings that have evidently been carefully and pointedly added in this paragraph!)

Nineteen Adjective Suffixes

Directions: Memorize this list of adjective suffixes, with their meanings. Study the examples and jot down any additional examples you can think of.

Adjective Suffix	Meaning	Examples	Your Examples
1. *-er	comparative (of two)	naughtier, tenser	
2. *-est	superlative (of more than two)	naughtiest, tensest	
3. *-able, -ible	able to be	durable, incorrigible	
4. -oid	in the form of	anthropoid, ovoid	
5. -esque	having the nature of	picturesque, romanesque	
6. *-ic, -ish	having the nature of	phonic, manic	
7. *-ish	having the nature of	feverish, reddish	
8. -ose, -ous	having the nature of	morose, glamorous	
9. *-tious, -cious	having the nature of	nutritious, suspicious	
10. *-ive, -ative	having the nature of	restive, curative	
11. *-ant, -ent	having the nature of	redundant, effervescent	
12. -ac, *-an, -al	having the nature of	maniac, partisan, abdominal,	
13. *-ar	having the nature of	solar, familiar	
14. -some	having the nature of	winsome, loathsome	
15. -fic	having the nature of	specific, soporific	
16. *-y, -ly	having the nature of	earthy, scholarly	
17. *-ful	full of	fanciful, artful	
18. *-less	without, free of	restless, artless	
19. -ward	direction	homeward, leeward	
	One Adverb Suffix		
20. *-ly	in a certain manner	humanely incorrigibly fancifully winsomely picturesquely	

Note: While most *-ly* endings are adverbs, a small group of words ending in *-ly* are adjectives: homely, brotherly, friendly, lively, leisurely, and so on.

*Also presented in *Reading Faster and Understanding More, Book I* and included here for review.

Exercise 1 — Adjective Suffixes

Directions: Choose the best adjective suffix for the word in parentheses and write the entire word in the blank, changing the spelling if necessary. Example: that (moment) momentous day

1. her (girl) ________________ charms

2. a (cellulose) ________________ film

3. a (democracy) ________________ organization

4. the (fruit) ________________ endeavor

5. his (continue) ____________ resistance
6. an (unforget) ____________ character
7. a (destruct) ____________ kit
8. a (mourn) ____________ sound
9. an (impression) ____________ young man
10. the (smart) ____________ brother [comparing two]
11. a (fever) ____________ pace
12. a (fire) ____________ temper
13. a (back) ____________ glance
14. the (weary) ____________ task
15. a (without *fear*) ____________ attitude
16. a (scholar) ____________ essay
17. an (amateur) ____________ performance
18. a (love) ____________ lass
19. a (specify) ____________ song
20. a (burden) ____________ undertaking
21. (commune) ____________ living
22. the (able to *restore*) ____________ powers
23. a (nutrition) ____________ repast
24. a (seduce) ____________ look
25. an (admire) ____________ cathedral
26. an (elude) ____________ quality
27. the (witty) ____________ sister [comparing three]
28. a (care) ____________ remark
29. a (knight) ____________ quest
30. a (quarter) ____________ report

Exercise 2 — Adverb Suffixes

Directions: Attach the adverb suffix to the word in parentheses and write the entire word in the blank.* In some cases the word in the blank is a noun and must first be given an adjective suffix before the adverb suffix can be added.
Example: to write (fancy) fancifully

1. is (athletic) ________________ fit
2. inquires (full of *purpose*) ________________
3. kisses (loving) ________________
4. is (hypnotic) ________________ charming
5. to be (instant) ________________ regretful
6. to admit (public) ________________
7. to be rude (period) ________________
8. was (impossible) ________________ true
9. will (like) ________________ rain
10. to address (similar) ________________
11. a (nutrition) ________________ prepared meal
12. an (incredible) ________________ easy problem
13. to speak (hurry) ________________
14. please (kind) ________________ forward
15. a (time) ________________ topic
16. he talks (matter-of-fact) ________________
17. he (witty) ________________ comments
18. (without *fear*) ________________ charges ahead
19. to sweat (continue) ________________
20. she is (happy) ________________ married

Check the answers with your instructor and record your score below.

% CORRECT ________

*Spelling tip: If you add *ly* to words ending in *y*, usually you change the *y* to *i*. Example: *busy* + *ly* = *busily*.

Posttests

COMPREHENSION AND RATE POSTTEST

LENGTH: 1628

Read the following selection as rapidly as you can but with good comprehension. Wait for a signal from your instructor before you begin reading.

I Was a Speed-Reading Dropout

J. M. Flagler

If, since beginning this article, you have already finished it, you are a speed reader.

In the past few fast-paced years, courses in rapid reading have spread throughout the land, both on campus and off. Human word-devouring machines have been churned out by the hundred thousand. As I see it, all this bodes no good for writers. When I do an article, I prefer the reader to hang around it for a while. Stay. Sift your fingers through the rare coin of my syntax. Gambol—barefoot, if you will—in the rich meadows of metaphor. Let's not race over my brilliantly (not to say painfully) wrought points.

The fact is, though, I am probably fighting the tide of history. Never has the eye been washed with a greater outpouring of printed matter, from new books (more than 30,000 a year in the United States alone) to thick reports by corporate subcommittees on *The Feasibility of Installing Plasticine Soap Dishes in Executive Washrooms.* At the same time, never has the eye been more loath to read. If television doesn't make words obsolete, the speed-reading movement may.

Most speed-reading systems seem to regard words as but pesky obstacles to reading. They advocate wolfing them down in clumps. "Why savor words?" said one speed-reading school executive. . . . Why savor words? Well, for one thing, some of them give a good deal of pleasure. The word "savor," for instance. Roll it around on the tongue. Savory, isn't it? Still, it must be conceded that the vast majority of printed pages are as indigestible as cold french fries. It is also undoubtedly true that the method by which we are taught to read in grade school serves many of us poorly in our attempt to keep up with the flood of required reading, let alone reading for enjoyment and personal enlightenment. There are almost as many reading theories as there are reading experts. However, most seem to agree that the traditional reading-aloud system so long and so securely established in schools leaves many of us with the bad habit of subvocalization. In other words, later in life, we continue to "read aloud," but under our breath. Insecurely, we also tend to read back over words; 10 to 14 "regressions" a page is typical. Emotional hang-ups caused by early reading anxieties may help slow us even more. The national reading-rate average is 250 words a minute; the average for college graduates only 350.

We are for the time being stuck with the printed word as the chief instrument for transmitting knowledge. It therefore stands to reason that we could do well to read faster (except when reading articles about speed reading). Some college-based reading-improvement experts believe 600 to 800 words is a realistic national average goal. On the face of it then, a speed-reading course is as logical a response to a felt need as a hat factory. With this wisdom in mind, I recently signed up for a course myself. As a writer, I can sulk all I want about words getting short shrift, but the fact is that I am also a reader, and not a consistently fast reader. . . .

I decided to sign on with one of the [Evelyn Wood's Reading Dynamics] institutes, partly because of the name, with its suggestions of Charles Atlas and "Dynamic Tension." No longer would 98-pound weaklings kick literary sand in my face at cocktail parties, simply because I was lagging behind in reading. . . .

. . . I have always been puzzled, not to say chagrined, by the curious flaw in my reading ability that made me take an age to get through any book read for pleasure and nonprofit. Since I started *War and Peace,* there have been three wars and even a few periods of peace, and I'm still slogging through the book. Speed-reading success stories served to inflame my interest. I knew of one graduate who tossed off a novel every morning on his bus ride to work from uptown to Midtown Manhattan. Riffling through pages like a gambler through a deck of cards, he had the satisfaction of astounding his fellow passengers, as they barely groped past page one of their newspapers. . . .

. . . [Reading Dynamic's] guarantee—to triple reading rate or money back—seems like a fairly safe bet, as far as I am concerned. By the end of my first class, I had jumped my achievable word-per-minute rate from a measly 345 to 1,300!

Actually, classwork plays a minor part in the speed-reading time-work schedule. You pay largely for the privilege of doing homework—an hour a day minimum, six days a week, for the two and one-half hour weekly class. The Evelyn Wood course takes eight weeks to complete, and is conducted in a typical bare classroom. . . . A shirt-sleeved young male instructor with an antiseptically modern, brightly lit teaching style presided over a class of 20, largely salesmen and students. From the first moment, he plunged us into our subject at a cheerlessly relentless pace. "It hurts, but it works," he said of the course.

In short order, I could see what he meant by the first part of the statement. For one thing, the basic tool of speed reading is the hand. (A slew of paperback books, a pencil and/or pen, a good deal of self-discipline and free time, and anywhere from $150 to $275 are among the other prerequisites for the usual triple-your-speed course.) . . .

"Use the hand as a pacer," we were urged—seemingly at every turn of a page—either to underline or to make sweeps, loops, "lazy L's," or "G whorls." All these gestures are designed to hasten the sluggard eye down a page or column. After the first class, my hand began to develop reader's cramp.

The two and one-half hours flew by, but not the demanded hour of homework for each of the next six days. Homework involves more than simply practicing with a different paperback book each night. I found also that a considerable amount of time was required to digest the mess of directions that I had bolted down in class. Then, too, homework required written comments on each segment we read from the paperback books. Conceivably, if normal academic contemplation were employed, the course could have taken a college semester. As it was, an hour's homework invariably came closer to two for this long-time refugee from scholastic discipline. The curdling of my disposition was correspondingly doubled by the end of the week.

Not that the technique didn't begin to pay off. In fact, I had gone through only three class sessions when laboring over home studies one evening I found myself racing through *Moby Dick* at 5,000 words a minute. Since my previous practice high had been someting like 2,700 words and faltering, I assumed that I had misread my watch. A careful recheck proved that I *was* reading at 5,000 words.

At that point, the realization crept up on me that for the first time in my scattered academic life, I would not make the grade. I was heading hell-bent to becoming a speed-reading dropout. For, as my reading rate escalated, comprehension seemed to fall rapidly. (Classroom tests indicated that it was no worse than standing still, but I was having more trouble recalling details for my written homework reports than a witness at a five-car accident.) I even became alarmed that, as the rate approached the rapid-reading equivalent of the speed of light, perhaps knowledge already accrued would be drained out of my system. On top of that, I was reading more but enjoying it less. Both nerves and muscles tensed as I whizzed a frozen clawlike hand through the pages. It was a matter—in humorist Gordon Cotler's phrase—of coiling up with a good book.

Finally, my conscience as a writer began to creep into play. It was all well and good to race through J. Edgar Hoover's *Masters of Deceit* at a four-minute-mile pace. Hoover has a job other than writing to fall back on. But when I found myself completing John Steinbeck's *The Pearl* in 11 minutes, I felt like a traitor to the cause. If a fellow professional puts in months, years, on a book, who am I to dishonor the effort by tossing it

______ **34.** People with the gift of gab are seldom *articulate.*

______ **35.** I am *complacent* in my job and am not looking for another.

______ **36.** Michael, an avid party-goer, loves to *fraternize.*

______ **37.** When she is motionless, she *gesticulates* frequently.

______ **38.** Filled with *remorse,* she promised not to break the law again.

______ **39.** He certainly is an *adept* surgeon; eight out of ten patients he operates on die.

______ **40.** The dress was too *gaudy* with its loud colors and rhinestone trim.

E. Roots, Prefixes, and Suffixes—Matching, 41-50

In the blank at the left, write the letter of the best definition for the root, prefix, or suffix.

Roots

______ **41.** cult	**(a)** war
______ **42.** bellum	**(b)** to lead
______ **43.** mono	**(c)** to stretch
______ **44.** tend, tens	**(d)** to care for
______ **45.** duc, duct	**(e)** one

Prefixes and Suffixes

______ **46.** -arium, -orium	**(a)** to make or cause to be (verb)
______ **47.** mal-	**(b)** on both sides, around
______ **48.** ambi-	**(c)** direction (adj.)
______ **49.** -ize	**(d)** a place for (noun)
______ **50.** -ward	**(e)** bad, wrong

Check your answers with your instructor and record your score below and on the progress chart in the Appendix.

% CORRECT ______

Finally, contrast the results of the Pretest and the Posttest.

Appendix

The Process of Reading

Reading is an advanced and relatively recent development in the history of language. The total reading process is very complex. It involves the whole self of the reader: memory, experience, brain, knowledge, language ability, psychological and emotional states, and, of course, the sensory input through the eyes.

This last, a purely physical act, is probably the best known of any of the factors that operate during reading. Vision, movements of the eye muscles, and movements of the lips or throat are fairly easy to study. But how can you process words, thoughts, and images that occur in the vast computer that is the human brain? In the description that follows, you should bear in mind that the physical part of reading, while essential, is only a small part of the total process of reading. Usually, faulty eye movements are not the cause of poor comprehension. Rather, the reverse is true! Poor comprehension and lack of purpose cause faulty eye movements and poor reading techniques.

However, the physical process by itself is interesting because most of us have misconceptions about what our eyes are doing when we read. We all know in a *general* way what we are doing. For example, we all know that we are decoding—translating a code made up of twenty six imperfect squiggles into English sounds that we've heard since infancy. We know that in reading English we unravel the code from left to right across the page, move down to the next line, decode from left to right again, and so on. We know that spaces, capital letters, headings, indenting, and little marks called punctuation help us translate the familiar words into thought units. These thought units range in length from one single word, such as "never," to longer units, made up of phrases, clauses, sentences, paragraphs, chapters or articles, and novels.

Also, if English is our native language, it is natural for us to process the words in sequence from the beginning of the sentence to the end, left to right. It is natural to grasp ideas from the *way* words are arranged. For example, words form patterns. One is the noun-verb combination. Another is signal words (a, the, big, pretty) before nouns and another is helper words (will, are, has) before verbs. It is natural to sense the difference between important or key words (nouns and verbs) and unimportant or function words (articles, prepositions, conjunctions).

But as we are doing all this, we are probably unaware of the *specific* movements of our eyes. How do our eyes work as we are decoding? Do good readers sweep their eyes smoothly across the line? (We can hardly feel the tiny movements in our own eyes, nor should we. Too much self-analysis simply makes us feel cross-eyed—to say nothing of causing a comprehension loss.)

One way to find out how our eyes work is to watch another reader closely as he reads for meaning. For example, watch him as he silently reads any of the paragraphs below. You can probably see the reader's eye muscles make tiny jerks and stops as he reads across the page. Then his eyes make a longer jerk back to the beginning of the next line. You may even see a slight jerk backward on the same line. The eyes do not read when they make these jerks, but see only a blur or streak. The eyes function this way for either poor or good readers. The correct terminology for some of these eye movements and other activities is contained in the following list.

Fixation is the point along the line of print at which the eyes stop for a fraction of a second. The eyes now actually "see" the letters. We read when the eyes fix. Fixations take up about 90 percent of our reading time; therefore we should practice to make the most of each fixation or "stop." The more words we can see at each fixation, the fewer we need make along the line, and the less we strain our eye muscles. Acuity, or sharpness, is best at the point of focus. Acuity decreases from that point outward. But healthy eyes can recognize many surrounding letters through peripheral vision.

Peripheral Vision is the ability to see around the point of focus. Both our vertical (above and below) and our horizontal (left and right) peripheral vision is useful. We use it to combine *what was just read* with *what is now seen* with *what is going to be read.*

Eye Span is the entire field of recognition. It can be increased by doing eye exercises. The maximum eye span at near point, such as in reading a book, is about twenty-nine letter spaces, or 2¼ inches in diameter. To test your own peripheral vision and eye span, draw a circle (larger than a half dollar) in the paragraph below. Make an *x* in the middle of the circle. Then fixate on the *x*. Without moving your eyes from the *x*, notice how many letters within the circle are clear, how many are recognizable, and how many you must guess from their context.

Return Sweep is the long eye movement from the end of one line to the beginning of the next. Accuracy is essential, to avoid skipping or repeating a line. And speed is important to increase rate.

Regression is the term for the tiny eye movement backward to a part of the print already read. It is a fixation in reverse (from right to left). Some regressing is normal as we read difficult material. But constant regressing in average material means a slower rate, a lack of concentration, a low level of comprehension, low self-confidence, or just a nervous habit.

Vocalizing and Head Movement are reading habits that are unnecessary and tiring for all but young children. Vocalizing is mumbling, whispering, or moving the lips during what is supposed to be silent reading. It shows that you depend on spoken language to get meaning from written symbols. Head movement is wasted motion. Move only your eyes.

Subvocalizing is "inner speech" or "hearing the words in your head." Although no sound emerges, the tension in the throat muscles can be picked up by sensitive instruments. It is generally thought to slow the mental process in reading, but many excellent readers who read rapidly or skim at 800 words per minute and up state that they still manage to "hear" selected words.

Checklist of Observable Clues to Vision Problems*

1. Appearance of eyes:

______ One eye turns in or out at any time

______ Reddened eyes or lids

______ Eyes tear excessively

______ Encrusted eyelids

______ Frequent styes on lids

2. Complaints when using eyes at desk

______ Headaches in forehead or temples

______ Burning or itching after reading or desk work

______ Nausea or dizziness

______ Print blurs after reading a short time

3. Behavioral signs of visual problems

A. Eye movement abilities (ocular motility)

______ Head turns as reads across page or watches screen

______ Loses place often in reading

______ Needs finger or marker to keep place

______ Short attention span in reading or copying

______ Often omits words in silent or oral reading

______ Repeatedly omits "small" words

______ Writes up or downhill on paper

______ Rereads or skips lines unknowingly in book or machine-scored answer sheets

B. Eye teaming abilities (binocularity)

______ Sees double

______ Repeats letters within words

______ Omits letters, numbers, or phrases

______ Squints, frowns, blinks excessively, or covers one eye

*Adapted from a checklist prepared by B. C. Jander, O.D., College of Optometrists in Vision Development, P. O. Box 285, Chula Vista, California 92012; and a checklist from The Primary Visual Abilities Essential to Academic Achievement, Optometric Extension Program Foundation, Inc., Duncan, Oklahoma 73533.

_______ Tilts head extremely while reading book or on screen

C. Eye-hand coordination abilities

_______ Write crookedly, poorly spaced; cannot stay on ruled lines

_______ Misaligns both horizontal and vertical series of numbers

_______ Uses hand or fingers to keep place on page

_______ Repeatedly confuses left-right directions

_______ Must "feel" things to "see" them

D. Visual form perception

_______ Mistakes words with same or similar beginnings

_______ Reverses letters and/or words in reading, writing and copying

_______ Fails to visualize what is read, either silently or orally

_______ Whispers to self for reinforcement while reading silently

E. Refractive status (nearsightedness, farsightedness, focus problems, etc.)

_______ Comprehension decreases as reading continues; loses interest too quickly

_______ Blinks excessively at reading, not elsewhere

_______ Holds book too close

_______ Makes errors in copying from chalkboard to paper, or from reference book to paper

_______ Squints to see screen or chalkboard, or must move very near

_______ Rubs eyes during or after short periods of visual activity

4. General physical complaints

_______ Headaches, body tension, nail biting, etc., when reading for more than a half hour

_______ Tires easily when reading

_______ Gets car-sick

_______ Generally poor motor coordination

Perceptual Drill 1

1. Circle the *cl* combination each time you see it. (Example: claw.) Write your time and number of errors at the end of each drill.
   (a) climb call click casual callow cold calf collar
   (b) casual clench chorus clack cull climber lick
   (c) lull clam calorie calcium calendar clear cling
   (d) calm clearly walk clan close curl closet clef
   (e) club aisle acclaim clone acrid claim clothes clue
   (f) chick claw clasp clean crass class calk clumsy
   (g) chink clink cancel clap clamp clunker chorus acclimate

TIME ________

ERRORS ________

2. Circle the *st* combination each time you see it. (Example: post)
   (a) sting sat string past tryst mask astir sty strap
   (b) stud haste sister satrap straight Steve inset
   (c) astra fast finest misstep visit hasty studying
   (d) stone staple rest restaple restive host strange
   (e) worst slit instant insert resist step story just
   (f) restaple retain ask must story stain unspoiled
   (g) listen stampede asked trust often strength star

TIME ________

ERRORS ________

3. Have someone read out loud to you one word from line (a). Point to it as quickly as you can. Continue through each line in both drills.

Perceptual Drill 2

To expand your peripheral vision horizontally (left and right), fix your eyes on the dot in the middle of each line in each pyramid. Try to see the figures or words on each side of the dot. As your eyes move vertically down each pyramid, *stretch* your eye span until the outside corners of your eyes tingle.

1.

4
341
82453
9264516
827141623
91452438996

2.

b
s s
pr b l
y b ro
lk b e t
e y b n no s

3.

A
bi-
ped
is an
animal
that goes
on two legs
such as a man
or a woman or birds
or some trick horses.

4.

1
+ 1
= 2;
and two
rabbits
can make
more rabbits
than you ever wanted.

5.

A
gnu
is an
antelope
that is also
called a wildebeest.

6.

A
gnu
gets
its name
from the
Kaffir word
"nqu," or would
you rather call it
by its proper Latin name
which is a Connochaetes taurinus?

Perceptual Drill 3

To expand your peripheral vision vertically (above and below):

1. Fixate on the black dot and try to read the items above and below it.

				faster
		9	form	latter
	7	1	for	madder
4	2	0	if	harder
•	•	•	•	•
8	6	5	I	banner
	3	7	in	dinner
		8	mine	shiner
				winter

2. Fixate on each dot and try to read the items above and below it.

Yeung D S
Yewell Frank
•
Yglesias Terry
Yhookas Pancho
•
Yi Chung Loo
Yick James
Yim Archibald
•
Yinger Maryanne
Yip Kate
Ylanan Agonistes
•
Ynson Yolanda
Yodo Restrt
Yoga Kundalini
•
Yogurt International
Yoh H. I. Co.

Perceptual Drill 4

1. Take an index card (or a folded piece of paper) and cover up the bottom half of the first line in the following paragraph. Try to read the line even though you see only the top half of the letters. Repeat the process on the other lines, still trying to follow the idea presented.

Comprehension simply means understanding what you read. You not only have to understand each sentence, but you have to see relationships between sentences in a paragraph, between paragraphs in a short reading, between sections in an article or chapter, between chapters in a book. You must know what topic is being discussed. You must know the main idea(s) the writer is presenting about the topic. You must follow the organization of details as the writer enlarges upon the main idea. You must keep sight of the structural scheme, the differences between the large general ideas and the small specific ideas. And you must retain or remember all or most of this, or why bother to read at all?

2. Now take the card and cover up the top half of the first line and read it again. You will notice that you get fewer clues from the shape of the bottom half of the letters. There are more differences in the configurations of the top half.

Perceptual Drill 5

1. In the following paragraph from the Introduction of this book, note how the words are arranged into natural phrase clusters. Try to fix your eyes only once per phrase (on the dot in the middle) and still follow the meaning of the paragraphs.

A person   with a rate   of less than
250 words   per minute   almost always reads
word by word.   This method   is so slow
and inefficient   that it   actually hinders
comprehension.   In learning   to read
by meaningful   word groups,   a person
enables his brain   to function   much closer to
its capacity   and almost invariably
improves his comprehension.   No matter   how hard
some people   try to ignore   the fact,   reading is
a learned process,   in which   certain techniques
operate   more successfully   than others.   No one
is born knowing   how to read;   he must
be taught.   He can be taught   well or poorly.
What most   often happens,   however   —and this
seems to be   what the   "slower, slower" people
are fighting for   —is that   he is not   taught at all.
Left to   his own devices,   he typically develops
a surprising number   of bad reading habits,
among which   is the habit   of reading   too slowly
for maximum comprehension   or enjoyment.*

*Adapted from "How Fast Should a Person Read?" by George Guomo. Adapted from *The Saturday Review*, April 21, 1962. Copyright 1962 by the Saturday Review/World, Inc.

2. In the next paragraph, many of the functional and repetitive words are missing. Only the key words remain. Try to follow the meaning of the paragraph through reading these key words.

We should not forget obvious aids
physical process reading. One, good lighting spread
evenly room, not concentrated
desk or book. Two, good posture breathing permit
oxygen reach eyes brain, area of
body uses high proportion of
total energy. Three, get plenty rest; fatigue affects
eyesight. Four, have eyes checked for defects
near-point (reading) distance year two.

Perceptual Drill 6

Look at the key unit of shapes on the left and try to find the identical unit among the units on the right. Mark the repeated unit, and work your way through the drill as rapidly as you can.

	key unit					
1.	GDP	PDG	GDP	PGD	BGD	ODP
2.	wmuv	wumv	vumw	mwuv	wmuv	wnuv
3.	$\frac{1}{2}\frac{2}{4}$	$\frac{1}{4}\frac{1}{2}$	$\frac{1}{3}\frac{1}{2}$	$\frac{1}{2}\frac{2}{3}$	$\frac{2}{1}\frac{4}{2}$	$\frac{1}{2}\frac{2}{4}$
4.	hb$\frac{1}{3}$	hb$\frac{1}{3}$	hb$\frac{1}{2}$	bh$\frac{1}{3}$	hb$\frac{2}{3}$	hp$\frac{1}{3}$
5.	+%;	=+%	%+;	+%;	+%,	+%÷
6.	8968	9868	6898	8968	8986	8936
7.	27530	27538	27530	25730	27503	03572
8.	il2x4	li2x4	il4x2	ilx42	il2x5	il2x4
9.	xxxxxx	xxxxx	xxxxxx	xxxxx	xxxxxxx	xxx
10.	XXVII	XVII	XXXVII	XXVII	XXVIII	XXVI

Note which type of symbol you found most difficult to perceive.

PERSONAL VOCABULARY LIST

Record any words and their definitions here that you missed in the Word Comprehension or Phrase Comprehension exercises.

PREFIX—ROOT—SUFFIX

Alphabetical list of word parts studied in the Homework sections, Lessons 4 through 12.

Roots

root word	meaning
1. aequus	equal, even
2. anima	breath, spirit, mind
3. *ann, enn	year
4. anthropo	man
5. *astro	star
6. *aud, audit	to hear
7. *auto	self
8. bellum	war
9. *bene	good, well
10. *bio	life
11. cap, cept	to take
12. *capit	head
13. cede, ceed	to yield, to go
14. cent	hundred
15. *chron	time
16. *civ	citizen
17. cogni	to know
18. cor	heart
19. *crat, cracy	rule
20. *cred, credit	to believe
21. cult	to care for
22. cycle	wheel, circle
23. dem	people

---

*Also presented in *Reading Faster and Understanding More, Book I* and presented here for review.

24.	dent	tooth
25.	derma	skin
26.	*dic. dict	to say, to speak
27.	duc, duct	to lead
28.	*fac, fact	to make
29.	*fin	end, to complete
30.	*gen, gene	birth, origin
31.	*geo	earth
32.	*gram	to write
33.	*graph	to write
34.	hetero	other
35.	*homo	same
36.	hydra	water
37.	*jac, ject	to throw
38.	*log, logo	word, study
39.	loqui, locut	talk
40.	luc, lus	light
41.	mania	madness, derangement
42.	manus	hand
43.	*metr	measure
44.	micro	small
45.	*mit, miss	to send
46.	mono	one
47.	mor	dead
48.	ocul	eye
49.	*path	feeling, suffering
50.	ped	foot
51.	pel, puls	drive
52.	*phil, philo	to love
53.	*phobia	fear
54.	*phon	sound
55.	*photo	light

56. pod	foot
57. *poly	many
58. pon, pos	to place
59. *popul	people
60. *port	to carry
61. *psych	mind
62. rupt	to break
63. *scrib, script	to write
64. sect	to cut
65. *sens, sent	to feel
66. *spec, spect	to look at
67. spir	to breathe
68. tain, ten	to hold
69. *tele	distant
70. *tempor	time
71. tend, tens	to stretch
72. terra	earth
73. the	god
74. *therm	heat
75. vene, vent	to come
76. vers, vert	to turn
77. *vid, vis	to see
78. *viv, vit	to live, life
79. *voc, vocat	to call
80. volens	wishing, willing

Prefixes

prefix	**meaning**
1. *a-	not, without
2. ab-	away from, down
3. ad-	to, toward
4. ambi-, amphi-	on both sides, around

5. *ante-	before
6. *anti	against
7. arch-	chief, principal
8. bi-	two
9. circum-	around
10. con-, com-	with, together
11. *contra, counter	against
12. *de-	away, down
13. *dis-	not, without
14. *dis	apart
15. *e-, ex-	out, away from
16. extra-	outside, beyond
17. *in- (im-, il-, ir-)	not
18. *in- (im-)	inside, into
19. inter-	among, between
20. *intra-	inside, within
21. *hyper-	above
22. *hypo-	under
23. mal-	bad, wrong
24. mis-	wrong, ill
25. multi-	many
26. *non-	not
27. poly-	many
28. *post-	after
29. *pre-	before
30. *pro-	for, in favor of
31. pro-	before, forward
32. re-	again, back
33. retro-	back
34. semi-	half
35. *sub-	under
36. *super-	above

37. syn-, sym-	together
38. trans-	across
39. tri-	three
40. *un-	not

Suffixes

suffix	part of speech	meaning
1. -ac, -an	adj.	having the nature of
2. *-able, -ible	adj.	able to be
3. *-an, -ian	n.	one who
4. *-ance, -ence	n.	state of, quality of
5. *-ant, -ent	n.	one who
6. *-ant, -ent	adj.	having the nature of
7. *-al, -ar	adj.	having the nature of
8. *-ary, -ory	n.	a place for
9. *-ate	v.	to make, cause to be
10. -cide	n.	killing
11. -dom	n.	place, condition
12. *-ed, -t	v.	past participle
13. -ed	adj.	having the nature of
14. *-ee	n.	one who receives an action
15. *-en	v.	to make, cause to be
16. -eer	n.	one who
17. *-er, -ar, -or	n.	one who, a thing which
18. *-er	adj.	comparative (of who)
19. -ese	n.	inhabitant of
20. -esque	adj.	having the nature of
21. -ess	n.	one who, feminine
22. *-est	adj.	superlative (of more than two)
23. -ette (-ie, -y, -let -ling, -ule)	n.	little noun

24. -fic	adj.	having the nature of
25. *-fy, -ify	v.	to make, cause to be
26. *-ful	adj.	full of
27. *-ic, *-ish	adj.	having the nature of
28. *-ing	v.	present participle
29. -ing	adj.	having the nature of
30. -itis	n.	inflammation, disease
31. *-ive, -ative	adj.	having the nature of
32. *-ize	v.	to make, cause to be
33. *-less	adj.	without, free of
34. *-ly	adv.	in a certain manner
35. *-ment	n.	state of, quality of
36. *-ness, -hood	n.	state of, quality of
37. -ose, -ous	adj.	having the nature of
38. *-s	v.	third person singular, present tense
39. *-s, -es	n.	plural of noun
40. -some	adj.	having the quality of
41. *-ship	n.	state of, quality of
42. -ster	n.	one who
43. *-tious, -cious	adj.	having the nature of
44. *-tude, -lude	n.	state of, quality of
45. *-ty, -ity	n.	state of, quality of
46. -ward	adj.	in the direction of
47. *-y, -ly	adj.	having the nature of

RATE (WPM) CHART FOR LONG READINGS

Match the Long Reading with the time taken for reading it. The number at the point these two meet is your WPM.

TIME:	1:00	1:10	1:20	1:30	1:40	1:50	2:00	2:10	2:20
Pretest	1571	1347	1178	1047	943	857	786	725	673
LR 1I	935	801	701	623	560	510	467	431	400
LR 2I	1332	1141	999	888	799	726	666	614	570
LR 3I	1539	1319	1154	1026	923	839	769	710	659
LR 4I	1282	1098	961	854	769	699	641	591	549
LR 5I	1265	1084	948	843	758	690	632	583	542
LR 6K	1241	1063	930	827	744	676	620	572	531
LR 6L	1525	1307	1143	1016	914	831	762	703	653
LR 7G	757	648	567	504	454	412	378	349	324
LR 7H	1202	1030	901	801	721	655	601	554	515
LR 8I	1682	1441	1261	1121	1009	917	841	776	720
LR 9I	1542	1321	1156	1028	925	841	771	711	660
LR 10I	1008	863	756	672	604	549	504	465	432
LR 11I	916	785	687	610	549	499	458	422	392
LR 12I	1825	1564	1368	1216	1094	995	912	842	782
Posttest	1628	1395	1221	1085	977	880	814	751	698

TIME:	2:30	2:40	2:50	3:00	3:10	3:20	3:30	3:40	3:50
Pretest	628	589	554	524	496	471	449	428	410
LR 1I	374	350	330	311	295	280	267	254	243
LR 2I	532	499	470	444	420	399	380	363	347
LR 3I	615	577	543	513	485	461	439	419	401
LR 4I	512	480	452	427	404	384	366	349	334
LR 5I	506	474	446	421	399	379	361	344	330
LR 6K	496	465	438	413	391	372	354	338	323
LR 6L	610	571	538	508	481	457	435	415	397
LR 7G	302	283	267	252	239	227	216	206	197
LR 7H	480	450	424	400	379	360	343	327	313
LR 8I	672	630	593	560	531	504	480	458	438
LR 9I	616	578	544	514	486	462	440	420	402
LR 10I	403	377	355	336	318	302	288	274	262
LR 11I	366	343	323	305	289	274	261	249	238
LR 12I	730	684	644	608	576	547	521	497	476
Posttest	650	611	574	542	513	488	465	444	425

	TIME: 4:00	4:10	4:20	4:30	4:40	4:50	5:00	5:10	5:20
Pretest	393	377	363	349	337	325	314	304	295
LR 1I	233	224	215	207	200	193	187	180	175
LR 2I	333	319	307	296	285	275	266	257	249
LR 3I	384	369	355	342	329	318	307	297	288
LR 4I	320	307	295	284	274	265	256	248	240
LR 5I	316	303	291	281	271	261	253	244	237
LR 6K	310	297	286	275	265	256	248	240	232
LR 6L	381	365	351	338	326	315	305	295	285
LR 7G	189	181	174	168	162	156	151	146	141
LR 7H	300	288	277	267	257	248	240	232	225
LR 8I	420	403	388	373	360	348	336	325	315
LR 9I	385	370	355	342	330	319	308	298	289
LR 10I	252	241	232	224	215	208	201	195	189
LR 11I	229	219	211	203	196	189	183	177	171
LR 12I	456	437	421	405	391	377	365	353	342
Posttest	407	391	376	362	349	337	326	315	305

	TIME: 5:30	5:40	5:50	6:00	6:10	6:20	6:30	6:40	6:50
Pretest	286	277	269	262	255	248	242	236	230
LR 1I	170	164	160	155	151	147	143	140	136
LR 2I	242	235	228	222	215	210	204	199	194
LR 3I	279	271	263	256	249	243	236	230	225
LR 4I	233	226	219	213	207	202	197	192	187
LR 5I	230	223	216	210	205	199	194	189	185
LR 6K	225	218	212	206	201	195	190	186	181
LR 6L	277	269	261	254	247	240	234	228	223
LR 7G	137	133	129	126	122	119	116	113	110
LR 7H	218	212	206	200	194	189	184	180	175
LR 8I	305	296	288	280	272	265	258	252	246
LR 9I	280	272	264	257	250	243	237	231	225
LR 10I	183	177	172	168	163	159	155	151	147
LR 11I	166	161	157	152	148	144	140	137	134
LR 12I	331	322	312	304	295	288	280	273	267
Posttest	296	287	279	271	264	257	250	244	238

	TIME: 7:00	7:10	7:20	7:30	7:40	7:50	8:00	8:10	8:20
Pretest	224	219	214	209	205	201	196	192	189
LR 1I	133	130	127	124	121	119	116	114	112
LR 2I	190	185	181	177	173	170	166	163	159
LR 3I	219	214	209	205	200	196	192	188	184
LR 4I	183	178	174	170	167	163	160	156	153
LR 5I	180	176	172	168	164	161	158	154	151
LR 6K	177	173	169	165	161	158	155	151	148
LR 6L	217	212	207	203	198	194	190	186	183
LR 7G	108	105	103	100	98	96	94	92	90
LR 7H	171	167	163	160	156	153	150	147	144
LR 8I	240	234	229	224	219	214	210	205	201
LR 9I	220	215	210	205	201	196	192	188	185
LR 10I	144	140	137	134	131	128	126	123	120
LR 11I	130	127	124	122	119	116	114	112	109
LR 12I	260	254	248	243	238	232	228	223	219
Posttest	232	227	222	217	212	208	204	199	195

	TIME: 8:30	8:40	8:50	9:00	9:10	9:20	9:30	9:40	9:50	10:00
Pretest	185	181	178	175	171	168	165	163	160	157
LR 1I	110	107	105	103	101	100	98	96	95	93
LR 2I	156	153	150	148	145	142	140	137	135	133
LR 3I	181	177	174	171	167	164	162	159	156	153
LR 4I	150	147	145	142	139	137	134	132	130	128
LR 5I	148	145	143	140	137	135	133	130	128	126
LR 6K	146	143	140	137	135	132	130	128	126	124
LR 6L	179	175	172	169	166	163	160	157	155	152
LR 7G	89	87	85	84	82	81	79	78	76	75
LR 7H	141	138	136	133	131	128	126	124	122	120
LR 8I	197	194	190	186	183	180	177	173	171	168
LR 9I	181	177	174	171	168	165	162	159	156	154
LR 10I	118	116	114	112	109	108	106	104	102	100
LR 11I	107	105	103	101	99	98	96	94	93	91
LR 12I	214	210	206	202	199	195	192	188	185	182
Posttest	192	188	184	181	178	174	171	168	166	163

PROGRESS CHART—SHORT AND LONG READINGS

Short Readings	WPM % Comprehension	Long Readings	WPM % Comprehension
SR 1G			
SR 1H		LR 1I	
SR 2G			
SR 2H		LR 2I	
SR 3G			
SR 3H		LR 3I	
SR 4G			
SR 4H		LR 4I	
SR 5G			
SR 5H		LR 5I	
		LR 6K	
		LR 6L	
		*LR 7G	
		*LR 7H	
**SR 8G			
**SR 8H		**LR 8I	
**SR 9G			
**SR 9H		**LR 9I	
SR 10G			
SR 10H		LR 10I	
SR 11G			
SR 11H		LR 11I	
		LR 12G	

*Study-reading speed should be slower than the other speeds.

**Skimming speed should be double the other speeds.

PROGRESS CHART—PRETEST AND POSTTEST

Contrast your scores on the Pretest (taken when beginning this book) and the Posttest (taken after finishing this book).

I. Comprehension and Rate

Pretest:	How Fast Should A Person Read	% Comprehension	WPM
Posttest:	I Was a Speed-Reading Dropout	% Comprehension	WPM
Difference:			

II. Vocabulary

Pretest:	% Correct
Posttest:	% Correct
Difference:	